With
Love
and
Quiches

With Love and Quiches

A LONG ISLAND HOUSEWIFE'S SURPRISING JOURNEY

FROM KITCHEN TO BOARDROOM

SUSAN AXELROD

CHAIRWOMAN AND FOUNDER OF LOVE AND QUICHES GOURMET®

GREENLEAF
BOOK GROUP PRESS

Published by Greenleaf Book Group Press
Austin, Texas
www.gbgpress.com

Distributed by Greenleaf Book Group LLC

For ordering information or special discounts for bulk purchases, please contact Greenleaf Book Group LLC at PO Box 91869, Austin, TX 78709, 512.891.6100.

Design and composition by Greenleaf Book Group LLC
Cover design by Greenleaf Book Group LLC
Cover images:
Pie-chart: ©iStockphoto.com/alexsl-Alex Slobodkin
Cake slice: ©John Montana photography/www.jmontana.com

Publisher's Cataloging-In-Publication Data
Axelrod, Susan, 1941-, author.
 With love and quiches : a Long Island housewife's surprising journey from kitchen to boardroom / Susan Axelrod, chairwoman and founder of Love and Quiches Gourmet.—First edition.

 pages : illustrations ; cm

 Issued also as an ebook.
 ISBN: 978-1-62634-071-8

 1. Axelrod, Susan. 2. Love and Quiches Gourmet (Firm)—History. 3. Women-owned business enterprises—New York (State)—Long Island. 4. Businesswomen—New York (State)—Long Island. 5. Success in business. 6. Gourmet food industry—New York (State)—Long Island. 7. Quiches (Cooking) I. Title.

HD2358.5.U62 L66 2014
338.04082/09747/21   2014930283

Part of the Tree Neutral® program, which offsets the number of trees consumed in the production and printing of this book by taking proactive steps, such as planting trees in direct proportion to the number of trees used: www.treeneutral.com

Printed in the United States of America on acid-free paper

14 15 16 17 18 19   10 9 8 7 6 5 4 3 2 1

First Edition

TreeNeutral®

To Irwin, my "stealth editor"

Contents

PROLOGUE: An Accidental Business

Part I

1: Finding the Passion (Early Days–1973) 7

2: Getting Started (1973–1974) 27

3: Becoming Love and Quiches (1974) 43

4: The Transition (1975) 53

5: The Mini-Factory (1976–1980) 65

6: Freeport, Here We Come! (1980) 91

7: Spreading Our Wings (1980–1989) 103

8: Securing Our Position (1990–2000) 123

Part II

9: Adversity 139

10: From Overstuffed to Lean and Mean 145

11: The Next Level 153

12: Company Culture 165

13: Constant Learning 177

14: Marketing and Branding 187

15: You Can't Taste a Cheesecake over the Internet 197

16: A Global Perspective 205

17: Family Matters 211

18: A Look in the Mirror 219

EPILOGUE: Where Will We Go from Here? 237

ACKNOWLEDGMENTS 241

Coda

RECIPES FOR SUCCESS: My Accidental Business Primer 245

RECIPES FOR THE MIND: A Few Favorite Books 251

RECIPES FOR THE SOUL: Travel Abroad 257

RECIPES FROM THE HEART: A Few Favorite Recipes 277

ABOUT THE AUTHOR 307

Prologue

An Accidental Business

*Life is a great big canvas, and you should
throw on it all the paint you can.*
—*Danny Kaye*

W hen I sold my first quiche in 1973, I had no idea that my
fledgling operation would one day, decades later, be competing with the giants of the food industry. How could I
have known? I was just a clueless Long Island housewife who made
that first quiche in my kitchen almost on a whim. And yet here we
are today: With no preparation for business ownership whatsoever,
I was able to translate a passionate love of cooking and food into a
multimillion-dollar family business that ships top-quality quiches and
desserts to every corner of the country and now the globe.

I had absolutely no idea what I was getting myself into—a recurring
theme during the early years of my business life—but it is an eventful
story. So I've decided to tell it. I'm going to take you on a journey from

my kitchen, through my neighborhood, and to the global business that I have loved from day one.

My business came out of nowhere, an accident that I was not ready for. And so, for years, I would refer to it as my "accidental business." Everything I learned was in the line of fire, and I will share it all, both the pain and the glory, laced with plenty of advice that I only wish I could have had. If there was a "how to" manual, I never got it. I had neither role models nor advisors; nobody cautioned me about the hazards involved. Looking back across the decades, I'm glad I was so innocent about those hazards; otherwise, I might have lost my courage before I truly got started. Yet, once I *did* get started, I knew deep inside that I was going to do this thing, that I *could* do this thing.

In many ways this story is a cautionary tale of what *not* to do when you want to start a new business. Yet here I am. I have done it. My company has become an integral and well-recognized member of the foodservice industry, serving almost every segment of the trade from hotels to airlines to multiunit chain restaurants to supermarket bakeries. We are now primarily a dessert manufacturer, and we ship our products worldwide.

So why am I telling my story now? Well, recently there was a spectacular exhibit at the Metropolitan Museum in New York called The Steins Collect, displaying the astonishing amount of art amassed by Gertrude Stein and her brothers during their years in Europe. The exhibit's accompanying explanations were primarily focused on the Stein family and their glittering circle of compatriots, including Picasso and Matisse. One thing that Ms. Stein said resonated with me: "Somebody told me to write a book, so I wrote one." Simple as that. I am not comparing myself to Gertrude Stein, but that is what happened to me. Our marketing department told me to tell my story, so I did.

In Part I of this story, I'll take you on the wild ride that was the early years of my business. You'll see some of our biggest successes as we got off the ground—and witness some pretty hilarious mistakes.

In the first chapters of Part II, we'll pick the story up just after the events of 9/11, when I nearly lost the business completely. It was in the subsequent rebound that I learned some of the greatest business lessons of my career. I'll begin sharing those lessons in short chapters in the rest of Part II that offer insight and advice on topics ranging from company culture, to marketing and branding, to the trials and rewards of working with family. In other words, information that any small business owner can use.

It has been an arduous journey, with hard truths and some brutal lessons. I was able to conquer them, and, for sure, I have never, ever been bored.

Would I do it all over again? Oh yes, I would. In a heartbeat.

Part I

Chapter 1

Finding the Passion
(Early Days–1973)

The best way to predict your future is to create it.
—Patti LaBelle

I was born in Bensonhurst, a Jewish and Italian neighborhood in Brooklyn, where cooking aromas constantly wafted between the tightly packed houses. Throughout my childhood, the smell of delicious food seemed to follow me around. I was nurtured in a bustling kitchen and around a heavily laden dining table—food was the vital center of our household. Looking back to those days now, I have no doubt that these early culinary experiences planted the seed of passion that eventually grew into my accidental business.

When I was three, we moved from Bensonhurst to Neponsit, an exclusive enclave within a beach community in the Rockaways. Our new home was a big, beautiful house right on the ocean, with a rolling lawn and a gate that opened right onto the beach. My mother used to say we lived in "Neponsit, Long Island," because she thought that sounded fancier, but Neponsit actually lies on the Queens end of the island, near the Marine Parkway Bridge to Brooklyn, from where we came. I've remained an inveterate New Yorker throughout my life, always living very near or in the city.

At the end of the day, you could say I was born with a silver-plated, but not quite sterling, spoon in my mouth—privileged, but not overly so. But after the move to Neponsit, we went from a comfortable existence to one that was much more upscale. For one, we had a cook, a butler, and a laundress.

The cook, Evelina, was as wide as she was tall, only she wasn't tall, and I always smile when I picture her. I can't think about Evelina without remembering—and almost still tasting—the best Southern fried chicken I've ever had, bar none. She was also a superb baker, and once a week she baked never-to-be-forgotten bread, chewy yet tender. We used to devour thick slices of the loaves and the rolls, dripping in butter just as they came out of the oven. That bread could bring tears—it was *that* good.

I never had to help in the kitchen, but I watched all the time. Evelina was constantly baking cookies, and there were always two or three bowls filled with them. My mother had a few specialties too; one of them was blintzes, lightly sweetened, cheese-filled crêpes that have always been a Jewish staple. I would closely watch her cook up the delicate crêpes and lay them out on towels all over the kitchen, ready to be filled, long before Julia Child's books (and *her* crêpes) became my bible.

My mother kept a kosher home, and most of the cooking in our house was quite simple—not too many sauces and nothing exotic. Ketchup was often the only condiment in the pantry. Even peanut butter was a bit too "out there." Nevertheless, there was always a lot of very delicious food around—a Jewish tradition—and our extra refrigerator in the basement held the overflow of fruit and other goodies from the *two* refrigerators we had in the kitchen and pantry upstairs. Friday night dinners featuring two and sometimes three kinds of roasts weren't thought of as anything special. And it was a family tradition that we would turn on the record player and practice ballroom dancing before dessert. My parents were great dancers, and my brother and I followed suit; we would practice the mambo, tango, the Lindy, and even the Charleston!

In Bensonhurst, we had lived as one family with my mother's oldest sister, and after our move to Neponsit, the sisters pined for each other. So within a year or two, my Uncle Phil, Aunt Mollie, and cousin Syril followed us across the Marine Parkway Bridge and built a house just two blocks away. We were once again living as one big family, only now we had to cut across the lawns of the two intervening houses to get back and forth, sort of like a grassy hallway between rooms.

My Aunt Mollie, like Evelina, spent all day in the kitchen cooking and baking, but she always rushed and had no patience for the rules. When making butter cookies, for example, she would never form even rolls and chill her dough to allow for nice, neat slicing; she would just break off pieces and press them onto the cookie sheet at random. So Aunt Mollie's butter cookies always had crevices and thumbprints all over them when they came out of the oven, and because the thicknesses were so random, many of them featured dark little burns. But somehow Mollie's Burnt Cookies, as we called them, were delicious anyway. I hung around Aunt Mollie's kitchen a lot, as fascinated by her improvised methods as I was by Evelina's careful culinary masterpieces.

I had plenty of cooking to watch, and I was captivated by all of it. Everybody was always cooking. Eating out was only for special occasions (that went for most American families at the time, not just ours).

When I was still quite small, before air travel became commonplace, we would travel by train once a year to Florida. We would take a Pullman compartment where the seats were made up into beds at night; very fancy, I thought. Once we got down South, there were orange groves as far as the eye could see, and the delicious fragrance of oranges permeated everything. We took all our meals in the dining car, where the tables were set with crisp linens and fine china; it was another time, another world. Though touted as Continental, the cooking was largely Southern, and it *almost* rivaled Evelina's cuisine. Even at my young age, I knew this was all quite special.

The Rockaways were a good place to be a kid. I grew up around a large group of neighborhood children from all walks of life, but we saw no differences among ourselves. We ran around in gangs, not cliques. We swam in the ocean until almost November, when our mothers would start screaming.

Once we were all in high school, we would congregate on Friday nights in one of Far Rockaway's two movie theaters—either the RKO Strand or the Columbia. Far Rockaway was a good half-hour bus ride from where we lived, and on the way home, the bus driver would wait at each stop until we had all run down the block and into our houses. We were safe, but he did it anyway. A different world.

The Rockaways were so close to the city but a world away. Just across the Marine Parkway Bridge, in Brooklyn, were two nightclubs—Ben Maksik's and The Elegante—that used to book the likes of Harry Belafonte and Frank Sinatra. At Ben Maksik's, I once saw a grown woman crawl onto the stage to grab at Harry Belafonte's bare feet before she could be stopped, a forerunner to later wild behavior at rock concerts. This club also booked Judy Garland for a two-week stint and, to our delight, rented my Aunt Mollie's house for Ms. Garland's family. I assume Liza Minnelli, still a young child, was part of that entourage. Sadly, it took less than one week for Ms. Garland to break her contract and *total* my aunt's house. The nightclub agreed to pay for all the repairs and damage.

Many of my friends would one day have their Sweet Sixteen and engagement parties in these two nightclubs. The best one was my friend Cynthia's party at The Elegante, where the show starred the then-unknown Supremes, with Diana Ross singing her heart out. They took the house down, and the rest is history.

My parents would take my brother and me, and sometimes my cousin Syril, nightclubbing on occasion, too.

These and many other nightclubs in the city used to serve Chinese food exclusively. In the fifties, Chinese food always meant Cantonese cuisine: egg rolls, egg drop soup, spare ribs, egg foo young, chow mein—familiar Chinese "comfort food." When my friends and I started dating, we would go in groups to various nightclubs, including the iconic Copacabana and the Latin Quarter in the city. They all served Chinese food and we ate a lot of it, as much as we did pizza. No sophisticated palates quite yet. This was all before disco took over.

This was the environment in which I grew up—happy but insulated. I wanted for nothing, but I knew nothing of the world. And as preparation for real life, my sheltered childhood worked against me precisely because nothing was expected of me. I had no role models and nothing to strive for because everything had already been worked out. My parents had no aspirations whatsoever for me. I was merely a girl. Their expectation was that I would graduate from college, maybe teach for a few years, and then get married, have my family, and become a housewife. I don't blame them for this, as this was the norm nearly sixty years ago. Did it ever cross their minds that I could start my own business? Not in a thousand years.

Enter Irwin

I first laid eyes on Irwin Axelrod when I was thirteen and he was sixteen. I stepped into the school cafeteria and saw him sitting there, hair slicked back but with one long curl hanging down his forehead, T-shirt with a pack of cigarettes rolled into the sleeve near one shoulder, leather motorcycle jacket hanging off the other shoulder. I immediately knew he was the one. The only problem, as I soon found out, was that he had a stable of other girlfriends. To my chagrin, it took me a while to prevail; he had two other girlfriends and would only call me every third day. He would pick me up in his father's plumbing truck, and my favorite date would be to go to Coney Island or to walk the boardwalk in Far Rockaway with all its concessions. I liked Irwin so much that I waited out all the competition and finally got what I wanted.

Irwin and I at the prom (top) and as newlyweds (bottom).

Irwin was a rebel by nature, especially in school, but he always managed to get by through acing his final exams. But his work ethic was another matter. He'd gotten his working papers when he was fourteen, and he had a plum job at the movie theaters in Far Rockaway where all our friends hung out on Friday nights. It was the early fifties at the time (no computers), and his job was to take the train into the city with all the ticket stubs and bring them to the RKO offices in Rockefeller Center to be counted. He would sometimes be trusted to bring back the large cans of films to be shown that week, as well as the placards to be displayed out front with the coming attractions. He was also an usher. So we had undoubtedly crossed paths before we first met on that fateful day in the Far Rockaway High School lunchroom.

As Irwin's dating pool dwindled down to just me in high school, I got to know his family. He did not come from wealth; the welfare kids had better baseball gloves than he did, and he would tell me it was hard to find a pair of socks that his brother's feet hadn't already been in. His mother was a very colorful character, a true eccentric, and mundane parental responsibilities like a supply of socks simply didn't resonate with her. She didn't own an iron, and once she even decided to break all the dishes rather than wash them. If Irwin got in trouble in high school, her idea of discipline was to go to the dean of boys with a bottle of scotch—a strategy that actually worked very well.

Looking back after many years of marriage, Irwin and I realized with great amusement that his family was in the food business long before I was. His grandmother was widowed while quite young, and she opened a kosher chicken market on Prospect Place in Brooklyn to support herself and her eight children, seven boys and one daughter. Thanks to her product, she earned the nickname Bubby Chickie.

Her husband had been a tailor and worked in the garment district in New York, but he never contributed much to the household. Decades after his death, a granddaughter asked Bubby Chickie for details about the man she had married but about whom so little was known. Through a relative who translated for her, the matriarch frankly replied, "He drank, he played cards, and that's all you have to know."

Bubby Chickie's language was Yiddish, and she never learned or spoke any English at all. She was still in the poultry business when Irwin was a young boy, and he would hang around in her shop or in the horseradish stall next door, where the pungent odor of the freshly grated vegetable was something of an intoxicant. Once, Bubby Chickie allowed him to try his hand at flicking a chicken (i.e., plucking it). He got into big trouble because he broke the skin on the breast, a very bad thing to do because it rendered the chicken unsalable at full price and it had to go into the discount bin. The memory of the crime remains with him to this day.

Bubby Chickie with her eight children, circa 1950.

Long after Bubby Chickie's shop had become an institution, Irwin's father also opened a chicken market, Louie's Fresh Killed Chickens, in East New York, another part of Brooklyn. Bubby Chickie had given him $100 of seed money to get started. That business didn't last too long, though, and Irwin's father eventually became a plumbing contractor. More successful was the pickle truck owned by one of Irwin's uncles; he would always allow Irwin to climb into the truck to choose any pickle he wanted out of the lined-up barrels. It was a long-ago forerunner of the current food-truck craze.

Regardless of his family's experience in the industry I would adopt as my own, I remain eternally grateful that I met Irwin. His sense of humor is legendary, and through all that was ahead of us, he always kept me laughing.

Young, Married, and Cooking

Irwin and I married young. That wasn't unusual in those days, but when I announced to my parents that Irwin and I had gotten engaged, they fought me tooth and nail. From the beginning, they had lobbied very hard against our match. I was rich and he was poor: it was as though I was marrying out of my religion. Of course they were right about me being young, but I knew I loved Irwin, and I was ready to marry him no matter what anyone said. I stubbornly argued my position and got my way—and I wouldn't change a minute of it.

My parents finally gave up arguing, and just a few weeks short of my turning twenty, they gave us an elegant wedding in the grand ballroom of the famed Plaza Hotel in the city. Inevitably my father and mother came first to accept and then to love Irwin *almost* as much as I did. I had always known they would. I wouldn't let anything get in the way of the end game, a stubborn streak that has always served me well—especially later, during my business life.

Irwin and I moved into our first one-bedroom apartment in Far Rockaway, a mixed neighborhood near to but a world away from exclusive Neponsit. In little more than two and a half years after the wedding, our family was complete; one boy and one girl had joined us in our 450-square-foot apartment. This was quite a bit sooner than we had planned. Little Andrew took the living room, and we joked that we kept his little sister, Joan, in a kitchen drawer. That actually wasn't far from the truth: we kept her bassinet on the kitchen table except when we were eating, at which point Joan got moved to the linoleum floor. I had just gotten my undergraduate degree, but with the arrival of the children, my plan to teach high school English had to be shelved for the time being.

In the first years of our marriage, Irwin and I did what was expected of us. We became junior members of an exclusive country club on Long Island by virtue of my parents being members there. (We would

withdraw eventually, years later, after we realized our schedules, budget, and temperaments weren't in tune with the country club life.)

When our lease on the tiny apartment was up, we bought our
first small home, a bit further east on Long Island in a nice suburban
neighborhood, but we moved back home to my parents' house for six
months during the transition. That meant six more months of Evelina's divine cooking, with a side benefit of occasional babysitting from
Mom, Dad, or Evelina. Strictly speaking, it wasn't the same house I
had grown up in. As I mentioned at the beginning of this chapter, in
that house, my childhood home, we had an ancient refrigerator in the
basement. When I was away at college, an electrical fire started in it,
and our home and almost everything in it were destroyed. It was a true
tragedy, but my parents rebuilt it exactly as it had been. (Years later, I
would come to see this as the first in what would become a long line
of freezer-related disasters.)

But once Irwin and I had finally settled into our new home, I found
myself fairly grounded. This was during the early to mid-sixties; we
were part of the Woodstock generation and were semi-hippies—or
at least we pretended we were. But in reality, our life together looked
pretty conventional. I'd accepted by then that I would probably never
get to teach high school, and I was okay with that. I was happy staying home to raise my children, having no real desire at the time to do
something outside the home.

But as months turned into years and the children grew out of
infancy, I found myself feeling increasingly stuck at home and bored. I
was cooking, but not in a particularly creative way. In keeping with the
era, I made plenty of casseroles with string beans bathed in Campbell's
cream of mushroom soup and topped with O&C onions. Another ple-
bian creation was Swedish meatballs stewed in a mix of half grape jelly,
half ketchup. I soon realized that this wasn't working for me. It was
against my innate style, and something needed changing. Fortunately,
I had plenty of time on my hands, so I started reading cookbooks and
cooking magazines from cover to cover. Slowly but surely, I felt my

passion for all things culinary rekindling. Then I started cooking—*a lot*. And so it began.

During that time, I eagerly collected *Gourmet* magazine, which had been around since 1941. I used to mark up each issue as if I were studying for an exam, and I kept a notebook where I noted where to find what in the various issues. (Since I never parted with even one issue, I ended up with a forty-five-year collection that I kept until we sold our house and moved into an apartment. I couldn't bear to throw them away, but neither eBay nor the local library would take them, so we finally had to put them out at our tag sale.)

I also discovered Julia Child's *Mastering the Art of French Cooking*, first published in 1961. I became obsessed with both. Starting in the sixties, Time-Life Books published a fabulous series of cookbooks called Foods of the World, with each book written by an expert in the cuisine of a different region of the world. There were at least twenty books in this series with titles such as *American Cooking, The Cooking of China, The Cooking of the Caribbean Islands, The Cooking of Vienna's Empire*, and *Classic French Cooking*. I collected them all and used them until most of the pages were dog-eared and stained with all manner of food.

As was popular during that era, we started a gourmet dinner club once a month with our other young married friends, where we each brought a different course for the meal. It wasn't as boring as it may sound because my friends were *really* good cooks. Exposed to the talents of others, my passion for food kept building.

In this time (and, honestly, ever since) I was more of a chef than a baker. Racks of veal, potatoes Anna, beef tenderloin with bordelaise sauce, ratatouille, mushrooms in a myriad of ways—these were the dishes that had my attention. To this day, I have never baked an apple pie—or any covered pie, for that matter! I have never personally baked a layer cake, never made a traditional frosting, never made any of the all-American kinds of desserts. Instead I did mousses, dessert soufflés, tarts, homemade rich ice creams, and sauces.

Just like Julie in the film *Julie & Julia*, I learned most of my techniques from Julia Child. I read *Mastering the Art of French Cooking* as if it were the Bible. Every recipe in that book, in my opinion, is perfect. All the advice in it is invaluable, and I still know and unconsciously use those principles to this very day. *Splendid Fare: The Albert Stockli Cookbook* is another source that I relied upon. In it is an exquisite *tarte à l'oignon* and a perfect Cumberland sauce, made with currants and port—a great sauce to serve with almost anything, and it lasts forever in the fridge. Albert is a famous chef I knew, if only because Irwin and I made a pilgrimage once a year to his restaurant, Stonehenge, in Ridgefield, Connecticut. Albert once told me during one of our dinners there that ketchup, in his opinion, was one of the most perfect sauces ever created.

I learned to cook before the world was aware of cholesterol. The over-the-top richness of some of my dinner guests' favorites (and mine) takes my breath away. One recipe was homemade crêpes stuffed with brie, dipped in beer batter, and deep fried in a cauldron of clarified butter! Another dish was my Crêpes Soubise, which were plate-sized homemade crêpes laid flat and alternately layered with a béchamel sauce to which caramelized sweet onions and grated Gruyère had been folded in; I would keep going until the tower of crêpes and sauce was at least ten layers high and then bake it until it was bubbly. I would serve this in wedges as a first course. My friends would nearly swoon as they ate it. My liver pâté, made before I had ever heard of foie gras, had more butter and heavy cream in it than liver.

My most sought-after dessert was homemade almond tuiles: crisp, crackly, plate-sized cookies that I would alternately layer with my homemade deep-dark bittersweet chocolate ice cream. Like my Crêpes Soubise, I would also serve this dessert tower in wedges with Crème Anglaise and berries. I believed then, as I do now, that overindulging once in a while is one of the great pleasures in life.

In 1970, we moved from our first house into a lovely Tudor home in Hewlett Harbor, on the south shore of Long Island. Our dark oak-paneled dining room was very dramatic and much like a movie set. During our very first dinner party there, twelve of us were seated around the table in this baronial setting when my dear friend Jack looked up and said, "Maybe we better eat quick and get the hell out of here before the real owners come home!"

It was in our home in Hewlett Harbor that dinner parties became more than just a hobby. I now had the perfect setting for a real affair. I loved to plan, shop for, and prep for these dinners. I loved the orchestration and the whole week leading up to them. By then we had a housekeeper, a woman from Belize named Bridget. Tall and elegant, with a regal bearing, Bridget served as sous chef while I cooked. It was serious business: I *never* bought anything prepared and even made my own crackers for cheese; I kept voluminous records of what I served and to whom; and I never repeated a menu or dish unless my friends begged me, which began to happen with more and more frequency. Eventually, my dinner parties became so highly anticipated that my friends started trading invitations to them.

The attention to detail I honed at this time, along with many other skills, served me well once the story of my business began.

My First Paycheck

I was having the time of my life throwing dinner parties, yet there was something else tugging at me even then. As I played the part of young society matron, volunteering at charity events, playing tennis, and so on, a hollow feeling crept in. I felt as if I were merely playing a part. Something whispered to me: I didn't feel genuine; I needed something more. Yet for the moment, I just kept cooking and entertaining my friends.

As I honed my skills, I was inadvertently building my reputation as a very good cook among a wider audience than just my friends. Consequently, I was invited to give demos at Macy's, other local department stores, and the local library, where I once found myself side by side with Jacques Pépin (when he was not yet "the" Jacques Pépin, celebrity chef and sidekick to Julia Child).

This all led to an invitation to teach a series of cooking classes on the north shore of Long Island to raise money for charity from ORT America, an organization that promoted Jewish values through educational programs all over the world. They offered to pay me! I wanted this so badly that I could taste it. I hoped it would be a remedy for the hollowness, that my time had come. I couldn't type and had no résumé since I had never had a job, so I *hand wrote* a laundry list of everything I loved about food and wanted to demonstrate in my classes. This is what I submitted as my application.

When we sold our house a few years ago, I came across that "application," and the list was quite hilarious. Tears of laughter ran down my face as I read it. The language was so flowery and overly dramatic! And the scope of what I said I would cover in the nine sessions was breathtakingly overambitious. I even called the participants "girls." (This document did land me the job, however, at what I thought was a very impressive $150 per cooking class!) Here are some excerpts:

> I create an analogy between painting and cooking. I love to cook and find it creative, challenging and really satisfying. A fine dinner or dish must balance color, texture, form and taste. Its final presentation in its very own way combines all of these parts, as a painting does. What we choose to serve and how we present it helps create the atmosphere for any gathering.
>
> I have learned during my years at serious cooking that there are some very basic principles and techniques that, once mastered, can give us the necessary tools for improvising and inventing things on our own that are unusual or express our own personalities. I will try to be representative in the foods I choose to demonstrate using as broad a spectrum and basics as I have the time for and I feel the girls taking the courses are ready for. I'll also keep in mind

that we, as hostesses, want to be able to enjoy our own parties as well as our guests.

French cooking techniques form, for me, the basis for expert cooking in any type of cuisine (Spanish, Italian, etc.) though, of course, any national cuisine has parts to it uniquely its own. Some French foods are very delicate, elaborate, classic and some more robust, peasant.

There are five basic sauces from which practically all other sauces are drawn (Espagnole, Béchamel, Velouté, etc.). These incorporate use of stocks and wines.

For hors d'oeuvres I will choose perhaps a classic cheese soufflé with lobster sauce. Soufflé techniques, once mastered, can be adapted for sweet or savory dishes, and can be done in advance by several hours if done properly. Quiches and crêpes can be used for gaining knowledge of custards, Béchamel and Hollandaise sauces.

I do a lot of Italian cooking, especially for my closer friends. Italian cooking is probably more fun but can be quite delicate and subtle, too. A very good dish, very fine, is veal in Marsala wine with prosciutto, eggplant and fontina cheese.

For hors d'oeuvres, my favorite is Pizza Rustica, an extraordinary Italian quiche; sausage in pastry; caponata, a cold eggplant dish that is fantastic when homemade.

Pasta is easy to make, even easier with a pasta machine: fettuccine Alfredo with white truffles, spaghetti carbonara (love it, the best pasta creation, I feel), ziti Siciliana, homemade marinara sauce, light northern Italian meat sauce, clam and lobster sauces. We can work with risotto and make gnocchi or polenta.

One of the most important techniques, included in so many varieties of desserts, is a successful pastry crust. They can be made in many ways, some crisper, or sweeter, or more short, or with overtones of wine or including pulverized nuts, or other spices. We can make a poached fruit tart with a frangipane cream, or a pecan tart, or tarts and pies with creams and mousses and other fillings.

Custards and creams, Bavarians and pastry fillings are a course in themselves. We can make a bread and butter pudding with a fresh raspberry Melba sauce, or a crème brûlée or a chestnut Bavarian with a chocolate sponge, sauce Anglaise, or some elaborate bombe.

Dessert soufflés and crêpes served with special fillings and sauces are always spectacular. Chocolate is good for the soul. I make a very special French torte called a trianon, which can be served with a praline crème, or sauce Anglaise or sandwiched with a rich pastry filling.

We will also make some candies. For example, a macadamia or mixed nut brittle and chocolate truffles, which are both easy and elegant.

If it is preferred, I can substitute the last course for a potpourri of dishes, such as Chinese Peking duck, cassoulet, a very special Spanish paella or Spanish sliced pork or veal with almond sauce and saffron rice, South American or Greek specialties.

While packing up our home of thirty-seven years, I also found all my recipes and notes for those classes in addition to the application. My handwritten recipes and the handouts I distributed to students are also quite hilarious, a combination of useful and *woefully* inadequate. One sheet, for instance, was called "A Well Equipped Kitchen," and in it I listed wire whisks, wooden spoons, cheesecloth, pastry brushes and feathers, a mouli grater, a food mill (ricer), a fourteen-quart stockpot, a huge mixing bowl, a mortar and pestle, a candy thermometer, and carbon steel knives as essential kitchen elements. Yet I never mentioned saucepans, frying pans, rolling pins, measuring cups and spoons, slotted spoons, spatulas, pitchers, strainers, cookie sheets, or dozens of other things that even the most basic kitchen would need!

Also on that sheet was a list of "necessary" ingredients; I did only a slightly better job in that one. I deemed meat extract paste, sweet almond oil, and truffles as necessary, but neglected to list salt, butter, canned plum tomatoes, and a dozen other staples.

Perhaps my favorite is my "Hints" sheet, a veritable potpourri of advice, some of which I seemed to have taken out of thin air! (The bracketed comments are my present-day responses as I reread the Hints.) Try not to laugh too hard when you read this sampling.

- Never forget presentation; garnish dishes in wine sauce with toasted buttered bread triangles. [Funny because sauce isn't a garnish, and I would never use ordinary toasted buttered bread triangles.]

- Egg whites; the older the better—freeze in ice cube trays.

- Don't use more than one rich sauce per meal. [This is achingly obvious!]

- Assemble all ingredients beforehand and measure accurately. [This one is good advice.]

- Onion—grip the onion, not the board. [What? I'm not even sure what I meant here.]

- Oil—must be room temperature for sauces. [How else?]

- Beurre Manie—knead 1 tbs. butter with 1 tbs. flour to thicken sauces. [A good basic technique, and simple to use for almost any sauce, sweet or savory.]

There were about twenty-five items on that list, and although many were right on, I don't mind making fun of myself for the more misguided hints of my first foray into professional cooking.

Also among the memorabilia I found while packing up our house was my original Quiche au Fromage recipe as it first appeared in my handouts for the ORT class. It doesn't include the method for the crust (because I was demonstrating it), and the crust need *not* be pre-baked for sure. This quiche would, of course, become a staple of my business, and the product today has not changed all that much from the original. (Please note, though, that my instruction to bake in the upper third of the oven is dead wrong: the bottom third is better, giving you a browner bottom without burning the top.)

I found a lot more when packing up the house before our move to the city: I had been a compulsive recipe collector, and I had torn literally thousands of recipes out of magazines and other publications, recipes that I then saved for decades. I hadn't looked at these recipes for many years, if ever, yet I had them spilling out of drawers, shopping bags, and cartons. I tossed them all, and it felt very good to do so. Cathartic to get rid of all that baggage! But all my notes and lesson plans for my cooking classes? And my cookbooks? They all came with me, even the overused and mildewed ones!

It's hard to believe how unsophisticated I was when I taught those series of cooking courses. Many of the recipes and techniques I taught were taken from the elaborate dinners that I used to serve my friends, and teaching that material cost me a fortune in terms of both time and money: thirty to forty hours of preparation for each three-hour weekly session, and God only knew what I spent on all the foodstuffs I needed for each class, together with what I spent for other needed supplies, travel costs, and the additional hours in front of a copy machine preparing my giveaway materials for each participant. Yet I thought the $150 per session pay a princely sum—clueless as usual. It worked out to all of about ten cents per hour after my ingredient and supply expenses, but I had "tasted blood" for the first time and was ready to do something more important. The time to do something other than solely entertaining my friends had arrived.

My Accidental Car Pool

Chance and serendipity are a recurring theme in my life, and the origins of my company are no exception. In junior high, I'd followed a friend to Woodmere Academy, a tony private school that at the time seemed far preferable to the public school in my neighborhood. One of my classmates there was a boy named Peter Davison, who I got to know but wasn't particularly close with. After some time at Woodmere, I realized that I wasn't the private school type, and I transferred back to Far Rockaway High School for my freshman year—which is a good thing, too, since that's where I met Irwin.

Almost twenty years later, though, when we moved to Hewlett Harbor, I found out that Peter Davison's sister lived in the neighborhood. I was looking to join a car pool for the children, so I called her up and told her I knew Peter. We found that our children had a few activities and interests in common and that we did too—primarily a passion for food. Jill and I worked out a car pool and soon became good friends.

One day after Jill dropped Andrew and Joan off, she asked if I had a little time to talk. At the kitchen table, over coffee, we chatted about mundane topics of the day for a few minutes before Jill paused and asked me a question. "I'm thinking about starting some kind of business," she said. "Something food related. Would you be interested?"

Well, as you can imagine, *that* gave me something to think about.

Chapter 2

Getting Started (1973–1974)

There are times when you want a bull in a china shop.
—Somerset Maugham

O nce I had processed what Jill asked me that day in the kitchen,
my answer was immediate: "Yes." I was game. Why *not* start
a food-related business together? Jill was a great cook, and
her mother had run a small but successful business selling Christmas
decorations to the exclusive department store Henri Bendel, so Jill
had always hoped to start a business of her own. To Jill, I seemed like
a natural choice for a partner. I agreed.

Over the next few weeks, our planning commenced. Without giving it too much thought, we decided to call ourselves "Bonne Femme"
(Good Lady). We thought it had a good ring to it, and we'd both
always leaned toward the French style of cooking.

Our start-up was both very funny and bittersweet. It should be
written in stone that no business, however small, should be started

without *some* kind of rudimentary business plan, but that's exactly what we did. We had no idea what kind of food-related business we even wanted: Would we eventually run a small café? Sell food we'd cooked to restaurants? What kind of food should we sell? Instead of answering any of these basic questions, we just started taking step after step, somewhat blindly. We started with no business plan. We simply started.

The first step we took was a good one, at least: we contacted the New York State Department of Agriculture to have my house licensed as a "Bakery/Food Processing Plant." Lots of people illegally sold food to restaurants from unlicensed home kitchens, but not me; I was brought up to always do the right thing. Somehow we got the license from the state, though I still have no idea how we managed to pull it off—for starters, my water heater surely wasn't hot enough to qualify! I imagine we took them by surprise because not many people had asked before. Today, home kitchens are rarely, if ever, able to obtain such licenses, instead having to rent space in licensed commercial kitchens, but back in the early 1970s it must've been easier. We got a pass, and we still have the same plant number to this day.

So off we went, my partner and I, charging blindly forward. Now the next question: What to do? We started off with a stab at catering. By virtue of our culinary reputations, Jill and I were able to take on a half-dozen jobs in the neighborhood before we decided that catering was not for us. Neither Jill nor I liked walking in through the back door of events as hired help. (Little did I know that catering would have been a walk in the park compared to the path I'd take over the next few years—"Humble Pie" would become my middle name for a very long time.)

Now that catering was out, what next? I don't remember exactly where the idea of quiche Lorraine came from, but once we happened upon it, it simply felt right. We looked at each other and said, "Let's give *that* a try." Our first quiche may have been an amateurish effort, but I still consider it to be one of the best I have ever tasted. Without realizing it, I was marching into my destiny—and in that offhand manner, Bonne Femme was off to the races.

With a name, a license, and a product, all we had to do now was persuade somebody to buy our quiche. In our first attempt, we took a few samples to our local gourmet supermarket, the Windmill Foodstore of Hewlett. As regular shoppers there, Jill and I both knew the owner. Our plan was to sell our quiche Lorraine to the store frozen raw, but we baked some off for the owner to sample. He ordered on the spot—our first sale, and it felt *very* good! Even better, he reordered, and then reordered again. Now we had our first repeat customer, and the journey had officially begun.

Our second regular customer followed soon after. I had the idea that we could make up some of the wonderful sauces I used for my dinner parties and sell them to the fish market just next door to the Windmill for use in their prepared foods section. I figured their customers would appreciate being able to pick up a delicious Newburg or cucumber-and-dill sauce with their purchase of fresh fish. The owner agreed, apparently, and soon Jill and I were cooking up and delivering the stuff by the gallon.

As owner-operators of Bonne Femme, we were truly clueless. We had no plan, no capital, kept our books in our heads, had no idea how to price our products, didn't realize that our own labor was actually worth something, and operated in just my kitchen with equipment gathered from both of our homes. Despite our ignorance, at the end of a three-month period, we had ten or fifteen customers, all local. Most of our new customers were restaurants, and they were selling our quiches as fast as we could make them. The company had started to take shape.

Our days at Bonne Femme started at five in the morning, when Jill and I would have a phone call to plan the day. As soon as the kids left for school, Jill would come over and we'd get started—rolling dough, frying bacon, grating cheese, and all the rest. (I very often grated my fingers along with the Swiss cheese, but even back then I had the sense to know I had to toss the cheese, not just pick through it to remove the bloody bits.) Everything was done by hand in tiny batches, and we were busy all day.

In the afternoon, I would run out to make deliveries while Jill, while doing her share, would typically pursue other interests. Somehow she still found time to run out for golf tournaments and things. After school, all of our children would get home, and we'd put them to work cracking eggs for the next day's production. Things were beyond hectic, but I loved it.

With things up and running, Jill and I started asking questions of anyone who would listen. We got some good advice from a master baker who, with his father, owned and ran an old line European pastry shop two towns over. He taught us useful and practical things: for example, that water was a great binder, and free! He stored quiches for us as well and sold us pie pans at his cost.

I also had an old friend whose family owned a very successful local supermarket chain, and he offered to sell us ends and scraps of bacon in fifteen-pound packages really cheap! Prior to that we had been clearing local supermarket shelves of their most expensive bacon in very small packages. Of course this added to our labor and waste, but what did we know? Buying from my friend was a tiny step forward. He would even drop off the packets of ends and scraps for us on his way home from work. And we found ourselves buying quite a bit of it as we got more and more customers. I might add that frying all that bacon played havoc with my kitchen. It took years to finally clean out all the vents, which were almost completely blocked with the accumulated grease, and I am quite thankful that I didn't burn my house down.

For all of our non-bacon ingredients, we were still raiding the local supermarkets and throwing off all their standard ordering patterns. We piled our grocery carts to the top with a hundred five-pound bags of flour, and we'd clean out their shelves of Swiss, Gruyère, broccoli, spinach, and everything else we needed for our quiches. It fascinated the other shoppers and infuriated the management. The managers used to say, "Here they come again—hide everything!" So we had to keep changing supermarkets.

So far, we were still only selling frozen raw quiches, which we stored at my house, Jill's house, and then all over the neighborhood. Then one of our customers, a local hamburger joint, asked if we could make them a pecan pie. That we could do! We had the pans, so why not? The dessert was a hit with the customers of that establishment, and our foray into desserts—our first line extension—was born. Soon we were also selling pecan pies to *all* of our restaurant customers.

Wholesale? What's Wholesale?

The unbaked quiches needed to be frozen before we could pack them in plastic bags and stack them at our friends' houses around town. We had come up with a system: we juxtaposed blocks from our children's toy sets to add as many levels as possible in my laundry room freezer and the extra freezer in my garage, in order to freeze as many quiches at a time as we could. And by now we had *two* sizes: six inch for retail and nine inch for restaurants.

Once we started making desserts, we couldn't exactly sell them frozen raw like our quiche (although we *tried* with the pecan pie), so we had to find a way to bake them efficiently. We came up with a similar system for baking desserts in our standard double ovens so that we could sneak in a few extra pies at a time. Nine per oven! Both of our houses! We started ferrying pails of pecan pie batter between houses. During one trip, a teenage hot-rodder came barreling out of a side street and slammed straight into my car, practically folding it in half and causing a veritable tsunami of batter all over the place. We repaired the car, but six months later the odor of very old butter and eggs was still so strong that dozens of scrubbings couldn't erase it; we gave up and got rid of the car.

Bonne Femme was not yet quite a full-time enterprise for either Jill or me, and I still had time to cook for friends. One evening, Irwin and I had our across-the-street neighbors and their children over for dinner. During the meal, we were discussing my little business, and I became the inadvertent entertainment, the butt of jokes and good-natured laughter, when I explained where we were buying our supplies.

"How about wholesale?" my neighbor said. "Wholesale?" I said. It had never occurred to us that we could buy such small amounts at wholesale. But we could, my neighbor told me, and we did! The very next day, Jill and I pulled out the Yellow Pages and found a ton of local suppliers.

One was a fresh egg supplier who would break the eggs for us and sell them to us by the pail. He would deliver them, too. It amazed me to learn that a case of extra large eggs (thirty dozen) would weigh *exactly* forty pounds every time! Only problem was that we were sure he had a habit of putting his finger on the scale, so I suspect that we rarely got what we had actually paid for.

I found myself with an enterprise that seemed to have a will and a pull of its own. We were getting busier, and needed help. By now we had a few friends and neighbors coming in on occasion, some for two hours every Tuesday and Thursday, others maybe for one hour every Monday and Wednesday. They rolled dough, grated cheese, packed the frozen quiches, and tasks like that. I don't even remember whether we paid them at first. But Jill and I still did all the mixing. The extra hands gave us some relief, but I couldn't help noticing that my kitchen was feeling more cramped by the day.

The Keystone Kops Quiche Factory

In the first year of Bonne Femme, I learned loud and clear that I wasn't going to stop—not until what we had started became real. A spark had been lit inside me. We already had our tentative market identified, so, to my thinking, all we needed to do was reach *more of it*. But to do that we needed more product, along with more storage space and better equipment. Little by little we began to segue from my kitchen into my garage, our very first move. My kitchen, by now a complete wreck, must've been relieved.

We had the garage fitted out with 220-volt outlets and bought our first commercial equipment. We found a local restaurant equipment supply wholesaler who sold us a life-altering commercial-grade freezer that was three times the size of our current one, a huge commercial fridge, and a miraculous freestanding double convection oven with six shelves in each. We could bake up to thirty-six pies at a time in each one! No more toy building blocks for us. No more ferrying batter between houses, either. We now had room to buy a few bakers' racks, several dozen bun pans, and some other wonderful kitchen aids. Our work table was made up of two sawhorses and a huge plywood slab, and we felt we were luxuriating in space!

In the months after our move to the garage, we gathered a few more customers, widening our sales area by a few slightly larger concentric circles. How fast we could grow was limited because I was still the only delivery guy. I had a little freezer truck going in the trunk of my car. Did you know that newspaper is the quintessential insulator? It was my secret to keeping the raw quiches from melting and the pecan pies from wilting.

Bonne Femme's customer count grew to about twenty-five. We concentrated on the pubs, yogurt shops, and sandwich shops: no place too fancy because we didn't yet have that much to sell. We were preparing maybe 150 products a week, but at an average of about $3 each, it didn't amount to much. Notice that we did not list any weights on our very first price list:

Still clueless, we continued to operate in the Keystone Kops tradition: two steps forward, three steps back. Nevertheless, the garage was our first mini-factory, and we started to think of our little enterprise as more of a business and less of a hobby.

We met up with a dealer in secondhand bakery equipment who served as somewhat of a mentor to us. The owner of another local bakery right in our hometown of Hewlett introduced us to him. That bakery—another place where we learned a great deal—is still there to this day and has been thriving in a world where most independent bakeries are a dying breed.

This dealer introduced us to the Comtec Pie Press. With the press of a button on this miracle laborsaving machine, we could stamp our dough into the pie pan, fluted border and all, in two seconds! Prior to that, we often felt as if we were spending our entire lives rolling dough by hand. We used to stand side by side in front of our worktable and have rolling contests set to music—Frank Sinatra, Tony Bennett, Ray Charles, and some rock and roll—to help pace us and get the work done a little faster. The pie press was revolutionary for us. The dealer also sold us two twenty-quart mixers, and so, *finally*, we graduated from our original kitchen Mix Masters (with ten times the capacity). Every single thing he sold us was secondhand and reconditioned, but it all worked just as if it were brand-new. He also taught us a lot about the bakery business, pointing out where we could go to find potential new customers and for better sources of supplies, as well as encouraging us to raise prices a bit.

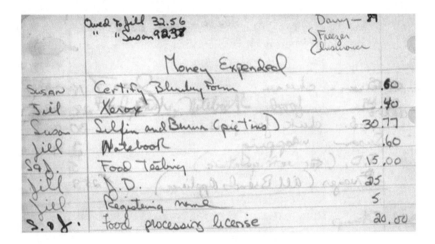

What we had going was still embarrassingly rudimentary, however. We *did* start keeping records several months in, but they were just running lists that we jotted down on whatever paper we could find.

We called our receivables "owables," our term for "those who owed us"! Of course, we had no "payables" because we had no credit and had to pay for everything up front. Nevertheless, we were coming up on the end of our first year in business with a grand total of $23,597 in gross sales! On our tax return we showed our cost of labor for the year as being $222, so we must have paid somebody for something, but for what, I can't recall. We were still unaware that our own labor even counted; we were just feeling our way.

Up to that point, even with Jill's and my discounted labor of $0 per hour, we still had no profit. Businesses exist to make a profit, not to fill up the day. We had yet to figure out that simple tenet. (About that time we hired a young accountant fresh out of school. Ours was considered a "shoebox business," one in which all receipts, sales, purchases, employee records, notes, etc. were kept on scraps of paper in a small box that we would hand over to him at the end of the year. It was our hope that he would make some sense out of it all.)

Nevertheless, some patterns began to emerge. At first Jill and I generally shopped, baked, and developed new products together, but little by little, Jill became more the inside person holding down the fort, and I became more the outside sales "expert." By now we were paying our friends for their time, and Jill did the payroll each week. As she confided to me recently, at that time this was an agonizing learning curve. *Still* we continued to grow, and the garage began to get really crowded. We were in the second half of our first year, a transitional period for us.

At that point we were still selling only quiches and pecan pie in about equal amounts, but we were definitely ready to add to our repertoire. We started by adding other desserts. We would try out our recipes on our friends during the weekends to see which ones they liked best. This was a lesson in learning from your customers! We started producing a delicious cheesecake in a nine-inch pie pan because that was still the *only* pan size we had, and then we added a few apple slices to make an apple cheesecake. One day we dropped an entire pail of cheesecake batter on the floor, but we had all these lovely apples prepared already, which prompted the accidental birth of our Swiss Apple Tart. There was just enough cheesecake batter left in which to bathe the apples, so—*voilà*—our third product! I assume that we added a chocolate dessert shortly after this, too, because there was still chocolate on the ceiling in my kitchen for the next fifteen years until I got around to redoing it.

Keystone Kops antics kept up all throughout the early days. First, we experienced what we termed our great Pecan Pie Disaster. Classic pecan pie filling is extremely dense, and if there is the slightest flaw in the crust, the batter will seep through during baking and the crust will rise to the surface, just under the pecans. The result is upside-down pecan pies—not exactly salable. (Even we knew that!) As usual, we found this out the hard way. Once was bad enough, but when it happened a *second* time, we needed to do something about it. We laid out all thirty of the ruined pies on the table and started picking off the pecans to see what was just under the surface. To our dismay, it was the crust, not the filling. We started absentmindedly eating the caramelized pecans, one by one, until we had eaten *at least two pounds* each. Not a very good thing to have done. We didn't quite get sick, but we examined the prepared crusts a lot more carefully after that, closing any gaps before filling them with batter. Unfortunately a few errant pies slipped through, prompting our very first customer complaints.

Then there was the Pâté Disaster. In our desire to round out our offerings, we started producing a very elegant liver pâté for our very first account, the Windmill supermarket. But we had only a *bakery* license from the state; to make products with meat, you need to be USDA inspected. Our bakery inspector went crazy when she came in for a visit and saw the pâté in the fridge, and we went running to the Windmill to clear it all off the shelf. The inspector gave us a pass, but we should've known better. We *did* use bacon in the quiche, but after the pâté fiasco, we were careful to keep it to less than 3 percent of the total weight so that the USDA requirement wouldn't apply to us.

We still had no scales; everything was poured by eye. I suspect, now, that we always gave more, not less, so maybe that's one of the places that our hoped-for profits went. It should have been easy to figure out by the sad lack of growth in our bank account. Our friends still kept coming to help us out as we grew, and our kids still had to show up after school to help out. It was about then that my housekeeper, Bridget, my regal sidekick from my dinner party days, started spending a few hours a day in the garage with us. She was Bonne Femme's first real employee, even if she was only commuting from inside the house. She was our efficiency expert and would point out obvious ways to speed up our methods, making us feel somewhat silly.

Putting Quiche on the Map

After our first year in business, things started to accelerate at an almost dizzying pace. Our quaint little kitchen business, which hadn't even been my idea in the first place, was taking on a life of its own. For me, a former bored housewife, the process of growing into something big was exhilarating.

One of the most important steps in the process was meeting Marvin Paige. He was a well-regarded New York City restaurateur, and the brother of my college roommate was kind enough to introduce us. Marvin looked just like Santa Claus, had an outsized personality, and was very giving. He didn't know me from a hole in the wall, but he had the patience to spend countless hours on the phone teaching me all about the restaurant business before we even met in person. Meeting him changed everything!

Marvin introduced me to the manager of O'Neals' Baloon, a highly visible establishment across from Lincoln Center, and I was able to convince him to try my quiche as a lunch special to be served with salad. It proved so popular that it went onto the regular menu.

The rest is pretty much history. Pub after pub tried out our quiche and started ordering from us. Restaurant managers all over the city shared their ideas, and Bonne Femme picked up many more accounts, all by word of mouth.

I was running all over the city hawking my wares, and almost everywhere I went, the restaurant manager would try out our quiche. We were still the only quiche company around, so we had a head start before the field became crowded. This was between 1973 and 1974, a recessionary period during which you could shoot a cannon through a white tablecloth restaurant and not hit anybody. We, of course, did not invent the quiche, but we started the trend that popularized it as pub food. Jill and I began to realize that thanks to Marvin's introductions and the relative novelty of our product, Bonne Femme had a tiger by the tail.

We were still operating entirely out of my garage, and I was still delivering in my car, driving as fast as I dared, my trunk still stuffed with newspaper (my secret insulating material). I was making sales calls between deliveries, up Third Avenue and down Second. I had this ridiculous paper sign reading "*DELIVERY—5 minutes— BONNE FEMME*" that I would put on the windshield of my Chevy. All the police in the city must have been scratching their heads—"Who *is* this crazy lady?" But I never got a ticket, not even once!

The success of our quiche in restaurants across the city marked the beginning of the end of the Keystone Kops Quiche Factory. By now we had fifty or more accounts between New York City and Nassau County, where we started. We found ourselves out of space again, with no place to keep our finished inventory, so we started stashing it in our friends' freezers all over the neighborhood—a logistical nightmare.

Our fame was growing, and I was on the road at least three days a week. At this point Jill and I were definitely defining our roles and dividing the labor. And it looked as if we would reach almost $65,000 in sales by the end of our second year, maybe even $75,000.

I smile to myself when I recall the names of our original accounts, some of which are still going strong and have become icons in the city; others that are now known nationally and internationally, with many hundreds or thousands of units. More and more restaurants were trying out the quiche and our desserts. I already mentioned O'Neals' Baloon, which was owned by my new friend Michael O'Neal and his late brother, the actor Patrick O'Neal; there was Charlie's, P.J. Clarke's, J. G. Melon, the Wicked Wolf, Puffing Billy, Proof of the Pudding, the Grand Central Oyster Bar, and the iconic Copacabana nightclub. Another was the Peartrees, owned by Michael "Buzzy" O'Keeffe, who went on to open the River Café, today considered one of the finest restaurants in the country.

And then there was T.G.I. Friday's, long before it was sold and became the omnipresent global chain it is today. Besides Friday's there was also a Tuesday's and a Thursday's, also owned by Alan Stillman, as he began his long career as a successful restaurateur. I remember the delivery to Thursday's was really frightening, located as it was in the bowels of a building on 58th Street with dark, endless corridors that never ceased to scare the daylights out of me. I also remember with a smile that the manager of Friday's told me he always kept one of my pecan pies at home on top of his refrigerator; every night when he got home at three or four in the morning, he rewarded himself with a slice before falling into bed.

Our packaging was still quite rudimentary. We did not yet have boxes in which to pack our products since we simply would have had no place to store them. So we were still using plastic bags—and, I am embarrassed to admit, in some cases tinfoil. How I carried them into the restaurants I cannot imagine, but I am quite sure it must have made me look pretty foolish and unprofessional, which I, most definitely, still was.

During the process of our initial expansion, I learned one of my very big lessons in business. We were selling our newest product, a Chocolate Mixed Nut Pie, to a restaurant called Gertrude's on East 64th Street. It was one of those restaurants that was very hot—all the celebrities and beautiful people flocked there almost before the expression "beautiful people" existed. I got a call from Gertrude at one in the morning telling me she needed four more pies right away.

"Gertrude, do you realize what time it is?" I asked wearily.

"*You have to*, Susan!" she said. Of course, she was right, and it only took me a moment to realize it. Even back then I began to understand that customer service is as important as the product. I dragged myself out of bed, packed up the pies, and began the hour-long drive to Gertrude's.

By then I was getting some help with my deliveries; hardly anyone in our neighborhood left for the city without making a delivery—even people we hardly knew, friends of our friends.

We still had no real profits, but our reputation was growing, a fact that began causing problems. It got to the point where we had lots of retail customers driving up to the house to stock up on our products, and large delivery trucks were pulling into the driveway to bring us ingredients all week long. Once again, desperate for space, we also began a slow creep back into the house—back through the kitchen and into the dining room, the library, the sun porch.

Our neighbors were proud of us, and very protective, but the village was another story. We lived in an exclusive residential community, and finally we got the letter I had figured would show up eventually. In not-so-polite language, it suggested that the village thought it was time for Bonne Femme to move its operations elsewhere.

The next leg of our journey was about to begin.

Chapter 3

Becoming Love and Quiches (1974)

I didn't fail the test; I just found a hundred ways to do it wrong.
—Benjamin Franklin

With pressure from the village to move our burgeoning business elsewhere, we started to look for our first real space. We wanted a small building close to home, preferably somewhere our children could walk to after school and help us out. It had been just a little over a year since Bonne Femme got off the ground as not much more than a whim, but by April of 1974, we had located our first little shop.

The place we found was on Franklin Avenue in Hewlett, a small street across from the local firehouse and next to the train station. It was six hundred square feet of space, plus a big basement, and it was less than five minutes from where we both lived. Plus, the rent was only a few hundred dollars a month. To us it was pure paradise!

We actually had a little business going. We had a good starting base of customers, we had all of the New York metropolitan area open to us, and we were excited to see where we could take it. Jill already had a few misgivings—the amount and scope of work we were putting in was a bit more than she had bargained for—but I did not. I was all in.

Since we didn't want to sign the lease personally, we went to incorporate under the name Bonne Femme. Much to our dismay, the name was already being used by a beauty shop; as a result, our application was automatically turned down by New York State. We needed to think of another name—fast. Jill's aunt had bought us a gift of something she had run across in an antique shop; it was a framed embroidery sampler simply saying "Love and Quiches" in a lovely script. As a joke, and because we had to act very quickly, we decided to incorporate under the name Love and Quiches. We actually loved the name, so that was that. (We also recognized that this was a great name, and so we trademarked Love and Quiches in June 1976 when the company really started to grow.*) Jill and I each invested $6,000 to outfit the store. That might not seem like much, but it's amazing just how much you could buy for $12,000 in 1974. We certainly could have used more equipment, but what we already had would have to do for the moment. We designed the place on a scrap of paper, just like we kept our books, but we now had a little front office and retail space, a decently sized work space with a seven-by-eleven-foot walk-in freezer, a second Blodgett convection oven, a second big double-door Traulsen fridge, a small scullery, and storage space. We brought our pie press machine with us from the garage, and though I can't swear to it, there is a good chance that secondhand machine is still in use for small runs at our plant to this very day. We also bought two forty-quart Hobart mixers to complement the two twenty-quart mixers we brought with us from the garage.

---

* In 1995 we renamed the company Love and Quiches Desserts, and in 2013, Love & Quiches Gourmet. To simplify matters, however, I have used Love and Quiches throughout the book unless the historical context required me to use one of the other two names.

We decorated the front office by ourselves—even sewed up the curtains—but I must admit that our effort was pretty feeble, with no real style. Not exactly high end, but at the time we were very happy.

Some of the first visitors to our new shop were the firemen from across the street asking if they could get some "quickies." After a few bewildered moments, Jill and I realized what they meant. *Quiche* was not exactly a household word at the time, so there is the possibility that they were serious and not being snide. As we started getting our first walk-in buyers, mostly commuters on their way to or from the nearby train station, we picked up some other comical pronunciations; my favorite was the customer who kept coming back to get some more of our delicious "qui-SHAYS." We also sold "kwishes" and "knishes"!

In the shop we had only one desk, which Jill and I shared, but at first we had it facing the wall, with our backs to all the action. We sensed our error, and with one quick turn, a whole new world opened up! Now we could keep an eye on everything while we worked. Next, my father insisted that we buy an adding machine *with* a tape; without it, I always had to add everything twice to make sure of the numbers. Of course I resisted, like I resisted all of his advice, but he won that round, and my accounting work was cut in half. This was long before the age when computers came into universal use. Businesses at the time used the general ledger to keep their books. But we hadn't even gotten *that* far yet.

What remains a mystery is how we kept it all going. Though business with our restaurant customers was brisk, we still had no clue how to price our products properly, there was no profit, and a salary for each of us was out of the question. Every penny went to keep Love and Quiches afloat. Regardless, our little start-up seemed to take on a life of its own and we grew. What we should have invested in was some solid professional advice, but that never occurred to us. We just kept baking, and I continued to run up and down the streets of Manhattan collecting more customers for our quiches, pies, and cheesecakes.

Encouraged by my taking his advice about the adding machine, my amazed and proud father started hanging around almost nonstop as my accidental business developed. One day he would suggest we concentrate on only a few products, and then the next day he would come in with a huge folder spilling over with articles, recipes—everything from muffins to raspberry cakes to pizza—and new product ideas. He was disruptive and sometimes a nuisance, but welcome anytime.

The Silver Bullet

Now that we were out of the garage, I wasn't living over the store, and we were able to keep all of our inventory under one roof rather than having it dispersed all over the neighborhood—much easier to keep track of. But it was getting to be too much to deliver out of the trunk of my Chevy. It was exhausting, and because the number of stops I had to make was growing, delivering product to our customers without everything softening around the edges was becoming much too tricky. While newspaper worked just fine as an insulator when I had very few stops to make, it was only taking me so far.

Serendipity intervened. We bought all of our new equipment from the same supplier that we had used in the garage, and we recognized the young man who made the deliveries to our new shop. When Jill and I reminded him this was his second time around with us, his eyes got very wide, and he called and quit his job on the spot! Now it was *we* who were wide-eyed as he turned to us and asked for a job, explaining that he had a personal policy of not staying at any job for more than a year. The timing was perfect; Jill and I had been talking about hiring a driver. We hired Don, and soon after hurried out to buy our first truck! (Don ended up disobeying his own rule: he worked for me for *many* years, and he became plant manager just over two years after we hired him.)

We equipped Don with a secondhand truck from Avis. It was a well-used, slightly banged-up silver refrigerated van we dubbed the "Silver Bullet." With our first driver, I could expand my sales arena to include Greenwich Village and further downtown Manhattan, as well as Brooklyn and Queens.

Thanks to our young accountant, we kept simple but real books. One of our friends became our part-time bookkeeper. We had two other production workers to help with packing, cleanup, and the like, but Jill and I still did all the product development, mixing, and baking ourselves.

One of the very first smart things we did as business owners was to raise our prices just a bit shortly after we moved into the new shop. Nobody complained, and that should have signaled to us that our prices were too low to begin with, but we were just happy with the very-much-needed extra income. Now we had time to expand our customer base and our product line at a steadier pace.

I could almost still taste some of Evelina's scrumptious desserts from my childhood, and three of her specialties were the inspiration for some of our next dessert products. Her lemon cream and chocolate cream pies and her sour cream coffee cake were largely the inspiration for our Lemon Mousse Pie, our Chocolate Mousse Pie, and our delicious Evie's Coffee Cake. We didn't have her recipes, but Jill and I were good enough by then to replicate them closely enough, and maybe even a little bit better. From Jill came our spectacular brownies in a half sheet pan, and together we developed a Raspberry Glazed Bread Pudding.

It began to dawn on us that we needed to make some changes—some subtle, some a bit larger—in order to move forward and compete on a more level playing field with other products available in the marketplace. Our customers were done with the plastic bags, a fact they let us know quite forcefully. So now that we fortuitously had the space, we *finally* started to pack our cakes for delivery in corrugated boxes. The basement at the shop was filled to the brim with cake boxes. Boxes then could not be made to customer specifications as they are today, so we had to find ones from local suppliers around town that "almost" fit the bill. Anything was a vast improvement over the bags, though.

We also realized that if we wanted to sell more cheesecake, we would have to change to a ten-inch straight-sided pan, such as was being used for *all* the other cheesecakes available in the marketplace. Up till then, we were only offering our *one* nine-inch size for all of our quiches, cheesecakes, and pies. We continued to roll the dough by hand for our six-inch quiches, which were intended for our limited local retail business, but because our original secondhand pie press came with only one die, we still offered just that single pan size to our restaurant accounts. Obviously, we had not yet been demonstrating very good marketing, a word not yet in our lexicon. As usual, still clueless, we had not realized that we could order additional dies to use on our pie press, from three inches to fourteen inches, with either straight or sloping sides. One phone call and we could have learned all this. With the introduction of our straight-sided ten-inch pan, we were learning the lesson of competition, of answering the needs of our customers rather than the other way around.

Selecting from the new array of pans available to us did result in one big mistake, though. We went out and bought a few dozen ten-inch springform pans at the hardware store, but it never occurred to us that they were not intended to be used commercially. They became so flimsy from repeated use that the pans became misshapen; more and more of the cheesecake batter would leak onto the bun pans beneath them, so the cheesecakes became thinner and thinner as time went on. We still had not awakened to the fact that our products needed to be the *exact weight* we said they would be. We were delivering cheesecakes with weights that were all over the place, some of them tissue thin!

All this led to one of my more embarrassing customer-supplier moments, one that I will never forget. One of our good customers was a seafood place called Nodeldini's. The owners had another restaurant called One Fish Two Fish, still there on Madison and 97th, and at one point there was a third place also. Around this time, Nodeldini's stopped taking orders from us, citing problems with the products we were delivering. The owner at the time knew that I'd be back once I got my act together. A few years later, when I made an appointment to try to resell him my desserts, he took me into his office where he had a small freezer. He lifted out the last cheesecake I had delivered, so thin it practically disappeared when held sideways! I was nonplussed, but thanked him for saving it all these years to show me. We both burst out laughing, and I got the account back! I was *always* good at sales.

As we successfully transitioned from Bonne Femme to Love and Quiches, I somehow spontaneously became known as "The Quiche Lady," a moniker that follows me to this very day, even among our most prominent national and international clients (despite the fact that we now sell mostly desserts). Our roster of restaurant customers kept growing: the All Star Café on West 72nd Street (only very recently closed); the Barking Fish; Rusty's, owned by the famous baseball player Rusty Staub; and Daly's Dandelion, owned by the bandleader Skitch Henderson and his wife, Fay Emerson, a popular actress and performer. In Greenwich Village there was the Riviera Café, the Buffalo Roadhouse, The Elephant and Castle, and the Lion's Head (where Jessica Lange was waitressing) before its current incarnation as the superhot The Lion. And so many more. All of these hark back to a lifetime ago, far from where we are today.

With all these customers to please, our new driver Don had to really hit the road early each morning in the Silver Bullet. More than once the van broke down—it was, after all, on its last legs when we bought it. On one of these occasions, we learned that . . . let's just say that Don still needed to grow up a little. True to form, he abandoned the stopped truck on the side of the Van Wyck Expressway. But he took the last couple of orders with him and managed to get them delivered; don't ask me how.

Jill and I had another set of keys and went to rescue the van. As it happened, just in front of our truck sat another abandoned truck being looted by two very large and unsavory looking characters. The truck thieves assured us that they were *only* interested in the truck they were in the midst of stealing, and that we could proceed to steal ours in peace! Incidents like that happened to us all the time, but at least we kept our sense of humor, and we could laugh as these crazy—sometimes dangerous—events occurred.

More Products, More Growing Pains

Another one of our customers requested a product that in later years precipitated one of the most pivotal leaps that Love and Quiches ever made. We were servicing Ellen's, a very exclusive gourmet shop on the Upper East Side, and the owner was catering a dinner party for Jacqueline Kennedy. He asked us if we could bake our delicious brownies *in the round* rather than in the traditional oblong pan. Thus was born our famous Pecan Brownie Pie, which he served on beautiful plates in wedges adorned with whipped cream and berries. Peter, the owner, was also our first customer for Frozen Lemon Soufflé. (These were prepared in the infamous springform pans, but by then we knew better and lined the pans to prevent seepage.) Shortly thereafter we transitioned to heavier weight commercial cake and pie pans, and we ordered more dies for our pie press. Little by little, we were evolving.

This was still just in our second year of operation, but we also had added a Mocha Cheesecake in our line that Frank Sinatra had apparently been served and loved. Somehow the dessert was traced back to us, and we were asked to deliver one to the Westbury Music Theater when he was performing there. Funny how certain small memories stay with you.

Then we introduced our Trianon, an exquisite bittersweet chocolate truffle cake (from a recipe I had used in my cooking classes) that we still produce today, more than forty years later, in several shapes and sizes. It remains one of our premier desserts, and it's among my favorites.

Our products were superb, but this fact alone didn't turn us into businesspeople. There were still no profits. Jill and I continued doing all the baking, and I had dozens of burns in uniform stripes all up and down my arms, like badges of honor. Jill must have been more careful because I don't remember her having quite as many burns as I did, but I do remember having to wear long sleeves (even in summer) to cover them when I went on sales calls. The scars finally faded, but it took twenty years.

We'd been in our new shop for about six months when some-thing changed for both Jill and me. We had started the business as a lark, but this was no longer a hobby or a part-time enterprise where we could show up if and when we felt like it; it had become very hard work. Love and Quiches seemed to have its own momentum and life. It seemed we weren't having fun anymore—or at least, as I learned, Jill wasn't.

Chapter 4

The Transition (1975)

*We cannot solve our problems with the same thinking
we used when we created them.*
—Albert Einstein

One day in the early spring of 1975, I was tramping up and
down Third Avenue making sales calls in the city. I was following my usual procedure: I would knock on any door that
looked as if my products would be a good fit, and I left a price sheet
and a sample or two. If the manager was in, I did my pitch then and
there; otherwise, I would call back for an appointment. After a couple
of meetings, I rounded a corner and there was a friend of mine and a
business associate of Irwin's—David—walking with a neighbor of his.
David introduced me to his friend, and we got to talking about Le
Snac, the fast-food café he'd just opened. It had a French motif, the
only problem being that he had nothing French to offer but the mustard. When David told his friend about my business, he expressed his

disbelief at the lucky coincidence and ordered two hundred quiches on the spot. He wanted them delivered very soon. For Love and Quiches—which at this time was still selling "eaches," not cases—this was a gargantuan order, our biggest so far.

As soon as we parted, I found a pay phone and called Jill. "We've got an order for two hundred quiche Lorraine—and he needs them before the end of the week!" I told her. "Start making dough and frying the bacon—I'll be right back."

When I got back to the shop in Hewlett, she'd started all the prep, and we worked on the quiches all through the night: me driven by excitement, Jill going through the motions, frustrated.

The next week, when Le Snac placed its second order—for *four hundred* quiches—the gulf between my approach to the business and Jill's became more apparent. Where Jill saw our endeavor as a side pursuit, I *needed* to make this work. In the short span of time since we had started Bonne Femme, I'd started to feel ambition growing inside me, and I wanted to keep going. Another big difference between Jill and me was the fact that I had the support of my husband. For a traditional suburban housewife in the early seventies, this was important. Even in the early days, I realized with great certainty that without Irwin's unfailing support, I would never have been able to build this business. Jill's husband, on the other hand, advised her against continuing, as did the rest of her family. She had more children than I did, as well as more social responsibilities, and although she really loved what she was doing, she could not devote the necessary time to take the steps to make the business profitable.

In other words, she couldn't get serious about Love and Quiches, even though I was very much ready to. With our visions of the future so out of line, I often found myself alone in the shop at the end of the day holding the bag. Out of sheer frustration at this, I would sometimes eat coffee cakes straight from the freezer, a practice I would not recommend to anyone else—especially since it doesn't solve anything.

So, Jill and I found ourselves at a crossroads. We still had no real business plan or vision and, more importantly, there was no profit, although by that point we were doing just enough volume to cover our overhead. With no profit, a business cannot survive. We were learning that growth does not solve problems; it merely amplifies them if you're not ready. We were not ready. Most small or start-up companies suffer from the same shortcomings: a lack of effective planning and enough capital to get through the first year or so. We had continued to make pivotal leaps forward, but all the while we were still doing *everything* wrong. We were so busy *looking* but *not seeing* where we were going. We didn't recognize growth opportunities, make relevant decisions, or act on them. Luck can only carry you so far. Then it's over. We had thought our venture would be an extension of our love of food and cooking, but experience proved us wrong.

Shortly after our two giant Le Snac orders, Jill came to me and said she wanted out. For her, it was over. Love and Quiches was going nowhere, and now my partner had cried uncle. The prospect of losing her overwhelmed me, but what could I do? I understood. It *was* over.

In March 1975, I bought Jill out for $12,000: $6,000 for her conception—the enterprise was her idea in the first place, and I will always be grateful for that—and $6,000 for her half of our expenses in fitting out the shop.

Jill and I remained friends during her departure and are still friends all these many years later. Shortly after she left, Jill started another business making rugelach (rolled cookies with various fillings in a cream cheese pastry dough), which she ran for a while out of her home. The work was just as hard, since the cookies were all handmade, but she could at least control the hours. No more all-night quiche-making sessions. (Many years later, after Love and Quiches had grown up, Jill told me that somebody at a party had once asked her if I had bought her out for $5 million!)

On My Own

As I surveyed the state of Love and Quiches in the weeks after I bought out Jill, I saw that I needed to shift my strategy. We had been gaining assets, buying more equipment with the proceeds from our sales, but we were also incurring liabilities. On balance, we were making no money, and ultimately we ran short. We weren't far removed from the days when we'd kept records in our heads—we even kept track of our receivables that way. Incorporating should have lent structure to our enterprise, or at least made us aware that we had a commitment to succeed, but we never really took that next step. We "appeared" to be organized: our accountant set up our books, we did payroll, we ran the Silver Bullet, and we increased our sales to over $75,000. But we still didn't know where we were going or how we were going to get there. I wonder, on occasion, why it took us so long to come to grips with our potential. Every time it became apparent that we'd better sit down and think, we'd be anxious to "get back to work"—as if planning ahead wasn't work, but frying bacon was!

We hadn't defined our goals and we weren't controlling our costs, buying well, or pricing our products properly. We paid no attention to vital details that virtually define success: we didn't realize that pennies counted, and we didn't know that we were also a service business and therefore had better provide good service along with our products. By now we should have been polishing our image, but instead we had remained in our original mindset: clueless.

The wholesale food processing business, as with any business involving production and service, is a full-time commitment, especially when there is established competition. It takes a tremendous amount of work, and we weren't good enough. We had started losing accounts at about the same rate as we were getting them because our service wasn't very good and our quality was uneven. The taste was there, but as I pointed out earlier, the weights were anybody's guess.

Our problems were those often faced by small businesses: we lacked capital, we lacked management and technical assistance, and we had no formal technical training in our particular field. We had no understanding of finance, and we were inexperienced about marketing and buying opportunities. In sum, we *still* had no preparation whatsoever for business ownership, which put us at a great disadvantage.

Now what? I found myself alone in the enterprise. It was a lonely feeling at first, but exciting too. There were a lot of possibilities ahead, and I wanted to stick around to see how the story ended. I was *way* out of my comfort zone, but I had bought my own business, and I had to assess what I had bought. I knew I might be in for the ride of my life, along with plenty of potential heartbreak—yet, at the very least, I wanted some payback for all of the burns I had suffered up and down my arms.

We were a young married couple with two children, a big house, and very little money. Yet, this recessionary period during which we rolled our first dough provided Love and Quiches with its start; we saw the rise of the pub without a pastry chef. This became my motivator.

With Jill gone and a few rudimentary business lessons under my belt, I knew I needed to turn things around. This is the point at which I launched the real business. I stopped dead in my tracks and made a fresh beginning. The very first step I took was to create an informal business plan. I outlined the scope of my operation: what I hoped to achieve, and what I needed to do. A more formal plan followed, detailing both the big picture and the smaller ones. This more formal plan detailed my rudimentary strategy and tentative marketing plans. I realized that even without Jill I could rely on a strong network for help: I had my accountant, my family, my friends, my mentor Marvin Paige, and anybody else I could get my hands on to answer my questions. I was learning fast and furiously.

The one constant of my endeavor was my own ability to sell. I had to develop an organization that could meet the demands created by my sales out front. This was true even in that first small shop on Franklin Avenue where we were operating. I was virtually starting again. I had so very much to accomplish in a dozen areas, and I had to do it right away or I would lose the momentum we had most definitely created but could not control.

I knew I had to gather the cash to get me through the next year or two, until I could develop a positive cash flow. (Yes, I finally knew what the term "cash flow" meant!) And I simply knew, with innocent clarity, that I wasn't going to *allow* myself to fail. I broke a lot of my own rules along the way, but I did what I had to do. I'm still here.

I was also mindful not to invest more than I could afford to lose, however little that was, just in case I was wrong and couldn't pull it off. And unlike Jill's and my initial mindless ideas, I would be doing it for the *money*, not the *glory*, which could carry me just so far.

Even though I was still using handwritten index cards, I now knew my formulas and all my costs. I borrowed $15,000 from my father (the only time he directly helped me financially) to give me some breathing room, and little by little, I righted the ship. My capital limited my participation in the marketplace. I developed the ability to know those limits and to rely on my budget. And then my business did begin to grow, and then to grow again.

I was working twelve- to fourteen-hour days, but I was thinking and planning all 24/7. I had my one or two employees and Don, my driver, who would pitch in with production when he wasn't on the road. Soon after Jill left, Bridget started coming with me to work in the shop almost every day, just as she had done when we ran Bonne Femme in the garage. But now she wanted to know when "we" were going to get someone in to clean the house!

In spite of all this, there *was* a home front, and I needed to keep at least a semblance of order while all this was going on. I will discuss how we kept it all together later in my narrative, in chapter 17, "Family Matters."

At this point I was still the baker, salesman, and chief bottle washer; yet the business by mid-1975 had grown to well over $100,000 per year in volume. Our reputation came through the turmoil of my partnership breakup intact; our products were still delicious; and, more importantly, they were always consistent. I was now able to breathe a little easier and have some fun, too.

Then someone new walked into my life, and everything changed again.

Jimmy the Baker

Shortly after Jill left the business, an acquaintance of mine called me to ask if I would be interested in meeting the husband of her housekeeper, who was a trained baker. The husband, James Gilliam, was out of work due to an injury, but he was looking for something he could do for a few hours a week. It was this chance introduction that brought the man who was to become Love and Quiches' head baker into the fold.

Jimmy the Baker, as he will be called from here on in the book, was a black man who got his professional training in the navy. At the time, a man of color, at least in civilian life, was not often given the chance to be considered a head baker. We were still in the mid-seventies, and this was the reality, even if it was the North. Instead, bakeries had employed Jimmy merely as a benchman. Yet I was told by many of my suppliers during those early years that Jimmy always *ran* the local bakeries in which he worked. He was a legend in the regional bakery industry.

Jimmy came to work for me in 1975, and I found out very quickly that old-fashioned bakers are strictly nocturnal beings. He worked only at night, dressed in his crisp whites, no matter how hard I tried to convince him otherwise. I soon got used to arriving in the morning to find all the day's production completed and perfect. Gone were the days of tissue-thin cheesecakes! We still were making the quiches during the day, but Jimmy took on all the desserts. Now I was able to introduce a variety of layer cakes from Jimmy's recipes, chocolate and carrot to start, then a few others, in this tiny shop.

Jimmy was also a superb bread baker. And although we have never sold any yeast products commercially, just to keep in practice he often baked a few racks of the most wonderful French breads—including, sometimes, brioche—for the staff. We devoured it all, slathered in butter, within minutes of starting our day. I was always reminded of Evelina and *her* bread when Jimmy treated us to *his* bread.

Jimmy was stubborn and had a quick temper, but everybody loved him. He was all business, but he had a soft side if you sought it out. He lived a few towns over, and his house was by far the most well kept on the block, with not a twig out of place. This is the same way he handled everything in our little shop. When I arrived in the morning, everything was sparkling, and, if he had not already left for the day, I was always amazed to see that he had not a drop of chocolate on his crisp whites.

Onward and Upward

By mid-1976 I knew a lot more about running a business, and with Jimmy's help, experience, and knowledge, we were really moving ahead. Love and Quiches was doing several hundreds of thousands of dollars in volume and generating a profit for the first time in its short history!

We were gaining ground every week in our little storefront. Jimmy the Baker was turning out gorgeous desserts every night, our sizes and varieties of quiche were growing a little, and Don was maturing by the minute, taking on some management responsibilities inside the shop in addition to making deliveries a bit farther afield, from Staten Island to Brooklyn to Long Island and every place in between. Also by mid-1976, we had about seven or eight full-time employees (one or two of whom would stay with us for decades).

Our roster of customers continued to grow, though we were still a local supplier doing "store door" deliveries in our own trucks. We had no distributors yet; I'm not sure I even knew then what a distributor could actually do for me. We still had most of our original customers—including our first, the Windmill—but we now had many more *in* the city, where I had concentrated my sales efforts. One of our newer customers right in Manhattan was a café opened by "society" restaurateur George Lang in the new Citicorp building. George was also the proprietor of the venerable Café Des Artistes (which has only recently closed), and his lavish apartment was famous for its spectacular green jade bathtub. George moved in rarified circles, but it didn't stop him from beating me out of $1,700 in receivables when they folded the Citi-corp Café. I was outraged, but when I protested, my only answer from his management was, "Grow up, girlie!" This turned out to be a fairly cheap education, because since then we have kept a very tight rein on our receivables.

We were also polishing up our image with sturdier packaging and more professional labeling. The resultant improved handling provided savings in labor and also eliminated waste. We moved to printed ingre-dient labels, eliminating our rather childish practice of filling out our labels by hand, running them off on a copier at a local stationery shop with ink that smudged and ran, and then cutting them out one by one. How ridiculous was that? Turned out that our hand-cut labels cost us more than our new printed ones once you counted in the labor, which we were finally beginning to do.

Chocolate Mousse Pie

The Pastry flour, butter, sugar, vegetable shortening, water, ground walnuts, grated chocolate, baking soda, spices.

The Filling heavy sweet cream, sugar cocoa, rum, pure almond extract, and LOVE.

SERVE CHILLED!

NT, WT,

We retired the Silver Bullet and bought our first real freezer truck. It was hot pink this time, and printed on its side in professionally drawn white letters were our address, our telephone numbers, and our newly stylized logo. We had appropriated the lady with the rolling pin (part of our logo until recently) from an image my college roommate found for me in a children's coloring book. Trucks are great "vehicles" for advertising! Losing my homespun style and image gave me further entrée into some larger foodservice organizations.

An Accidental Favor from Jill

Once again, something accidental that proved pivotal precipitated our move to our first industrial space. On January 17, 1976, Jill was written up in a human interest story by the *New York Times*. It was an article about a woman who had started a business from scratch but decided to leave it, returning home to find a much smaller enterprise in which she could control her time, rather than the other way around.

From that *Times* article I received a phone call from the foodservice director at Columbia University. Columbia did a tremendous amount of catering and became a very large customer of ours. As was often the case with my customers, the director and I also became good friends for many years, until he moved out of the state after accepting another position.

The article also attracted the attention of the buyer who ran the restaurants in Bamberger's department stores, later bought and absorbed into Macy's. This was my first large multiunit account; the company had fourteen stores from the New York metro area all the way down to Maryland. For the first few months, my patient and supportive husband made the delivery run (fourteen hours!) in our shiny new truck once every other week, until the buyer put us together with his meat and produce supplier. This supplier became our very first distributor and "delivered" Irwin from his grueling ordeal!

Just as Bonne Femme had in my garage, Love and Quiches was straining at the seams. Stuff was piled up everywhere, there was no room for much-needed new equipment, and we had no real bakery ovens. Far worse, there wasn't nearly as much freezer storage as we now needed in the wake of the article—and we were, after all, a frozen foods business! Although this little storefront in Hewlett had served us well, I knew I wouldn't miss the cluttered place for a second. We were at the end of our rope, and I knew we had to get out of there— and fast!

Chapter 5

The Mini-Factory (1976–1980)

Whenever you take a step forward,
you are bound to disturb something.
—Indira Gandhi

I didn't want to move far, no more than five or ten minutes from home. Irwin, always ready to help me, was my sidekick in my search for new space. We started by driving in small concentric circles around the Hewlett location in our Chevy, zeroing in on commercial areas in nearby towns. One day we were cruising around Oceanside, two towns over and about ten minutes from our shop, when we noticed a For Rent sign that looked promising. It stood in front of a neat-looking one-story building with a brick façade. Though the building had no loading dock, it did have a wide garage door that would allow our truck to back up close to load up in the mornings. The building was on a wide boulevard, a main route to all the beaches—including Jones Beach—and we realized that this spot, if it worked out, would help us pick up a lot more retail walk-ins even as we kept our current customers, since it was so close to the old space. It was perfect!

Irwin and I knocked on the door of the building and met my soon-to-be new landlord. He invited us in, and I was immediately struck by the vastness of the space before me. This building was five thousand square feet, but coming from our tiny shop, it might as well have been a hundred thousand. The rent that went along with the giant building—$1,200 a month—seemed a princely sum for us in 1976, but we felt we could swing it. By this point we were doing over $300,000 a year in volume, and expansion to a bigger facility was mandatory. But could we afford to outfit such a cavernous space?

Within a week we'd decided to go for it, and we signed the lease for the Oceanside facility for five years with the right of renewal. For this move, I needed some working capital, and I managed to secure a $200,000 loan from a bank that my father, albeit grudgingly, introduced me to. Love and Quiches wasn't yet considered bankable. My father also grudgingly put up securities as collateral, which was the *only* way I could secure the loan. He wasn't very happy about that, and neither was I.

We were, at this juncture, still a do-it-yourself organization with extremely limited resources, so we designed the shop floor ourselves with some advice from our equipment suppliers. My father-in-law, a retired plumbing contractor, did the plumbing work, and we used local electricians, carpenters, handymen, and other assorted characters to do the other necessary remodeling. We had a few mini-disasters, including one that involved a handyman named Willie and bright, raspberry-colored paint all over our sidewalks and window glass. ("I told you, I *cain't paint!*" was Willie's defense.) Finally, up went our great big Love and Quiches sign, and we were almost ready to move in.

In Oceanside, we could handle real equipment. The secondhand bakery equipment supplier whom we had met when we bought our first pie press for the garage sold us a Middleby Marshall rotary oven. It was a reconditioned twenty-four-pan gas oven with six shelves that rotated like a Ferris wheel so that the product was constantly moving through the heat. (Later, we added a second rotary oven with an eighteen-pan capacity.) The installation of our first Middleby Marshall was a major case of taking my company to the next level for me, but it was business as usual for Jimmy the Baker; he was used to real machinery.

My mentor Marvin Paige introduced me to another equipment supplier—a guy named Jack Harris, who became a mentor to me himself—who sold me a very large storage freezer for the baking side of our new workspace. Shortly after, he sold me another freezer— this one for the packing side—that made the previous one look tiny. It was about eighteen feet by twenty-four feet, almost the size of our first shop! This holding freezer enabled the staff to operate more efficiently by providing them with a place to store longer runs and to stage orders for shipping each morning. We were still delivering directly to our restaurant accounts, which meant we had a lot of very tiny orders to pack daily—two of this, one of that, and one of the other thing. (Yes, we were still selling eaches, not cases. The thought of cases hadn't yet occurred to me. Still clueless!)

We bought plenty more racks, more mixers—some holding 180 quarts!—and more pans. Finally, we were ready for a *real* education in the industry. I had a feeling that *this* facility would be my proving ground, and I was right.

Love and Quiches Begins to Grow Up

Our years in Oceanside gave us time to grow both as a company and as an organization. We were rounding out the company with a growing number of support staff as the company began to take on more shape. With Jimmy the Baker to help, our product line was still growing. He was training our young recruits in mixing, baking, and cake decoration (or "deco" in bakery manufacturing parlance).

At first the front office was run by my friend who had moved with us from the first small shop across from the firehouse. After she announced that she had not intended to be working so hard and was leaving, she was followed by a more experienced head bookkeeper, Mildred, who stayed with us for the rest of our time in Oceanside. She was an old-fashioned bookkeeper who was ardently committed to her manual ledger and had no use for the encroaching wave of computerization. We also hired a customer service rep who called our customers weekly, sometimes daily, for their orders. All of our invoicing was still done by hand, but at least we wrote them out on printed triplicate forms. This was an important baby step for us, one among many others that had begun to add up. We also started to do a bit of almost embarrassingly rudimentary advertising in local newspapers to attract more walk-in retail customers, and we set up a tiny area in the front office as a retail counter.

Pictured, a few of our early advertisements.

Purchasing responsibilities were shared by whoever was around and had some free time in the front office, since this function did not warrant a full-time position as of yet. We were still a fairly small business, but even so, we used quite a few suppliers. Under Jimmy's tutelage, we always compared prices to keep them competitive. Jimmy the Baker was familiar with all the local distributors, so he compiled the list of needed supplies, and the rest of us pitched in to make sure he got what he wanted.

We bought another truck; this one was white with raspberry lettering instead of the other way around, because the hot pink on the first truck had faded pretty quickly into a really dull color. Naturally another truck meant another driver—actually two because Don finally moved inside full time as the day manager, while Jimmy the Baker ran the night crew.

We had an endless supply of young people who wanted jobs, all of whom were friends and had grown up together in the neighborhood. They became our drivers, and soon we bought another and yet another truck. The new employees also became production workers, cake decorators, packers, cleaning crew, and all the other roles that evolved as we grew. We used to call them the "Motley Crew," and I loved them all dearly. Many of them stayed with us for many years, growing up and into management positions before moving on.

You'll recall my earlier comment that we tried our best to keep our sense of humor, but running our own trucks was, admittedly, a headache. Today we have strict inventory control and can account for every brownie, but back then, we had a few entrepreneurial drivers who would, on occasion, help themselves to a few cakes with the hope of selling them on their own. Luckily we had loyal customers who would call to let us know about this. One driver, still just a kid with a license, approached Marvin Paige, of all people, offering him our quiches at a great discount. Big mistake—end of job. Another time, two of our drivers had an accident—with each other! On the highway! When one of them called to inform us, we asked, thinking they were doing a route together, "Who was driving?" The sheepish response: "Both of us."

My favorite driver story features a young man who was tall, very handsome, well muscled, and tattooed. Most of the time he wore a torn sleeveless T-shirt, even when it was cold outside. He was, at heart, a very gentle person in spite of his tough appearance. When he wasn't making deliveries, I used to have him drive me around to my sales appointments in the city. He had this knack of maneuvering behind emergency vehicles and then speeding along when all the other traffic was stopped along the sides of the street. I would slide down in my seat with my hands covering my eyes, but I didn't stop him from doing it because, I must admit, I was able to make more than twice as many stops as I did when driving myself around. I was able to make at least ten sales calls on the days when *he* drove me around, and he was also good company. One time we stopped for lunch at one of our customers' establishments. Once we sat down, I noticed that half a dozen women from my neighborhood who knew me from my former life were seated nearby, and all of them were staring at me with this hunk with decidedly dropped jaws. All I did was smile and wave, happy to give them something to gossip about.

Then there was Jimmy (not the baker), another driver who used one of our trucks to go out on dates because he didn't have a car of his own. He also used it to go upstate with his father to pick up a load of Christmas trees during the holidays—only he never asked permission.

On occasion we found ourselves bailing one or two of our drivers out of jail. Nothing too heavy, all minor stuff, but we were all part of the Love and Quiches family, and I felt responsible for them all! We always gave our employees the benefit of the doubt whenever possible, saying, jokingly, that you had to practically be a murderer to get fired from Love and Quiches. Of course, now we hold our employees to another standard, but in those days, we were all learning together and things were quite a bit more casual.

But what we still didn't know could fill volumes. I remember so very clearly that workers were *smoking* on the production floor! I have never smoked, but almost all young people at that time did. It was cool to smoke, and I didn't know enough at first to stop them. And we would keep the doors open on hot days, another great sin. This was obviously before stricter rules became the protocol. Yet we were getting regular unannounced audits from the New York State Department of Agriculture, and we always got good scores. It is hard to fathom how we could have been so ignorant of how things should have been done, given how we operate today. Now we spend as much time cleaning and sanitizing as we do producing, with the production areas all separated from outside areas with curtains, doors, and anterooms. I am grateful that my instincts finally took over, and I put a stop to what had been going on.

Our accounts now numbered more than 250, and we were holding on to them because our quality stayed high—in spite of everything just confessed—and our service, *finally*, had become quite good and reliable. Our reputation as a high-end supplier was growing.

Restaurant managers all over the city unselfishly shared their secrets, so a lot of them helped me grow the company by spreading the word about our products. I admit that I was beginning to have a lot of fun selling despite its grueling aspects. I was meeting tons of people and becoming an accepted member of the restaurant/supplier community. Our minimum order was only $50; needless to say, we had to make a lot of deliveries. Our only out-of-town account was still Bamberger's, and it was serviced through our one and only distributor.

Our primary product line remained quiche, though the dessert line would surpass it in volume within a few years. To our foodservice customers, we offered quiches already baked, no longer frozen raw. We had quite a few sizes of quiche in at least fifteen varieties, from the usual broccoli, spinach, and Lorraine to asparagus, artichoke, and smoked salmon. Our dessert offerings grew with the addition of Black Forest Cake, German Chocolate Cake, Lemon Raspberry Cake, and other cake varieties. I now see that we had too many varieties in our lines given our setup at the time; we hadn't yet learned about "product rationalization," whereby products are analyzed by comparative sales and the slower movers are eliminated.

Our base of supermarket customers was growing, too. Shortly after the move to Oceanside, we managed to complete a sale to a group of markets called Mel Weitz's Foodtown—about fifteen stores, our first supermarket sale since the Windmill. We were also selling our quiches to Waldbaum's (now part of A&P), partly because Mrs. Waldbaum had been one of our customers from as far back as my garage days.

Sadly, though, I got a phone call from Ira Waldbaum himself one day to inform me that they were dropping our product line. He explained that retailing was a different animal, one that required extensive marketing dollars (which we did not have), and he apologized more than once during our conversation. (Actually, we didn't care about losing the account that much. Our deliveries to their hectic warehouse were always an ordeal; our little trucks were dwarfed by the tractor trailers all lined up. Our drivers cheered when they heard the news!)

As we got settled into our new home, we felt secure in our growing number of customers. But very quickly I realized that I would *really* have to hit the road selling if we wanted to keep it up. It was becoming increasingly apparent that we weren't the only ones out there. We had competition, and plenty of it.

Enter the Competition

Our core business was still comprised of restaurant accounts, so I spent most of my time selling in that arena. But I was not alone. By now several other companies had entered the scene, including companies dedicated to quiche and others that just sold desserts. There was Quiche and Tell, Food Gems, and Miss Grimble. (This last one is still around, I think, after several changes in ownership. The original owner was a woman named Sylvia Hirsch, and I clearly remember the scandalous story of how she sued her daughter for publishing some of their recipes in a cookbook without permission.) There was also Umanoff & Parsons and Country Epicure (sold early on to a Japanese croissant company Vie de France). There were others, but these are the ones with whom we constantly found ourselves going head to head while still in the local arena.

The original founder of Food Gems, a quiche company that has gone through ownership and name changes, used to actually follow our trucks. He would wait outside while our driver made the delivery, and then he would wave to the driver and laugh as he headed inside with a sample in his hand. This went on for quite a while. Needless to say, our drivers weren't too happy about this and explained to him exactly what they were likely to do if he didn't stop following them. We received a letter shortly thereafter accusing us of "hooliganism" of all things! Nothing ever came of it; he finally stopped because our drivers were big guys, and I guess he weighed the risk/reward factor.

Competition from other dessert companies located all over the country also grew and kept us on our toes. This never changed, and the battle continues. It took a while, but I eventually learned from all of this that there is enough business to go around if you stay calm and focus on what you do best.

New York Stories

Deep down in my heart of hearts, this will always be a New York story, even though for most of its life Love and Quiches has been a national, and, ultimately, a global supplier of bakery products. After all, we honed our skills supplying quiches and desserts to many hundreds of foodservice establishments in the New York metro area.

At this juncture, we also joined a few industry organizations, including the New York State Restaurant Association and the Eastern Dairy Deli Association. Joining the former brought us quite a few steps ahead because I showed up at *all* of the meetings, even board meetings. (I wasn't on the board; I simply didn't know any better.) Even after I realized my mistake, they asked me to stay. As a result, I met many more restaurateurs, among them Vincent Sardi of the iconic Sardi's, so well known for its star power if not for its food, and Stuart Levin, who owned Top of the Park atop the Gulf and Western Building, which is now the Trump International Hotel on Columbus Circle and houses my favorite haute cuisine restaurant, Jean Georges. Stuart Levin became another close friend and mentor. Love and Quiches also exhibited for the first time in the New York State Restaurant Show in 1978. We were slowly making a name for ourselves with the New York power players within the foodservice industry.

Our first trade show with the New York State Restaurant Association in 1978.

One such player was the owner of Proof of the Pudding, which closed its doors owing me $700. About that same time he opened the very exclusive Palace restaurant in an exclusive apartment building on 59th Street overlooking the East River. There, well ahead of his time, he invented the hundreds-of-dollars-per-person dinner. He honored his debt to me with a due bill to the Palace, and Irwin and I enjoyed a spectacular meal on the house!

My best New York story is the "Taste of the Big Apple," a major event held in Central Park in 1976 that was organized as a fundraising event by the New York State Restaurant Association. Nearly a hundred restaurants and suppliers set up booths, and, incredibly, hundreds of thousands of people showed up, many more than we had bargained for. The association sold script at the event entrance, with 25 percent of the revenue promised back to the vendors so we could cover our costs. We were to hand in our collected script at the end of the day.

We sold about five thousand slices of quiche before we ran out, and then we started selling our decorations: fruit, hunks of cheese, chopped chocolate, hard-boiled eggs, bowls filled with nuts, rolling pins, whisks, and the like, until our booth was completely denuded.

The association had run out of script, yet one lady insisted that we sell her our very last apple for cash. We told her we absolutely could not; it was against the rules. Suddenly she hit Irwin on the head with her pocketbook, grabbed the apple, and ran! Although we were all really tired and out of patience, we chased her and took back the apple just on principle.

Me (front and center) at the Taste of the Big Apple.

Molly Ivins, a prominent columnist and *New York Times* bureau chief at the time, wrote up the successful event, and to our surprise, we were mentioned among very good company. Love and Quiches was even singled out ahead of quite a few other popular venues, including Sardi's, the Grand Central Oyster Bar, and Benihana. And we all made a mess of the park. Though hundreds of Hare Krishna volunteers had it cleaned by the very next morning, the city would never allow us to hold another festival.

Within the next year or so, as we continued along our journey, new areas of growth presented themselves. I was knocking on doors *everywhere* and not confining my efforts just to restaurants. I went to hospitals, universities, caterers, gourmet shops, and corporate feeders—the people who fed the employees within the gigantic skyscrapers. I even went to the UN, where I just called for an appointment and handled it no differently than I would a pub on Third Avenue, except for the intense security checks required just to enter the building, which included opening every sample cake box. (They eventually recognized me and would let me walk right in.) The UN had a lot of dining venues and did a lot of catering, as you can well imagine. They turned out to be a very good customer, both for our quiches and our desserts. I was never shy to knock on any door that was in my path, though it took a while to learn how to gear my sales pitch to the venue I was targeting.

The Love and Quiches crew (Taste of the Big Apple, 1976)
with Irwin (#41), me, and our son, Andrew (far right).

Airline Stories

One of our biggest and most exciting areas of Love and Quiches' growth was in the airline industry. JFK was on my route to and from Manhattan, and one day I decided to go in and knock on some doors. All those passengers had to eat—why not our quiches and desserts? I made my way to the hangars on the periphery of the airport and spotted a Marriott sign on one of the doors. Marriott used to be an in-flight food caterer that prepared meals to be served on planes, along with all the other things for which they are now known. They provided this service at La Guardia and Newark airports as well. At the time, airline catering was Marriott's largest division, with facilities across the country. Once again, I made a sale. My original buyer at that facility, now an old friend, thinks that Marriott had actually started buying from us in a small way while Bonne Femme was still in my garage, but *I* think that story is apocryphal!

This was the beginning of a new area of growth for the company, and we continue to supply many major domestic and international airlines with our products. Now the strength of the entire organization is behind such sales, but back then it was limited to those airports that we could get to with our own trucks.

One airline we started selling to was People Express, a start-up that originated the first New York–to-Boston or -Washington shuttle. We sold them our first single-portion individually wrapped products, as a matter of fact. The products were fruit and veggie loaves, and included such varieties as Zucchini Bread, Banana Bread, and Carrot Bread, all of which we sliced and wrapped in cellophane. True to form, we did not yet possess the equipment to do this when we first made the sale— yet another example of the cart before the horse—but we fixed that situation pretty quickly. We had to; our first orders were already in-house! All we needed was a bread slicer and a small wrapping machine, readily available with so many equipment suppliers in our area. We went on to supply the various New York/Boston/Washington shuttles with these prewrapped slices for very many years, until they stopped giving them away to the passengers.

In those days we supplied many airlines that no longer exist— Eastern Airlines, Ozark Airlines, Pan American, and Braniff among them. The executive chefs of these airlines were extremely sophisticated, having worked in the best restaurants and hotels worldwide. (Two of these chefs became my mentors as well.) Within a year of entering the airline sector, we had our first airline distributor—a special breed that exclusively supplied airline-catering kitchens nationwide—to distribute our People Express products to Washington and Boston so that they would be available on the return flights to New York. This opened the possibility of expanding our airline customers across the country.

Best of all, passengers on these various flights seemed to love our product. At one point, Swiss Air accused us of using sugar in our quiche crust without listing it on the label, citing the fact that it tasted too good. It took some work to convince them otherwise. We have an entire archive of airline fan mail that we've collected over the decades, and these letters, many of them handwritten (this was pre-Internet, remember), never cease to bring a smile to my face.

WHILE FLYING— I WAS GIVEN SOME OF YOUR DELICIOUS BANANA NUT TEA BREAD— THEN WHEN I READ THE INGREDIENTS & SAW THAT Love WAS ONE OF THEM — I WAS OVER-JOYED!
I HAVE SPREAD YOUR RECIPE AROUND — EVEN FROM MY PULPIT.

One Day at a Time

Finish every day and be done with it. You have done what you could. Some blunders and absurdities no doubt crept in; forget them as soon as you can. Tomorrow is a new day; begin it well and serenely and with too high a spirit to be cumbered with your old nonsense. This day is all that is good and fair. It is too dear, with its hopes and invitations, to waste a moment on the yesterdays.
Ralph Waldo Emerson

*You know, I thought I made the best carrot cake
I have ever eaten. Then I tasted "Susan's Sweet
Talk - Carrot Bread"! It was so very delicious!
It takes first prize! Kindly let "Susan's" know.*

Past the Million-Dollar Mark

By 1978 we had grown to more than $1 million in volume.[*] We were now
servicing about 275 restaurants, and I finally got my first help with sales, a
tennis friend, Elaine, from the days when I still had time for tennis.

Our new freezer trucks were a good source of advertising for us
because they were all over the place all week long; plenty of restaurants
called us after noticing them while our drivers were making deliveries. Once, by sheer serendipity, we made the cover of one of the trade
magazines (see photo). We kept our drivers even busier once Elaine
started working—first two days a week, then three, then full time. She
scanned the trade and local papers for leads, made cold calls on the
phone, fed me leads, and also went out on sales calls.

---

[*] This number, like all others in the book referring to our volume growth, has not been
adjusted for inflation, so our trajectory was actually a bit more dramatic than the numbers suggest.

We also began to hire, one at a time, a rogues' gallery of salespeople who quite simply could not sell. Among them were a former fish salesman, a muffin salesman, and even some people who had worked for our competitors, all without success. I guess that is why they no longer worked for our competitors! We obviously had not yet honed our hiring skills.

Many of our decisions were still shot from the hip, but one by one we started to correct them, learning what *not* to do when running a business. Above all, we tried *not* to take the missteps too seriously and *not* to allow ourselves to be discouraged.

On the plus side, we continued to pick up some of the larger food-service accounts in the city, including one of the most prominent athletic clubs. One particular club had a tradition of supplying its members with larger-than-life twelve-inch double-crust mincemeat pies during the holiday season. The pies were specially packaged and mailed all over the country as gifts. The club had reached the point where it could no longer bake the pies in-house—it needed about fourteen thousand every year—and we were happy to take on the job. Each top crust was rolled by hand and decorated with a "flying foot" logo stamped out in pastry. The customer gave us the mold of its flying foot for safekeeping since it was the only one in existence. Like clockwork, every year we'd lose it and would be panic-stricken until the precious mold was located in our shop. We eventually gave up this athletic club as a customer due to the lack of fit: all those mincemeat pies had to be delivered fresh, but we were a frozen food supplier, so every December we wrestled with a logistical nightmare. Our lesson here was that if the fit isn't there, walk away. (I do believe we still have that flying foot someplace.)

Ever learning, we started offering products with price points at more than one level, enabling us to reach more potential customers. To accomplish this, we employed a simple strategy: use the same top-quality cake layers and frosting, but with varying amounts or types of decorations, less elaborate garnishes, a varied number of layers, and so on. In this way we could offer a simpler or less weighty cake, for example, to caterers and institutions that sold desserts as part of a buffet rather than by the slice at à la carte prices. It also resulted in extremely effective and seamless line extensions for our products.

Jimmy the Baker had his hands full, so the product development still fell on me for the most part. But I was rapidly losing my moxie in that department. My talents were more for cooking than for baking, so the process was rather painful, although I managed to come up with some good ideas and recipes that Jimmy then either vetoed or perfected. I was quite bogged down by it all, but I managed to pull off what needed doing, as usual.

We also started offering pre-cut cakes at this time for an additional fifty cents per cake. This was long before we had automatic cutting equipment like we do today, yet we managed, in Rube Goldberg fashion, to create some cutting tools that were quite effective. Using rods with handles and attaching pizza-cutting rollers spaced inches apart, we could cut our sheet cakes and brownies into twenty, thirty, or any other number of portions as needed. We also bought from a local company a rather ingenious device for pre-cutting round cakes into wedges; with it, we could pre-slice a cake in thirty seconds flat or faster.

Hitting the Road

In the late seventies we also made a sale or two to our first few out-of-town distributors. So, while hitting the road, I often chose to fly to my appointments. These were our first few forays outward, and they were dry runs for what came later. It was still only *me* selling, with Elaine helping, so I didn't venture too far afield; New Jersey, Philadelphia, Delaware, and Connecticut were about as far as I went, but I had learned about the world of distributors from the meat and produce outfit that serviced Bamberger's for us. I thought to myself: "Why not?" These distributors might be servicing five hundred customers, so they offered a lot more potential than my one-at-a-time search for new customers. Finding them was easy; by now I read the trade papers. We won our first few distributor customers this way.

Okay, new plan. We set our sights higher. I had been in business for less than six years, but our growth would soon begin to form two distinct areas: local on our own trucks and out of town through a growing distributor business. The local activity eventually grew to be a business within what was rapidly becoming our real business until we moved to distributors exclusively.

My teenaged daughter, Joan, helping out at the plant before joining our sales efforts.

It was when we started exhibiting in some *additional* local trade shows that we first came to the attention of a few more distributors in the tri-state area (New York, New Jersey, and Connecticut) than the first few I had originally gotten. For us this was a big leap from operating exclusively within the confines of the New York metro area.

We still didn't have much experience with distributors, but it occurred to us that the distributor sales force was, in a way, an extension of our own sales force, and it could help us increase our sales more quickly than we could do on our own. This was quite a revelation. We came to terms pretty quickly with the fact that we had to sell our products to the distributors at a discount in order for the products to land with the end user at a reasonable price. A whole new world opened to us! So I packed up my samples and hit the road with more of a plan. This time I was selling to the distributors, both farther north and south, and making sales calls with *their* sales forces to *their* best customers.

Until the mid-1990s, when we gave up our trucks altogether, we could never snag the more prominent distributors in our own back-yard—they thought we were competing with them. They held this belief even though we were selling our quiches and desserts at the same prices, or higher, than they would have done. We could never convince them otherwise. So it became easier to sell our cakes through a distributor in North Carolina—and, now, even Russia—than it was in New York, a very vexing problem that took a very long time to cure. Par for the course; nothing comes without its challenges.

As we started to have some success with our handful of new distributors, we widened our circle a bit, and approached distributors operating as far north as Boston, all the way down to the Carolinas, and places in between, like Maryland and Atlantic City. "We" still meant "me," and some of the planes I flew on were very tiny and very rickety indeed.

Rubbing Shoulders

I suspected that word of mouth and advertising in a minor way in the small local papers was not enough. As was usually the case, we had no idea how we should go about promoting the company, and we had no spare cash to do any real advertising. It didn't even occur to us to con-sider advertising in the trade publications on a very small level, which is where we should have looked in the first place. Mine was a business-to-business enterprise, but I didn't know what that was yet.

Nonetheless, in addition to our silly little ads with the funny one-liners that ran in the local papers, we did manage to attract some other media attention. I made an appearance once or twice on Channel 12

News, the local Long Island cable news station; they also aired a small two-minute piece they had filmed at our plant. Many of our products received favorable mention in various restaurant reviews, and we tried to capitalize on that wherever we could, although most restaurants wanted their customers to think their desserts were "house made."

One day I got a call from Barbara Rader, the chief restaurant critic for *Newsday* (the most prominent newspaper on Long Island). She was writing an article about prepared foods and asked if she could stop by. She had been a news journalist for most of her career, and admittedly she knew very little about food at the time. Hers was something like my story: I knew food but nothing about business; she knew nothing about food but could write! This was the beginning of our decades-long beautiful friendship. Irwin and I got to dine out with our new critic friend and her spouse, Tom Punch, at least once, sometimes twice, a week since eating out was now her full-time job, with *Newsday* picking up the tab. It actually *was* work, as we had to try to order almost everything on the menu without the restaurant realizing it was being reviewed, and many of the restaurants were not very good at all. We suffered through almost as many bad meals as good ones. This was still among my first brushes with networking, and I was enjoying myself.

Love and Quiches was also drawing the attention of some of the giants in our industry. During the course of my long career, I have been privileged to be invited to tour some of the largest state-of-the-art manufacturing facilities in the country. One such visit stands out because it came along so early in the game. One day a call came in to the Oceanside facility from Quaker Oats. They were considering adding quiche to their product line, and they wanted to discuss any mutual synergies that might exist. We couldn't imagine what they really wanted. They couldn't want to buy us—we were still so tiny there was nothing to buy!

We were invited to visit their plant in Tennessee, where they produced Aunt Jemima French Toast and Celeste Pizza, two other brands under the Quaker Oats umbrella. This plant was more than five hundred thousand square feet in size—massive in comparison to our five thousand square feet. The tour we had given them of *our* plant took ten minutes; this one took all day.

I saw a few things during that tour that I still remember vividly, thirty-five years later. First, the Celeste Pizzas were moving down the line almost too quickly for the eye to focus on, but as a result, a good portion of the toppings being sprinkled onto the pizzas from above were literally bouncing off the conveyor and landing all over the floor. It was a lesson in diminishing returns because of the inordinate waste, and I suggested they slow down the line. After a few moments of hesitation, during which they contemplated the simple logic of my suggestion—out of the mouths of babes—they actually thanked me and said they would consider it.

Second, along the never-ending sea of French toast moving down the grilling line, there were at least a hundred of what looked like store-bought spatulas, attached at twelve-inch intervals, moving periodically, and in unison, to flip the toasts so the other side could brown. When I asked about these spatulas, I was told they were indeed bought in a local hardware store—ingenious and highly effective! They also found a way to waste an unseemly amount of packaging by ripping open and discarding the outer boxes *after* they deemed any products underweight or otherwise imperfect. In this case, I kept silent.

The last vivid recollection I have of that memorable plant tour was when I inquired as to their most effective quality control systems. Taste testing is a vital step for any size food manufacturing business, and great fun. But Quaker told me that primarily *they eat a pizza every day!* Of course, obviously, they perform the many additional quality and safety checks and parameters dictated by good manufacturing practices, but taste testing is way up there for all of us.

Quaker Oats never did add quiche to their line, but that visit was another great chapter of my "on the job" training in the vast foodservice industry that my accidental business landed me in and that I truly love.

Reality Sets in

I was always working. It was relentless. My business had taken over my life, and fighting it would just have made things that much harder. But at least when I finally dragged myself home at night, Bridget had dinner ready (one of her creations, much to my chagrin, was lamb chop soup!). In later years, after Love and Quiches was well established and until she retired, she was the Love and Quiches doyenne, a matriarchal symbol who came to the office with me once or twice a week for many years, claiming she was bored at home, to stamp out shells.

Bridget Thurton, the L&Q doyenne.

Bridget was a very interesting character. Every year she took a trip with her church group—big-time trips. Years later, when Irwin and I were finally able to travel, there was hardly a place we visited that she hadn't been to before us! China, Israel, South America, and lots of cruises where she brought back photos of herself at the captain's table dressed in an evening gown, complete with elbow-length gloves.

My work-dominated life and the crazy events that came with it was the new reality, and I accepted it. On one occasion, Irwin and I were in the city to enjoy a rare evening out on the town when I made the mistake of calling the plant from the restaurant to see how everything was going. I was told that the roof had fallen in. Thinking this was a manner of speaking, I immediately became upset, thinking of every imaginable catastrophe that they might be referring to. But as it turned out, the roof of our eighteen-by-twenty-four-foot freezer had actually *collapsed!* Something wonderful also happened, however: my employees had taken charge, calling in the necessary parties, and by the time Irwin and I got back, the repairs were already well under way. Everything was under control without me! Without realizing it at the time, this was an important milestone, part of the process of learning to let go . . . to trust.

Trying to separate your personal and business lives simply doesn't work—not at this level, not until you have developed an effective organization with clearly defined areas of responsibility. We were nowhere near that point yet. I was exhausted all the time, still finding compelling reasons to spend time on my hands and knees in the plant scrubbing something that I felt needed scrubbing, responsible for everybody, worrying about everything, but knowing deep inside that I was going to see it through and move on to the next level. Too much momentum had already been created; there could be no turning back.

The 36,000 Pies

We continued in our efforts to expand up and down the East Coast, with me serving as sole out-of-town salesperson, and I can report that it is *really* cold in Buffalo in the dead of winter. I was dancing as fast as I could, and little by little, we picked up even more small distributors from New England down through the Carolinas, with occasional tentative forays further into the Southeast.

We kept growing in the New York metro area, too. We obtained our first co-packing contract, producing the original Lindy's Cheesecake for the group who held the license to market it as well as the recipe. We continued to produce for them for many years until they wanted the cheesecakes to be finished with various *fresh* fruits on top, which we could not do. We have always been a frozen food manufacturer, and fresh fruit simply does not freeze well. We were unhappy to have to walk away from this piece of business, but we learned, just as with the mincemeat pies for the athletic club, things change, and sometimes if the fit is not correct, you need to stop and walk away.

We started doing business with one of our longest-running accounts. Sandy Beall, the founder of Ruby Tuesday, had just opened his first gourmet shop and café on Hilton Head Island, and he was visiting New York with his wife to hunt for menu ideas. He spotted our quiches in Zabar's on the Upper West Side; they looked good, and so he gave us a call. We have been servicing Ruby Tuesday with various products for more than thirty years, from the time when there was only one, then seven, then a hundred, and now more than eight hundred Ruby Tuesday units! (Sandy recently retired as chairman and CEO of Ruby Tuesday, but we still keep in touch.)

Then came the biggest game changer of all. To our great surprise, we received a phone call from a very large restaurant chain with better than four hundred locations requesting a sample of a seafood quiche for a new brunch menu they were developing. I assume they found us because we were still just about the only company producing quiche at the time, certainly the only one with "quiche" in its name. We sent them the quiche sample, but we also threw in a ringer: our spectacular Pecan Brownie Pie, the same pie we had developed for Jacqueline Kennedy's dinner party. They called within minutes of receiving the samples, raving about the brownie pie and insisting that they simply *had* to have it for a six-week special. This may have been the very first limited-time offer, a marketing ploy that has become a standard in the restaurant industry. They said they planned on serving the pie warm, accompanied by ice cream and chocolate sauce. Then they asked how quickly we could produce six thousand cases. *Six thousand cases!* Our largest order to date had been maybe three or four hundred cases. And they wanted six pies per case, not our usual four—which meant an extra *twelve-thousand* pies!

After less than a second's hesitation—once we got up off the floor, having fallen off our chairs in disbelief—I said, "When do you need them?" "In six weeks," they replied. "No problem."

How we produced such a large order so quickly, with hardly a problem, while conducting all of our regular business in our small plant—which still had only our twenty-four- and eighteen-pan ovens, which translates to a mere eighty-pie capacity (two per bun pan)—was truly a testament to Jimmy the Baker's time management skills and supreme talents as a baker! Of course we baked all through the weekends for those few weeks. We were still, at that time, only a five-day operation, so that extra capacity on Saturday and Sunday was crucial. If I remember correctly, we also had our two original Blodgett convection ovens from the Bonne Femme days; we had hooked them up when we moved to Oceanside, just in case. Well, "just in case" was upon us. But in the end, it paid off: the Pecan Brownie Pie dessert special was such a spectacular success that the restaurant chain immediately put it on their regular dessert menu, where it remained for twenty-five-plus years!

As the seventies drew to a close, Love and Quiches flew past the million-dollar mark, and our volume between 1978 and 1980—a pivotal period—doubled and then some. We started to see that yet another move was inevitable, this one even bolder than the others (and fortunately our last). I also knew, with certainty, that there would be no more "me," that from now on it would be "us" and "we" for everything. I knew I did not want to go it alone anymore—nor could I. And so I asked Irwin to join the business officially.

Chapter 6

Freeport, Here We Come! (1980)

Why not go out on a limb—isn't that where the fruit is?
—Frank Scully

B y 1980 we had developed from our accidental and tentative beginning into a business with a fairly extensive line of
quiches and desserts, and we had secured our reputation as
a high-end supplier. We had won some important national customers, and now we needed a place from which we could continue to
grow. If we didn't, we could be in danger of losing them. We laughed,
recalling how we had considered renting out some of our five thousand square feet upon moving to our Oceanside facility in 1976; four
years later, the walls were once again pressed to their limits. We had
reached well over $2 million in volume, employed thirty-five people,
were servicing four hundred customers, and were running six trucks
daily that covered the tri-state area. I'd also finished paying back the

$200,000 bank loan that my father had collateralized for me. A part of me was still constantly asking, "Is this really happening?" even though I knew the answer very well.

But even given this level of success, up to this point the development of Love and Quiches had been, as our first seven years amply demonstrated, somewhat haphazard, with chance playing a much larger role than it would have had I planned it out a little more thoughtfully. That could have cut both ways—although fortunately, it didn't—but if the whole thing had gone down, we would have disappeared without too much disruption since our reach was still rather small. Of course, I was never going to let that happen, but from here on out the stakes would become much larger, and the consequences of any missteps more serious. Frankly, if I was not so confident of our current standing within the foodservice industry, I might have been embarrassed to admit to so many missteps and foibles up to this point. However, I have always had the ability to laugh at myself, and I've also been helped along by the knowledge that my audience is laughing *with* rather than *at* me. Building a business of our size is a very serious undertaking, and I needed to hold on to my sense of humor through it all. Otherwise, the tears could have easily taken over. And there were plenty of those.

As the decade of the eighties began, I realized that we had once again reached a point in our growth where no manner of reorganizing with the tools at hand would work. The floorboards were literally crying uncle under the weight of our business, and so were we. That meant another move, this time a big one, with professional help in the planning, and we needed a lot of money to do it right. We could no longer operate as a homespun, do-it-yourself outfit.

Irwin had always been there to help and advise me from day one, and I had constantly called upon his expertise and foresight, but I recognized that I needed his undivided attention from here on in if the company was going to continue to grow successfully. I'd asked him to officially join me in Love and Quiches, and now I pressed him for his answer. But although he had already become an integral part of the effort, the proposal remained on the table for the time being.

We all agreed that the time had come to launch our search for yet another new home. We were mindful of the logistics of our existing staff and didn't want to lose them, so we followed the same course we had when we made our move to Oceanside: concentric circles. We started our search across the street at a twenty-thousand-square-foot warehouse that one of our suppliers for pie tins, paper goods, cartons, etc. was moving out of. Even though it was four times the size of our current facility, we deemed it too small.

Next we looked at a defunct tennis center around a very long corner, which had the advantage of office space situated on a balcony overlooking what would be the production floor, but this building presented other problems. Although it was merely half a mile away from our present location, it seemed more like a world away. The building itself was extremely isolated, unappealing, and dreary, surrounded as it was by many huge oil tanks and a landfill. It was quite obvious why the tennis center had failed, and I wanted our staff to look forward to pulling up to the building in the morning, not dread it. This was definitely not the right move, even at forty thousand square feet.

Our current location was abuzz with plenty of activity, what with light manufacturing places, outlet stores, banks, coffee shops, and other services nearby. (There was also a butcher who had been selling us butter at a price that we should have known was a bit too good. We discovered that it was government surplus when one delivery arrived and he had forgotten to peel the paper off of the packaging—it was clearly marked as "Surplus" and "Not for Public Sale." So much for that.)

Those were the only two buildings of any size in the area, which made expanding our search a necessity. We hired a commercial real estate broker—a family friend—and in spite of his protests because of its reputation as a dangerous area, we found our way to Freeport, only ten minutes farther away.

Thirty years ago, the village of Freeport was an area of contrasts; poverty and racial unrest coexisted alongside a thriving waterfront replete with sprawling homes and a lively "restaurant row." Still a vibrant mecca today, Freeport draws both locals and tourists alike to the scenic restaurants, bars, and fisheries along its canals. An industrial park was built there on the grounds of what used to be a stock car racing arena, which was a popular place to take a date when we were teenagers. Irwin and I would go there with a group of friends a few times during the summer, and then we would all go down to the waterfront area for fried clams and shrimp.

We decided we would concentrate our search here. At the same time, Irwin officially signed on, as I had always hoped he would, and I was happy. The prospect of a partnership both in marriage and in business had given him pause, but we have had a good life, and it was the right decision.

A Lease Gets Signed

Despite so many people advising us against the area, I had a good feeling about Freeport from the very start. It felt open and calm. The area has always served us well, with a plentiful labor pool of fine and hardworking people, many of whom have been with us for fifteen or twenty years or more. Freeport generates its own power, offered at a much lower rate than the Long Island average. Added to these benefits, the town fathers have always bent over backward to help us whenever possible because we provide a great many jobs in the community. The building we were considering was directly on a canal. I love water, having been brought up in a community right on the ocean, where we walked the beach all year long. Freeport was perfect.

We drove around the industrial park and quickly identified what, in my opinion, would be the perfect building. It was thirty thousand square feet. The ceilings were considered low at fourteen feet, but in my innocence I thought of this measurement as simply more energy efficient. Now I wish we had some additional headroom for platforms, extra storage, and the like. However, there was quite a lot of room for expansion on the outside. As the years passed, we built many additions, one by one, as the business grew. We expanded our capacity in other ways as well. For example, we purchased some high-speed equipment that allowed for much greater output per hour—by that I mean production—within the same space. Very often, efficiency trumps square footage.

Negotiating with our potential new landlord was trying; it felt more like we were vying for one hundred thousand square feet of the most prime floor space in the Empire State Building! Lots of lawyers, lots of rewriting the contract, lots of arguments, and many weeks going by, but we finally ended up with a quite favorable lease with a right of first refusal *and* an option to buy, which meant that they could never sell the building out from under us. (We still do not own the building because of some estate issues on the landlord's side, but we continue to enjoy favorable terms, and we have an easy out should we decide to move on.)

After many marathon negotiating sessions, the lease *finally* got signed, and Irwin and I, our new landlord, and the lawyers from both sides all repaired to the legendary Algonquin Hotel for an after-midnight champagne supper. It was really that late, and we had earned it!

Actually, our new landlord reminded me a lot of my father. He had an opinion about everything, and he visited quite a bit more than he had to in order to check on our progress.

Quiche Factory #4

In the space of seven years, we had traveled from my kitchen, to my garage, to the little shop across from the firehouse, to our first commercial space in Oceanside, to our current home in Freeport. We were finally in a position to do some serious business. During this learning curve, we went from no dollars to just over $2.5 million—not too bad for a business that came from nowhere and started with nothing. We had put quiche on the map as an alternative to the hamburger, presenting it as a meal when accompanied by salad. Not quite Oreos, but still!

Incidentally, we found a tenant for the Oceanside facility because our lease was not yet up. We sublet it to the Knish Factory, run by a successful local kosher caterer. The man had been a friend of Irwin's older brother, and Irwin always admired him because he was the only one of his brother's friends who had a job. We sold him—and in some instances just left him—whatever equipment we would not be taking with us, including our rotary ovens, for $20,000 plus a $5,000 interest-free note due in five years. It was quite a bargain since the equipment we left behind was worth many times that. When the note came due, the tenant admitted he had been hopeful that we would have forgotten about it. Not likely. Anyway, he finally paid us.

I think that in the hope of continuing to attract some of our walk-in trade, he had done his street-front signage in the same colors and style as our Love and Quiches logo, calling it the Knish Factory instead of the Quiche Factory. Not *exactly* purposely, I don't think; but even twenty years later, people would remark to us, "Hey, I just passed your place on Lawson Boulevard!"

Our move to Freeport was very different from the others. In prior years, we had financed whatever equipment we needed with proceeds from the business, but fitting out this plant properly would require some major financing. Unless self-financed, there is no way around this for any start-up or newly established business. My father had originally counseled me to develop a good relationship with a small local bank, and we did our original banking with Peninsula National Bank. They were taken over by the larger Norstar Bank, which was in turn absorbed by Fleet Bank. It was with Fleet Bank that we sought our financing.

Nothing about the growth of my business came easily. The timing of this move coincided, with exquisite irony, with an unprecedented escalation of interest rates—just when we had borrowed serious money for the very first time.

During the recession of 1980, interest rates soared to 22 percent and higher, and we had projected, at most, 14 percent when seeking our million dollars of plant financing. This spike affected us profoundly, our biggest challenge to date.

Here we were, about to enter the next phase of our journey. We had our first really detailed business plan, our architectural engineer on board, our professionals and equipment suppliers all drawing up the construction plans—yet these unprecedented interest rates were looming above us. It was too late to go backward. Moreover, I was determined to move forward and overcome the obstacles in my path even if it meant I had to sign away my life in the process.

We approached Fleet Bank with our financial plan, which included our intended floor plan, the equipment required, an operating budget, and our somewhat vague sales projections. Our accountant, who helped us prepare the plans, was the same one I had originally worked with when I was starting out, back in 1973. The projections were sound enough for the bank and we were granted our loan. We financed everything, both the construction and the equipment, through this one loan. And *everything*, including the spatulas and my house, was put up as collateral. Needless to say, betting more than you can afford to lose is an extremely dangerous gamble, but in this case I disobeyed my own rules. The total package amounted to about $1.2 million.

We took a deep breath and got started. We had the luxury of having our Oceanside facility fully operational until moving day, which fell on Labor Day weekend of 1980. We had no major equipment to take with us, since we left almost everything behind. All we had to move was our meager office furniture, a few 80- and 120-quart mixers, our pans, various racks, scales, storage bins, a few tables, and inventory of raw and finished goods. We accomplished most of this with our own trucks and the Love and Quiches Motley Crew; the rest went with a local moving company.

We had hired an architectural engineer to draw up the plans both for design of the workflow and to provide the City of Freeport with required blueprints: plumbing, electrical, etc. He also ran the job for us. Jay was semiretired and elderly, but he possessed the energy of a twenty-year-old; we found him through a network of my father's friends. He really knew what he was doing, and working with him provided me with one of the most memorable periods in my business career. He was amazing.

Freeport, here we come.

As you'll recall from chapter 5, "The Mini-Factory (1976-1980)", my father-in-law, a retired plumbing contractor, ran this part of the job—just as he had for the Oceanside mini-factory. Considerable electrical work was required, and for that we used a local independent electrician. He worked for the town by day and moonlighted our job by night. He was Italian and was constantly bragging to us about what a great cook his wife, Rose, was, so I gave her my pasta maker—since by then my home cooking days were pretty much over. We also hired a local flooring contractor to quarry-tile the six-thousand-square-foot production area. Our jack-of-all-trades, Willie the handyman, was around for odd jobs despite the fact that he really couldn't paint.

The main heavy equipment—ovens, pan washer, refrigeration, and freezer—were built and installed by the manufacturers, as is customary, and training the employees on their use was included in the price. We had thought our eighteen- and twenty-four-pan rotary ovens in Oceanside were quite grand, but here we left them in the dust. We started out with two sixty-pan rotary ovens, then added two more, and finally added an eighty-pan oven as the years went by. Jay, our engineer, had included space in his designs for this type of expansion. We graduated to 140-quart, then 400-quart, and now much larger mixers and dough makers as well.

Yet we were still in some ways a do-it-yourself outfit. We recruited many of the Love and Quiches workers to help in the renovations, and they appreciated the overtime, besides wanting to be a part of it all. Both Jay and my father-in-law put my son Andrew and his friends to work, home as they were for the summer following their freshman year at Michigan State Hotel and Restaurant School. They performed a lot of the grunt work, just as son Irwin had done for his father when *he* was a teenager. I was one of the grunts, too. My mother-in-law was recruited to sit in the office all day throughout the summer to answer the one phone we had at the time. And *my* father hung around quite a lot, almost daily, as did our new landlord. They were enjoying themselves.

It was a long, hot summer. We all worked like horses; lots of "blood, sweat, and tears." But by summer's end, the renovations were completed, the equipment was up and running, and we were finally ready for the big move.

The Big Move

We accomplished the move in three days flat over the Labor Day weekend. All of our employees made the move to Freeport with us, and we were ready for business for the fall season of 1980, our busiest time of the year, by Tuesday morning with no disruptions.

Moving day!

Our new facility was so grand we were sure it would do very well until the end of time. We had *real* offices that were half the size of the entire Oceanside facility, an employee lounge, a separate retail shop (later converted into our test kitchen when we took some space across the street and moved the shop there), more than six thousand square feet of production space, a refrigerator bigger than our first house, and a freezer equal in size to the entire Oceanside mini-factory.

In fairly short order, however, six thousand square feet of production space became uncomfortably small. This was painfully evident when we needed to decorate our delicate Whipped Cream Cakes right next to the ovens, which generate a tremendous amount of heat. Sometimes the whole production area exceeded 100 degrees! Piping whipped cream rosettes and packing frozen cakes alongside the ovens was never fun. On some days, we provided the whole deco line with jackets and moved them into the refrigerator!

But on the plus side, with this move we also now had almost nine thousand square feet for packing, shipping, and storage, a mechanics shop, and, finally, a loading dock. *And*, all of this with a water view!

Despite the advantages of the new space, our first year or so in Freeport was brutal. We were struggling with the reality of that 22-plus percent interest rate, floating about two points over prime, during this hyper-inflationary period. The bank had serious doubts that we could survive this economic debacle, and for a little while we had our *own* doubts. We started to secretly call our bank officer "Black Jack Fagan." He was the prophet of doom and advised us either to give it all up and call it a day or to find a new bank. That, for me, was not an option. This very difficult period, among others that I will recount, almost took us down.

We found out pretty quickly that coming into this building with a bit less than $3 million in volume was simply not enough. We needed some quick growth, and happily, it started to come. I was on the road quite a bit, picking up more distributors in the tri-state area and beyond. Elaine started doing more outside sales too. We also moved one of our truck drivers, an original member of the Motley Crew, into local sales. Everybody agreed he was very "cute," and he turned out to be very good at sales. He ended up running our local direct sales department, and later, after he married, his wife also joined Love and Quiches, working in distributor sales up and down the East Coast for many years. (We have never discouraged nepotism; in fact, it has *mostly* worked very well for us.)

Most importantly, we still had our biggest customer: the restaurant chain that had ordered the six thousand cases of our Pecan Brownie Pie as a six-week special. Once it landed a place on their permanent menu, the Pecan Brownie Pie provided us with much-needed and steady volume, almost $1 million yearly, and that one account was instrumental in getting us through this trying period. Later, we provided products for other restaurant concepts the group developed and introduced. We had an excellent relationship with the buyers, and we were privileged to be invited to take a tour of their seafood processing plant on the west coast of Florida. It was fascinating, but much to our surprise, the workers peeling shrimp were paid by the piece, not by the hour.

Visiting with our biggest customer at the time.

After the tour, we stopped for lunch at the very first unit, complete with a "Welcome Susan and Irwin" sign! Much to my chagrin, they were serving alligator as an appetizer that day. Definitely not on my list, but I had to be polite and taste some.

So, we survived the move and increased overhead, the interest rates began to moderate, and we doubled our volume in the first two years in Freeport. We had reached just under $5 million yearly. We began to prosper.

Our office staff grew. We now had reps for customer service, accounts receivable, accounts payable, a warehouse manager, and our old-fashioned controller Mildred (who looked the part right out of central casting), as well as a small sales staff. We also contracted our first payroll service, ADP, and it was through them that we began our first simple foray into computerization, limited as it was to invoicing and rudimentary accounts receivable. Our accounts payable were still done by general ledger, as was our inventory, and there was nothing *yet* in the way of customer or product analysis. The early eighties and the computer age were still ahead of us.

We continued our growth into more restaurant chains and more distributors, and we further penetrated the airline industry. It was an exhilarating period, and for the time, I was breathing a bit easier.

Chapter 7

Spreading Our Wings (1980–1989)

I believe in luck, but you have to go out and find it.
—Oscar de la Renta

When we first moved into Freeport, our offices were still a study in catch-as-catch-can. The back of the house was equipped, all shiny and ready to go, but we still had no furniture in our offices. We sat all over the floor to do our work. The employee lounge had no tables and chairs for lunch breaks, but we *did* have a pool table and a ping-pong table, and there was always a game in progress. What we did have was in order, and we were ready to do business.

Today in the office at Freeport we still have a closet full of archives, and I recently discovered a treasure trove of information and examples of how we did things in the early eighties. What I suppose should be embarrassing is quite funny, in retrospect. The important thing is that the mistakes of our beginnings—which we were still making aplenty in Freeport—didn't keep us from building more business.

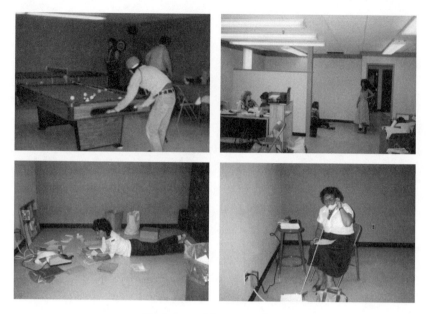

The first month in our new home.

Very few small companies were computerized back then, so the fact that we weren't was normal. Nevertheless, I can't fathom how our business operated in the early days of computerization in light of what we have at our disposal today. As I look back on the early to mid-eighties, I smile when I recall how our pricing was still done via a system of index cards and a calculator! We had a two-man team for this—a bright young employee, Molly, and me. It couldn't possibly have been more rudimentary. Hopefully we *mostly* remembered to use the most current price paid for our ingredients. We used three percentages to determine the price of our labor, choosing which to use based on whether the work was "easy," "medium," or "hard"! Amazing, but the system worked for us until later in the decade. On top of this, we were still doing our price lists on the typewriter since we were still quite a few years away from spreadsheets.

Our first foray into computerization through the payroll company ADP had been off-site, dial-up, and *painfully* slow. Very little else was computerized, but we had one employee who basically functioned as a human computer. Billy had previously been one of our drivers and part of the Motley Crew back in Oceanside, and he had begun to stand out as being extremely bright. He quietly took control of our finished inventory, participated in production planning, and took the lead in managing our drivers and trucks, assigning routes and other related responsibilities. He was able to accurately track *in his head* the exact inventory we held for each and every quiche or cake, even after we had hundreds of products in our line, and this still held true even after we became computerized. Billy was our computer brain. We would send purchase orders back to him, and he would then send all the trucks out with handwritten bills of lading, after which he would come into the office to let us know exactly what *did* ship. We would then—*after* the fact!—print the invoices. Laura—who started working for us while still in her teens and who's remained for more than twenty years—recalls that everybody in the office was afraid of Billy and had to remember three things: (1) Billy was always right; (2) Never say no to Billy; and (3) Billy took his coffee with cream and sugar!

We did know enough by now to upgrade our point-of-sale material, which we used on sales calls, at trade shows, and in mailings. We started using professionals to photograph our products and had our simple two-sided sell sheets typeset and professionally printed on glossy paper. But our product lines were constantly evolving, so we ended up with racks full of product brochures that were obsolete before the ink even dried.

With our first real bookkeeper, we had moved from our shoebox to a general ledger, which was maintained by our next two controllers even into the nineties. And our recipes, which we had yet to call "formulas," were still handwritten on the ubiquitous index cards. Once we moved to Freeport, we "upgraded" to loose-leaf paper as we finally started adding method instructions to the recipes. It was in the mid-eighties that we "graduated" to the typewriter for recipes! A few years later we would *finally* migrate to entering all our formulas, complete with subassemblies, into the computer. But even at that point the formulas were in a word processing file, which had to then be reentered into our integrated software as we initiated batch control, raw and finished inventory control, formula management, accounts receivable and payable, and so on. Doing things the hard way was one of our specialties, but as the years passed, we got better. *Very* much better.

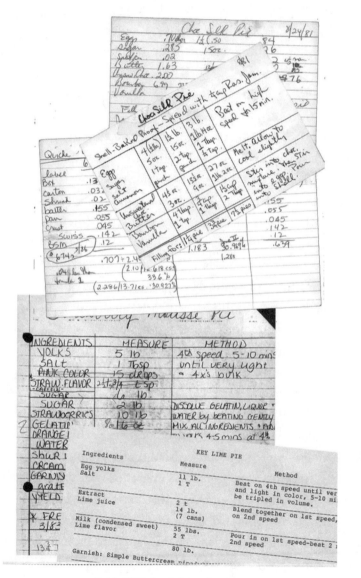

Early 1980, barely beyond crayons.

Through our ADP dial-up, we had been delivered from writing our invoices and statements by hand. Soon after, in 1982, we brought in our first general office manager, Dave, who had worked for our first airline distributor before joining Love and Quiches. He knew much more about computers than any of the rest of us did. At his prompting, we invested in our first in-house IBM server, which was truly monstrous and ended up being installed right in his office. But we were still keying in the purchase orders on two "dumb" terminals that could only communicate with the server and not each other. (This was before PCs became "smart" and could communicate with each other.) Still, it was much quicker, and it represented another step forward.

During his first years after coming on board, Dave purchased a software program, Cimpro, from a company called DataLogix, as well as another (smaller) server and two more "dumb" terminals from Unisys. Invoicing and accounts receivable was the first module of the software package to be put into use. Several years later, we brought in a new IBM-AIX server that was even smaller and a *lot smarter* than what we'd had up until then. We also started adding more terminals because we had more employees doing a lot more things.

All of our orders came in via the phone, so we did not yet have any real need for a fax machine. But on the rare occasion when we did, someone would have to go next door to send a fax! And most of our business was still local. Our customer service staff was armed with client information noted on—you guessed it—index cards! They would go through the cards—sorted Monday for Tuesday delivery, Tuesday for Wednesday delivery, and so on—to call each customer for their next day order. Theoretically, if an index card got lost, misplaced, or misfiled, we could lose the customer and not even know it!

We may have been a ramshackle operation in some respects in those days, but our key employees continued to produce top-drawer products. Jimmy's reputation as a legend followed us into Freeport. In fact, on many occasions an ingredient or equipment supplier would spend the night at the plant helping to incorporate a new ingredient or machine seamlessly into production. They would always comment in the morning that they had never seen anything quite like the way Jimmy orchestrated the night's production, moving his people around without a single wasted motion or moment. One supplier even likened it to a magnificent ballet performance!

Jimmy eventually had well over a hundred production workers under him. At the start of each evening, Jimmy always said he was "going up the hill" and toward the end he was "going down the hill." One thing's for sure, if we were out of an ingredient, he needed to be told in advance; otherwise, Irwin and I would likely get a call at two in the morning! Jimmy didn't take kindly to any sudden changes in his Love and Quiches ballet.

Jimmy the Baker.

As the years went by and our business became more computerized, we had to handle Jimmy very delicately, "making an appointment" in order to corner him in the conference room to wheedle all the details of a particular recipe out of him. Sometimes his description "about a handful and a half" was as close as we could get him to nail down a particular measurement, although his handfuls never varied; they were as reliable as a scale. He was extremely protective of what he thought of as *his* recipes and equally suspicious of them falling into the wrong hands. Occasionally he would leave an ingredient or two out; at these times we'd have to bypass him, getting the needed specs from his second-in-command, for inventory and pricing purposes. He finally did *get it*, and became more cooperative, but basically he was just Jimmy being Jimmy!

During this time, another member of our original Motley Crew began to stand out. One of our drivers, Tom, had also worked in inventory control and production alongside Billy. He was learning more and more about the operation of both the hardware and the software, and he asked for an opportunity to be our in-house IT technician. We sent him to school, and it turned out his computer skills were superb. Tom proved himself very quickly and would remain with us until 1998, when he landed a big job with the New York Jets. He remembers that our biggest challenge, among other big challenges, was keeping the inventory of ingredients. Billy would hand him the production list for the night, and Tom would enter it into the system. Each morning at six Tom would corner Jimmy the Baker to get a list of what had been made the night before. Then he'd sit with Bonnie, our buyer, trying to "back into" the materials that had been *used* so that she could reconcile materials *required* for future orders. Her "system" for keeping everything straight was to use sticky notes all over her desk—a step backward even from my pricing system of handwritten index cards.

As we put a few years in Freeport behind us, our general office manager and Tom helped us take some big steps forward, technologically speaking. We added other modules within Cimpro (in addition to accounts payable, formula management, batch control, inventory control already added), such as cash flow management and sales analysis, which allowed our processes to become much more integrated. DataLogix was sold several times, and support for the program became more and more remote, so most of the enhancements over the years were accomplished either by our own IT people or other consultants. There was still plenty of handwriting and typewriting, though! And, as you might imagine, our old-fashioned controllers were very distrustful of computers at first, and they were reluctant to let go of their general ledgers. They worked with the "dual" systems, just in case, but as time passed, they—along with the rest of us—learned to trust our technology and slowly join the march with the rest of the world toward meaningful computer systemization.

At some point in the mid-eighties, we implemented a time and attendance system that required employees to punch in and out using their hand, like fingerprinting. This system was better than punch cards because now no one could punch their friends in or out without their being there. One morning an employee came to Tom and, holding up his hand, which was now missing two fingers (*not* from an on-the-job accident, I am happy to report), explained that he could not punch in. The payroll company advised us to have the employee use his other hand, *turned over*! It worked, though I will never know how or why. Technology and Love and Quiches kept marching on, but it wasn't until the nineties that everything started to leap forward at warp speed.

Trade Show Days

In the early eighties, Irwin and I decided to see what all of these national industry trade shows were all about, so we flew into Chicago to take a look at the gigantic National Restaurant Association Restaurant, Hotel-Motel Show held there each May. We wandered up and down the aisles like nobodies and were amazed at the size of this show! No one among our competitors was yet exhibiting; it was just the Sara Lees of the world. We accepted and enjoyed dinner invitations from some of our suppliers who were exhibiting, and they started to introduce us around. The best of these meals was the one at Le Perroquet, where we dined on fine classical French cuisine. (Le Perroquet quickly became a favorite, and eventually, *we* were the ones taking *our* customers there.)

We also attended the International Flight Services Association's (IFSA's) yearly show, which was much smaller, more focused, and much more closed to newcomers. Because we had already done some airline business in the New York area, however, we met some of the menu planners more easily and picked up Ozark Airlines (now defunct), our first significant airline account. We started servicing them with desserts through the special breed of distributors that catered exclusively to the airline industry, one of which we had already picked up to distribute for us throughout the Northeast.

Winning Ozark prompted us to join IFSA as a member, and we started to exhibit at the annual show. In our first year exhibiting, we picked up TWA as an account, and we were making almost all of their coach desserts by 1984. TWA was a very big account! We were supplying them with eight-inch single-layer cakes in three flavors and precutting them into twenty portions. Since the cakes weighed only about eighteen ounces each, these had to be the world's smallest portions!

In 1985 billionaire financier Carl Icahn bought TWA, and the next year, TWA bought Ozark Airlines. We knew Carl prior to this, since he and Irwin had been army buddies and we were all from the Rockaways in Queens. We were friends, but working with him in his capacity as owner of TWA taught us a crucial lesson. Shortly after the purchase, Carl invited me up to his offices in Westchester as a supplier representative in a meeting with his head honchos. I soon realized I was more of a sacrificial lamb, although I don't think Carl had intentionally meant for that to happen. But he had hired a few killer sharks to cut costs to the bone, and soon after that meeting, we found ourselves in a bidding war with another small cake company from Chicago to keep this business, which already had a very thin profit margin. At first, we kept inching down our price, but we finally just said, "We are done here," and walked away. The small Chicago bakery kept bidding, but they didn't know they were now bidding against themselves. They got the business, but the company failed within the next year or two.

Once again, we learned this most important lesson: If you can't make a profit while working with a particular customer, you need to learn when it's time to walk away. Had we slashed our prices as low as Carl and TWA wanted us to go, we would've ended up in trouble. Fortunately, we could let the account go and not suffer too much because I'd learned another crucial business lesson: Never let any one customer account for more business than you can afford to lose, just in case you *do* have to say "no" one day. If a customer is dangerously important, that is your signal to go after new growth. It feels relentless, but that is the reality of almost any business.

We walked away from TWA, used the experience to become a little stronger and a little smarter, and went after other airline business to make up the loss. We had nobody but ourselves in our corner when this bidding war took place, and another lesson learned was this: if we wanted serious growth in this segment, we would need a strong and well-connected broker to help us do it.

We found our fit with McGuire & Associates in 1987, and we have partnered with them ever since. Little by little, as a major supplier we picked up just about every one of the domestic airlines and quite a few of the international ones as well. It took us about ten years to go from outsider to insider, but contrary to what the public may think about airline food, the buyers, executive chefs, and menu planners are *very* serious about the food they serve, and we have always had to do our best to live up to their standards and never lose their trust. The executive chefs of both Pan Am and Eastern became mentors and advisors to me in the airline segment, and of course we remained friends. In later years, as the original airline giants began to disappear one by one (besides these mentioned earlier, now TWA among them), some of the buyers moved to the other side of the desk, and several joined McGuire & Associates. Some of the original buyers I used to sell to are now professionals I am selling *with*! They brought a tremendous amount of expertise to the table, not to mention their excellent contacts.

Because we were making progress exhibiting at the yearly IFSA show, we decided to take a shot at exhibiting at the supersized National Restaurant Association (NRA) show in Chicago. At the time, the smaller booths were all crowded together on the lower level, and that's where we ended up. We didn't give out samples because we have always held the opinion that the trade-show freeloaders would elbow away the real buyers, preventing them from getting near the booth. But there was a lot of cooking and frying going on around us—not very pleasant—and the show was a very long five days instead of the current four. It was grueling, but we came back the next year, and the year after, and the year after . . . we've been exhibitors for about thirty years now!

And as I grew older and my crew grew younger, a tradition took hold at the Love and Quiches booth that always made my day. At 5:00 p.m., when the show closed, a group of us would change into our walking gear and walk back downtown to our hotel about five miles away. It seems like a crazy idea after spending the whole day on your feet, but it actually has always had the opposite effect—we were energized. Chicago is a great city, and I've always looked forward to this show just so that I could spend a few days there.

After our first year exhibiting, the NRA show in Chicago quickly became very important to our expansion. It has consistently provided enough leads to keep us busy all year long. Tens of thousands of visitors attend each year from all over the world, and it is at this show that we have attracted many of our biggest and most important clients.

Yet, looking back, I can't help comparing those days to where we are now. In our first few years at the show, we just piled our cakes on top of the boxes, but then, little by little, we started to display them much more artistically. By the 1990s, a photo of our booth made page one in the business section of the *Chicago Tribune*! Today our booth is much larger and we send our entire team of talented chefs, who spend two days setting up and decorating the booth with gorgeous platings of our desserts and quiches and artfully arranging our products in the refrigerated display cases, as well as setting up our backdrop, decorative touches, and seating area. Once again, we've come a very long way.

We expanded the horizon for our sales force, as well. We had always promoted people from within the company, and many of our employees grew into their roles, but we knew we needed to attract some outside talent to keep up the momentum. We recruited some experienced sales veterans from within the foodservice industry in the Northeast, but this time we hired ones who understood what needed to be done, and we were skilled at picking the right brokers to represent us along the Eastern Seaboard. One salesman came out of the Moore's Onion Rings division of the Clorox Company, for example, and he was experienced in operations and production as well.

During this time, in addition to attending these national shows, Elaine (who had morphed into our marketing director, among other things) and I went to some smaller distributor shows, where we also met some brokers who agreed to represent us and taught us how to work a show. Instead of standing behind the display waiting for somebody to stop, we learned to stand in front and lasso them in. We learned to work the aisles! We *had* to because hardly anybody had ever heard of us. If you wanted to network, you *had* to get out there to do it.

Despite all the conferences I've been to and all the people I've gotten to know, in my heart of hearts, I have never been comfortable with small talk, and I find it somewhat difficult to talk to strangers. But that doesn't alter the fact that networking is a crucial element in most businesses, and I have always done what I had to do. (As a result, by the way, I have met and forged relationships with people from all over the world, and I have found some *true* friendships in the equation.)

Another important chapter in my absorption into the industry centers came through the Roundtable for Women in Foodservice, which was formed with the help of a US Small Business Administration

(SBA) loan in the mid-eighties in New York to serve as a resource for women from all areas of the trade: restaurant owners, chefs, nutritionists, food writers, and the like. I was invited to serve on the founding board of directors. We held monthly meetings and instructional seminars, traded job information, mentored younger women, and provided other services. During the next few years, chapters of the Roundtable opened in other metropolitan areas such as LA, Dallas, and Chicago. We held an annual luncheon during the NRA show in Chicago to attract members and attention—in other words, *networking!* This was, to my knowledge, the first broadly based organization formed to help advance women in my particular industry. The Women's Foodservice Forum, which currently has twenty-two thousand members, would overrun us by the turn of the century (I am active in that organization, too), but the Roundtable was first to bring me together with many women whose passions, like mine, resided at the intersection of business and food.

We were still marching inexorably forward, but this was still long before everybody was walking around armed with laptops, cell phones, and BlackBerrys. Everything in sales moved along at a slower pace even as our computerization efforts speeded up. So it was at these shows that our relationships were forged, one by one. And now, today, we exhibit at shows worldwide.

Susan's Sweet Talk

By the late 1980s, thanks to our relentless pursuit of new business, we were doing about $6 million in volume, soon to grow to $8 million and more as we crossed over into the early nineties. We took a lot of steps and made changes during the second half of the eighties to help prepare us for the next decade. Some of them were deliberate; others, as usual, just happened.

We had our bakery kosher-certified when it became apparent that all retail in-store bakery departments, all airlines, most hotel chains, and many other segments of the industry demanded it for all baked products. I remember the certification process was very trying and costly. We had to send out all of our pans—thousands by then— to be re-glazed, or else we would have had to replace them. All of the equipment had to be scrubbed down and sterilized. The most frightening process involved the ovens: we were required to raise the temperature above 1,000 degrees and run them at that temperature for more than eight hours! I asked, "How about 800 degrees for ten hours?" No deal. The rabbi said "No!" Somehow we got through it, but it took an army of mechanics to ensure that we didn't destroy our ovens in the process.

(I recently read in the *New York Times* about the very same process being required in the White House for just one kosher event. In that instance, only one hour at 500 degrees did it. I guess the president has more influence and got a better deal.)

Becoming kosher-certified meant giving up our quiche Lorraine. It broke my heart at first, but since we were fast becoming more of a dessert company, I got over it for the greater good. As a matter of fact, desserts were gaining so much ground with us that by the early nineties, and as we grew nationally, the majority of our product development was in that arena. Sometimes at trade shows the same people would ask over and over again, "When did you people start making desserts?"

We decided that because the dessert segment of our product mix was growing by leaps and bounds, we needed a better name to connote our sweet goods. We knew that the name of a business is vitally important, so we thought about it carefully. We trademarked Susan's Sweet Talk in the mid-eighties and described it as a division of our company, printing it as a subheading on all of our boxes, sell sheets, business cards, and the like. But while the ink was drying, we began to realize that the name Love and Quiches had achieved significant recognition throughout our industry, and that, try as we might, it would be a struggle to get anyone to connect "Susan's Sweet Talk" with "Love and Quiches."

Good R&D Is a Very Good Thing

Another major development was hiring our first director of research and development (R&D). Out of the blue one day in 1986, a local suburban housewife—just like I had been, but this one complete with a *doctor* husband and two children—marched in with a carrot cake in both hands and asked for a job. Abby had trained as a nutritionist while in college and had worked in hospitals in that capacity. For the prior few years she had been supplying a local country club with exquisite desserts that she was baking at home in her kitchen. She hadn't bothered getting a license as I did when I first started; she was just *doing* it. Highly skilled product development is a vital component of a business such as ours, providing the ability to communicate on a level playing field with the executive chefs of our target markets. Abby was very talented, and because of her expertise we were able to work with all the restaurant chains in developing products tailored to meet their precise needs and requirements. This was a key factor in our growth.

When we first hired Abby, the office employee kitchen was doing double duty as the test kitchen, and she was doing double duty by also running our little retail shop in the front. It shortly became apparent that this was *not* going to work. As the organization grew, so did the number of our R&D projects, and we quickly found ourselves in desperate need of space for a real test kitchen. All eyes turned to the space occupied by our outlet store, at the front and across the hall from our offices. So we rented some space in the building directly across the street in our industrial park and fitted out a new retail outlet, which we hired someone to run. We didn't lose any of our loyal regulars; all we had to do was point when they knocked on the office door in bewilderment.

Now we had a *real* test kitchen, which we fitted out with all the necessary equipment. We even installed a seven-pan rotary gas oven for Abby to use so that what was developed in the test kitchen would more closely resemble what could be done on the production floor. This whole process is called *commercialization*, a term I didn't yet know existed, one of the primary functions that linked our R&D and the operations department.

A few years later we recruited Mary, yet another pastry chef, who had been an instructor at the Culinary Institute of America in Hyde Park, New York. Mary had *infinite* patience. She would try a recipe dozens of times, just changing one ingredient at a time by the tiniest measure until it was perfect. She once worked on a simple zucchini bread recipe for months, having us taste over and over, then over once again, what we thought each time was the same thing. We could never tell the difference, but she could and did, before we could transfer the recipe to the back of the house for production.

Little by little, lesson by lesson, Love and Quiches was coming into its own. We were better able to vet the opportunities coming our way because we now had some people on board who could, from experience, work out the logistics for production, oven time, labor hours, throughput, and so on. It gave us our first knowledge of the "constraints" (bottlenecks) that all manufacturers face, and by which many have been sadly defeated. Although we were not quite state of the art at this juncture, we were moving in the right direction. With more experience, we learned to read the industry with better results and to watch our competitors with a more practiced eye.

With our new status as more of a known quantity, we were approached by two industry giants to undertake R&D projects, which greatly added to our learning curve. The giants in the industry often turn to small companies like mine because we are flexible enough and have the expertise and time to work on R&D projects such as these. In other words, we understood baking and knew what we were doing. Consequently, we were very well remunerated for materials and our time and expertise.

One such project was from General Foods, before they merged with Kraft and while they still owned Entenmann's bakery. This was a "fresh refrigerated single serve dessert" project that General Foods planned to test in about thirty supermarkets in the Midwest. The project took months, but the formulas were too labor intensive, and the project ultimately went nowhere. Still, we learned a lot, and we met many important people way up the chain in our industry. Since this was General Foods, we were drowning in the required record keeping, and we were glad when it was over. (Fast forward to today: our record keeping is just as stringent, maybe more so.)

Because of this R&D project, we got to tour the Entenmann's plant, now largely closed, farther out on Long Island. I'll never forget some of the things I saw. For example, they had a brand-new high-tech line that sent the boxes down a conveyor belt facing in the wrong direction; they stationed someone at the end of the line just to rotate them manually. They also swept nuts off the *floor* beneath another line and then sterilized and re-toasted them for reuse! (Please remember this was twenty-five years ago, and I suspect, or rather I hope, this could never happen today.) Racks, pans, and supplies were all over the place. By the end of the tour, we were thinking that even *we* were better run than Entenmann's, although of course their volume dwarfed ours.

The other R&D project came from Rich Foods (still a private, family-run business), and it involved making ice cream cakes with a type of ice cream that didn't easily melt, could be distributed through normal frozen food channels, and did not need the special panel environment normally required to transport ice cream. And although this project, too, never moved forward, it was a lot of fun despite the unusually hot summer.

It was during the eighties that we developed relationships with several fledgling national chains, businesses that grew from just a few stores at the outset to hundreds and, in some cases, more than a thousand units. One was a chain that featured chicken; the opportunity came our way because one of the executives' wives was so fond of our brownies that she used to regularly drive down all the way from Connecticut just to get them. Another was an Italian pizza chain, whose executives told me to feel free to share this story. The family matriarch had been baking all of their cheesecakes in the original pizza parlor in Brooklyn for all twenty or so stores that they had at the time. As they developed their expansion plans, however, they knew this couldn't last. Getting the cheesecake recipe out of Mama was worse than dealing with Jimmy the Baker! She put her three sons, who were running the business, and Love and Quiches through hell until we finally received her blessing. We have been baking their cheesecakes ever since.

Then we had an opportunity to do a second product for the chain that had given us such a tremendous boost when they bought our Pecan Brownie Pie, knocking us out of the ballpark and into our next phase of growth. This story didn't have such a happy ending, though. The second product was a lovely frozen lemon mousse that we packed and shipped in four-pound tubs. The dessert was to be scooped and served with a berry sauce. None of the servers wanted to bother scooping the mousse and garnishing it, however; to them, it was too much trouble. Since the item was a special and did not appear on the printed menu, it needed server enthusiasm to push it. It failed rather spectacularly.

The company asked us to take it back, all $90,000 worth, and we *did* in order to preserve the relationship. We made the Salvation Army very happy that month!

Throughout the eighties we were setting the stage for the nineties. Our distributor business was becoming more distinct from our local business, but our focus was on building our multiunit chain account and airline business. And soon—export! Love and Quiches continued to grow and was poised to enter yet another new phase in its busy life.

Chapter 8

Securing Our Position
(1990–2000)

Get a good idea and stay with it. Dog it, and
work at it until it's done, and done right.
—Walt Disney

The 1990s brought dramatic changes to Love and Quiches. Many events of that decade reinforced the fact we were still, so many years after our beginning, an accidental business. We continued to make a few too many costly mistakes, but we had progressed enough to recognize them much more quickly and to use them to gain strength as we righted them. We were definitely making progress on the top line, but it's the *bottom* line, of course, that counts.

Love and Quiches was not just waiting for things to happen *to* us; we were, by now, constantly planning our growth, and we landed our first big export client as a direct result of our decision to exhibit at the NRA yearly trade show. One year an entourage from an international company—one that has thousands of restaurants worldwide, including in the Middle East—happened by our booth. They looked at our display of products, asked a few questions, and then moved on down the aisle. (The last thing on their minds, as they told me later, was desserts.) So, when they phoned just days later, we were astounded, and our astonishment grew as, within weeks, we were supplying them with cheesecakes and chocolate cakes. This unexpected and wonderful opportunity changed our image of *ourselves* and what we could become. If they hadn't turned into our aisle that day, I would perhaps be telling quite a different story. But when opportunity knocked, we opened the door and let it in. And in this case, the partnership has continued for twenty years.

Although this might sound as if we were getting in way over our heads, it was a logical next step for the company. Most freight, whether hard goods or frozen foodstuffs like our products, moves around the world via container ship. Located as we were on the East Coast near so many major ports, we were in an ideal position to enter the export market. We could easily contract for frozen containers, which our freight forwarders drop at our loading dock and then haul away when they are loaded and sealed (to measure temperature all throughout the voyage and to assure that no tampering has taken place). Then the containers are loaded onto vast container ships and plugged in to the ship's electrical system to keep the contents frozen until they arrive at customs at their final destination. This is a costly process, so our international customers only order full containers to help spread the cost across as much product as possible. But the integrity of the product is no different from what it would be if we were merely delivering it from Freeport, Long Island, to New Jersey.

Thanks to Love and Quiches' positive reputation in the industry, invitations to tour major facilities continued to pour in. One such tour that comes to mind was of the Hormel plant in Austin, Minnesota, where they produce everything from Spam to the finest prosciutto. The Hormel plant was so large that it took more than five hours to complete the tour. It was a marvel of efficiency: the animals coming in at one end and dozens of *perfect* products coming out the other—a vertical operation, nose to tail, and even the slaughtering done right there (the smell permeated the area for literally miles). Seeing—and smelling—that place was something I won't ever forget.

Why did we get all these invitations to tour gigantic facilities? Probably it was because the food industry giants were inviting us to a dance to see if we were interested in being acquired. We'd accept the invitations to tour, always interested in hearing what the giants had to say, but we remained a private company through it all. The giants move very slowly and cautiously; they are the tortoise to our hare. Love and Quiches was thriving on its nimbleness and quick response time, so a sale would dull our competitive edge. Our field is very R&D intensive, and to satisfy our customer base, we knew we had to be extremely flexible and constantly aware of that base's needs. As we fought our way forward independently, we watched as many of our competitors were acquired. Typically, the absorbed upscale brand either disappeared or the quality of its products became secondary.

Another phenomenon that swallowed dozens of our competitors was a gathering of dessert brands under one umbrella by venture capital groups with a mind to overrunning the Sara Lees of the world. They, too, were quite wrong; to be in the dessert business requires knowledge of the baking business, and these groups didn't have that knowledge. The majority of these experiments failed, and the companies—including, sadly, some very fine ones—have at this point mostly disappeared.

During this very busy decade, the business also segued into a family enterprise; both Andrew and Joan joined the firm in the '90s. I will discuss this in more detail in chapter 17, "Family Matters."

Stretching the Walls

The early nineties brought new energy to the business as the second generation brought their ideas forward. We quickly grew to $8 million in volume, and then to $12 million, and then way beyond that.

The building we occupied began to feel very small, and we started looking for ways to expand without moving. We found ourselves in the same position as with our prior smaller facilities, only now our inefficiencies had a much greater impact.

We were desperate for more space, so our next project was to design and build a five-thousand-square-foot holding freezer outside the building. (The old freezer had the same footprint but was inside, taking up valuable space.) This new freezer has a thirty-foot ceiling and four hundred pallet positions, and it is connected to the building through what we dubbed the "patio," an enclosed area with a loading dock for staging our orders. Because of its size and capacity, except for one ill-advised and short-lived period yet to come, we have never had to contract for outside freezer storage, which is quite costly.

The space the old freezer had occupied, which was next to the production floor with its very thick and insulated walls, was converted into manufacturing space that always remained quite cool. We literally doubled our production area overnight, *now* with both a baking area *and* a separate deco and packaging room.

While nothing ever happens at Love and Quiches without its bit of drama, the events surrounding the building of this new freezer were over the top even by our standards! It may sound unusual, but this type of construction involves building from the inside out. The entire racking system is put up first, and it is this system that supports the outside walls and roof. Essentially, the racking system holds up the entire building. The roof and compressors are the last to be built and installed.

Well, during the construction period, in the middle of the night, we received a frantic call from Jimmy the Baker inquiring—or more like howling—"Are you trying to scare me to death!" Something had gone terribly wrong, and the entire infrastructure, the racking system, had toppled over upon itself just like a set of dominos! Just imagine the sound and the fury of all that metal collapsing in a heap. After the initial shock, the refrigeration construction company jumped into action, and the project was completed with only a six-week delay. It seems that a collapsing freezer is a rite of passage, once per facility, for Love and Quiches. (And as you'll recall from the story about my childhood home burning down, refrigeration disasters have always played a dramatic role in my life.)

Over the next few years, we built other additions outside our Freeport facility to make more room inside: blast freezers and both flour and sugar silos with capacity for tens of thousands of pounds of those ingredients. We use a *lot* of sugar and flour, so we refill our silos very often. Almost fifteen years later, I still find myself amazed when I drive up in the morning and see the huge tanker trucks pumping the stuff in! The fact that we have silos at all is not something that I would *ever* have imagined. Not me, not here, not ever.

There was a time, back in the nineties, when I used to see trucks on the highway or lined up in front of our building as symbols—that is, symbolic of the relentless and never-ending responsibility, feeling as if my whole life was passing before my eyes. Now I just see them as trucks.

Forward Progress

Most of what we did in the nineties paved the way for what we faced and what we did in the first decade of the new century. We were growing, but we operated with the wrong business model for what we ultimately hoped to achieve. We just didn't know it at the time.

One of the most important decisions we made in that decade was to give up our trucks and move to common carriers for transport and distributors to sell our products for us. It took great courage because our direct delivery business represented several million dollars of our volume. But we had come to realize that that wasn't where our real future lay.

We decided it would be more profitable to devote our energies to developing distributors in the tri-state area to service our 450 local customers, who by then consisted of restaurants, hotels, cafés, colleges, employee feeding, and all the other usual suspects. Direct delivery for us meant having to maintain the customer service staff and warehouse crew—not to mention drivers, trucks, and parking tickets (for details, see the next paragraph)—to make at least 450 phone calls weekly, print hundreds of invoices, pack hundreds of orders mostly under $75, and have them delivered daily, with every account clamoring for morning delivery.

(If you did business in the city, you inevitably got a lot of parking tickets. In fact, we got so many that we qualified to have our own rep within the traffic violations department. An employee went up there once a month, by appointment, to plead the tickets and settle up at a discount. Very civilized, but we were glad it was over when we took our trucks off the road!)

And then to collect! We always knew there were plenty of fly-by-nights in the business, and we took that as part of our costs, but we diligently worked to keep bad debt to a minimum. Nevertheless, it was often quite aggravating. Our accounts receivable clerk's husband worked at the time for a debt collection agency. He was our formidable enforcer; this was, after all, New York, a very tough town.

Our local direct delivery business had been kept separate from the rest of the company; it had its own operating budget, sort of a business within the business. But we were fast segueing into a national presence as we expanded our reach and sought more multiunit customers. The local business was profitable and well managed, despite its difficulties, but it was taking way too many of our resources, and we needed to move away from it. Our focus moved outward.

During this era, Elaine retired, and we recruited some talented and highly computer-literate young people to take over the various functions she had managed. We also hired a PR firm exclusively aligned with the foodservice industry, and it was during this period that we designed and launched our first website, with their help. It featured a lot of pink stripes, but soon we upgraded the site to beige with green diamonds and lots of swirling slices, berries, and walnuts. This is also when, after ten or more years, we finally gave up trying to persuade the industry to recognize "Susan's Sweet Talk" as a trade name for our desserts, gave it up, and formally renamed the company "Love and Quiches Desserts."

Another project was our first gatefold brochure, a six-sided affair with a deep pocket in which to tuck sell sheets. This was major. We hired both a top New York City commercial photographer and a food stylist, rented freezers, and sent tons of products to his studio, along with countless cartons of props. Each morning a mob of us would descend upon his place: marketing and R&D personnel, me, and representatives from our PR firm, plus—I am chagrined to admit—a ubiquitous box of greasy donuts to sustain us.

What we thought would be a three-day project took almost a month, with each shot requiring a painstakingly slow process. By the time each slice or whole cake was fussed with and dressed up, not a crumb out of place, and the plates, props, and background had been selected, we were exhausted. But we loved every minute of it. One day Abby, our R&D chef, and I were dispatched to Macy's to pick up a certain sized plate since *nothing* among the myriad props we had brought satisfied the photographer for a particular shot! We found the perfect candidate, but it was only available as a set. We had no choice but to slip the display plate into my bag and quickly walk it out the door. Among our many other company roles, we were now thieves; my heart still skips a beat when I think of it.

We took dozens upon dozens of shots, including individual slice shots that did double duty by being printed as table tents. Our PR firm also worked closely with us on the copywriting. All in all, it was a fantastic experience and the brochures were gorgeous.

What we did at that incredible photo shoot we partially do in-house now, including updating and printing brochures only as needed. We even do some of the photography. But by printing to order, we have eliminated all obsolete sell sheet inventory, which used to pile up quickly in our storage closets.

Bigger Is Not Always Better

When we moved our retail store across the street to make space for our real test kitchen, we also took a lot of additional space in the same building for dry storage, meant to hold inventory such as corrugated packaging supplies, canned goods, label inventory, and such. We also created a sales office and an office for Irwin that he never used, *ever*, because it isolated him too much. In taking this space, we assumed that by buying larger quantities of supplies we would receive better prices, among other rationales. But we never considered the high cost of carrying so much excess inventory. This was space we absolutely did not need, and it was painfully brought home to us during the events of the next few years.

Just before the year 2000, we hired someone from one of our competitors, a man who had approached us to run the operations and production end of the business. He was an interesting guy—I'll call him X—good looking, with a long, blond ponytail. He commuted from the West Coast weekly because he preferred to be with his family on the weekend. We rented a studio apartment for him, but all he wanted in the way of furnishings was a bridge table, one chair, a mattress, a TV, and a hot plate.

To our way of thinking, X was the answer to our prayers. We were wrong. We already suffered from too much inventory, but his approach to best servicing our customer base's needs was to further build finished inventory to such an extreme amount that we found our four-hundred-pallet freezer completely inadequate to hold it all, which led us to take some public freezer storage from a third party for the only time in our forty-year history and to ship our orders from there. We built thousands of cases of product that then sat there waiting for the orders to come. The cost of carrying inventory in my industry is much higher than in many other manufacturing businesses: it takes a lot of energy to keep product frozen, and the shelf life clock starts ticking from day one. Material costs are quite high, as well, for our upscale products. It seems so utterly obvious, *now*, that we needed to be much more mindful that our products were perishable. Not to do so in this case was a big mistake on our part, as we'd soon come to find out.

We piled on the inventory and overhead on the theory that if we had everything we could possibly need (and then some!) we could fulfill orders more quickly as they came in. We were choking ourselves with everything that we absolutely did not need, and for all the wrong reasons.

The End of an Era

Still other events during this decade had a dramatic effect on the company. In early 1998, Jimmy the Baker—we will forever think of him by that name—started to complain about having constant headaches. He kept saying, "I think I need a new prescription for my glasses" and other things along the same line while trying to explain it to himself. He must have had a very high threshold for pain, because the sad punch line is that within ninety days he was gone, a victim of brain cancer.

We were devastated because *all* of us—over two hundred people at the time—loved and respected him. And it was a credit to his management skills that we never missed a beat after his passing. The very next day, his second- and third-in-command stepped up to the plate, and production continued as usual. Luckily, we had come a long way in developing our software systems by then; otherwise, many formulas for our very best products might have been lost when Jimmy died. The formula management modules in our software programs, by then, were well developed, so we had complete control of our recipes. That was hard won, because right up to the end Jimmy would *still* tend to cup his hand, hold it up, and tell us "about this much" or "about three handfuls" when we asked how much of a given ingredient was in a recipe. His well-trained heirs apparent helped us formalize it all, yet to this day we still recertify some of our original recipes to make sure all the information is correct. Even so, our chefs constantly look at our most original recipes with a critical eye to see if they can be improved upon, along with our constant parade of new product introductions.

Esprit de Corps

As early as our first days in Oceanside, when we had about a dozen employees, I knew that developing an orderly hierarchy was my next order of business.

In that mini-factory, we had taken our first rudimentary steps at building an organization by dividing management simply between the day crew and the night crew. This was developing an organization in plain vanilla. After that, we started to further divide areas of responsibility and function: the Deco Crew decorated, and the Packing Crew packed. At night there was a Mixing Crew and an Oven Crew. And so we evolved.

As our original Motley Crew began to move on, we started to promote others from within who showed talent, and then we started looking outside for operations managers just as we had for sales staff. Our organization began to take on a more formalized shape.

We also knew that developing a family spirit—an *esprit de corps*—would be a vital element in our future growth. There had been several attempts throughout the years to unionize our company, but our employees have never chosen to do so. I think it is because we have always treated them fairly and with respect, have always invited their input, and have always done as much as we could for them. We provide a good place to work, and we always give good people opportunities for moving up in the company.

As soon as we moved to our present home in Freeport in 1980, we started a tradition of celebrating the Christmas holidays with a fiesta right in the middle of the production area. We would push all of the equipment to the side; we brought in a caterer and a waitstaff; we hired a disc jockey. All family members or significant others were welcome, and we all had a grand party on a Friday evening about a week before the actual holiday. Today, no outside food nor anybody who is not all suited up in a lab coat, complete with hair and beard nets—much less all dressed up for a party—is even allowed anywhere *near* the floor. But back then we even had a wedding for two of our employees on the production floor, just as elaborate as our annual party!

But the Christmas tradition ended abruptly and with a bang. The party's allure was growing, and we had to set up gatekeepers, like bouncers at a disco, but each year the number of party crashers was growing. One year there was an altercation. We called the police, who were there in minutes—Freeport takes good care of its businesses— and *that was that!*

From then on we held our yearly bash in June at a local park in Freeport, and they got better and better. The park offered excellent facilities that could be reserved for a private event if you remembered to call on January 2, when they would book on a first come, first served basis. Eventually it sort of became "our spot" for the first Saturday in June, with no danger of our being shut out.

Fun and games at a Love and Quiches annual picnic.

In addition to the caterer and disc jockey, we hired a party planner to organize relay races and activities for the children, cousins, neighbors, and friends of our employees. They were wonderful parties, and over the years we kept adding more elements, such as a magician to perform, face painting for the kids, a row of concessions for amuse-ment park–type games, towering blow-ups for rock climbing and slides, miniature golf, bucking bull riding, and other stuff. We also held dance contests with small cash prizes, and we had a raffle where the first prize was a TV.

Eventually we had as many as four hundred attending as the Love and Quiches family, and *their* families, grew. I was the archivist and took hundreds of pictures at each June party; we made a photo album of each and every one. One entire shelf in my office is full of them in chronological order.

———

We continued to very carefully look for talented employees to promote from within, as well as to bring in some experienced people from the outside, people who could bring fresh ideas to the table. The demand for high-end gourmet products was growing; we had to position our-selves to compete on a level playing field.

Everything happens for a reason, and one door closing opens another. We had just hired Michael G.—almost right out of school at Johnson & Wales—as our pastry chef's assistant, and since he was too young to have had enough jobs to provide references, I called the school and spoke to the dean. I was told that on a scale of one to ten, Michael would score a fourteen. So, we never missed a beat when, shortly thereafter, Abby walked out the door after ten years with us and never came back—not even a phone call. Michael—who I'd fight to the death to keep—has been with our company ever since and now serves as VP of research and development. He works very closely with all of our larger clients and is recognized as one of the top pastry chefs in our industry.

Many of our other employees, even our line workers, have been with us for twenty-plus years. I have seen a number of them recog-nized for their promise by being promoted to positions such as line leaders, quality technicians, shift supervisors, warehouse managers, and so on. Their longevity has strengthened Love and Quiches. They are all part of our team, built from the bottom up.

But building our management teams—both top management and mid-level, with areas of responsibility and orders of command well defined to avoid duplication, waste, and conflicts—took a *very* long time, and we made quite a few mistakes. As I've said before, failure is definitely underappreciated as a learning tool. We brought in a series of operations directors until we found the right one. We brought in a series of quality assurance directors until we found the right one. We brought in a series of purchasing directors—some howlingly incompetent—until we found the right one.

We also brought in some whom we thought would be heavy hitter salespeople, but, once again, we made some very poor, and costly, choices. Finding the right sales force proved to be the longest process of all, because it is only recently that we have developed the high-performance sales team we have always needed.

During our early decades, we had constantly evolved, first in very simple ways and then in much more complex ones, but it has always been our willingness to roll up our sleeves and get *to* it that has enabled us to achieve our current place at the table. It had been a decade-long process just to begin to achieve an effective organizational structure, and we still weren't done as we crossed over into the 2000s.

Actually, the nineties, after the brutal 1991 recession precipitated by the First Gulf War, was a decade of strong and sustained growth in the overall economy. Love and Quiches was humming along at quite a robust pace at the time. Little did we know that very soon our business model would be completely transformed—suddenly and dramatically—as a result of one tragic day in our nation's history. Our accidental period was about to come to an abrupt end.

Part II

Chapter 9

Adversity

What does not destroy me makes me stronger.
—Friedrich Wilhelm Nietzsche

A ll New Yorkers know exactly where they were and what they were doing when the two airliners hit the Twin Towers on the morning of September 11, 2001. Our entire country and the world beyond stopped breathing as we watched it happen in real time. The images will never fade for any of us, but especially for New Yorkers, as well as for those near the Pennsylvania field and the Pentagon, there is a feeling of vulnerability and grave insult that just doesn't leave us. We could taste it, feel it, and smell it. And there are very few of us who don't know somebody who died that day, or know somebody who knows somebody who lost a loved one—a son, a daughter, a husband, a wife, a mother, a father, a friend, a relative. But we have learned to live with it. There was no other choice. For a very long time after that day, my heart would race each time I headed into the city and had to cross a bridge, enter a tunnel, or take a train.

That morning our friends from Kraft Foods were visiting Love and Quiches. We were supposed to spend the day in the Freeport facility working on a co-branding project, but we ended up staring at the screen of a tiny fourteen-inch TV in our small conference room. As many Love and Quiches employees as could fit into the packed room watched with us. It was so surreal that we found ourselves shaking our heads, trying to clear our eyes of these images. We thought it couldn't really be happening. But it was, and we saw it all.

Later that day, our traumatized visitors from Kraft eventually found their way home, but it wasn't easy. The disruption was monumental. Nothing was moving.

Our buyer was in Las Vegas for a big bakery show. She had to get back somehow, but there were no planes, of course, and no cars were available to rent. She approached a complete stranger who got the very last car at one agency—perhaps in all of Las Vegas—and was heading east; she offered to share the driving. These strangers spent almost three days traveling together—each thinking the other could very well be Jack the Ripper—before parting at the George Washington Bridge. Both of them were relieved finally to be near home and convinced they would keep in touch. But of course, they never saw each other again.

I have a friend whose daughter-in-law lived downtown; she literally ran uptown barefoot in her pajamas with her half-naked newborn, dust and debris everywhere, found her way out of the city, and never returned. She left behind her clothes, her furniture, *everything*.

New York had been brought to its knees, and so had Love and Quiches. We got clobbered, as did so many other businesses. Twenty-five percent of our business at the time was within the airline industry: obviously not a very great place to be just then. We suffered hundreds of thousands of dollars in canceled orders and hundreds of thousands more in losses due to what was now obsolete and irrelevant inventory, both finished and raw, already produced in anticipation of filling those orders.

We had hundreds of thousands of additional dollars tied up in inventory for our other channels of business, not to mention our lease for storage space across the street and the accompanying carrying costs. In short, our glut of inventory was a recipe for disaster.

Everything came to a dead stop. There was a mass reshuffling in our customer base, especially those segments we serviced that were heavily travel related. The phone stopped ringing. Long-standing contracts were canceled because of the severe disruption, and there was plenty of other collateral damage. Sbarro lost two units when the towers collapsed, although, miraculously, no employees lost their lives. Their hundreds of units in airports across the country suffered, however, which led to *their* distributor filing for bankruptcy. That hit us with a further loss of even more hundreds of thousands of dollars. This distributor had *never* been a good payer, and I often had to appeal to my friend Joseph Sbarro himself, who would call the distributor for us, raising his voice and demanding payment on our behalf, so that there would be no disruption of supply to *his* restaurants. But now the distributor had gone bankrupt altogether.

To add insult to injury, we were sued by the bankruptcy receiver for the last payment of about $250,000 we'd received from the company—only a *part* of what they owed us! Because of a quirk in the bankruptcy statutes, anything paid out within ninety days of the filing is deemed preferential. We ended up settling for $90,000, which we had to pay the court—and don't forget that our lawyers in this case did not work for free. Because we were a legitimate claimant we got some of the money back years later, once the case finished wending its way through the courts. But it came to about ten cents on the dollar! I don't remember ever being quite so angry.

Another of our distributors that exclusively serviced the airlines could never fight its way back to profitability and closed its doors, costing us $200,000. We were *not* happy people.

It was a devastating time for the country and for our business. Our reserve cash—so vital for carrying companies through downturns and slow periods—wasn't enough to help us weather this unfathomable storm. Our path ahead looked rocky and uncertain to say the least.

Indeed it was. With ironically superb timing, the bank that we had been with for many years leading up to 9/11, which was originally a Midwest outfit, decided to withdraw from the New York market. We found ourselves in the unenviable position of needing to find a new banking relationship at exactly the wrong time. We succeeded, but not very easily. It was another marathon, but the relationship with our current bank has grown, and we are still with them today, a decade later.

There was *one* bright spot along that path, however. We qualified for an SBA disaster (9/11) loan with an extremely favorable interest rate and a twelve-year payback because we were so specifically and negatively affected in so many ways. This helped us secure desperately needed funding. Still, once again, we had to put up our home as collateral; there are no free lunches. During this period, there were times when I feared 2001 might mark the end of the Love and Quiches story, but we did not, *could not*, give up.

Here is one of the very first lessons every entrepreneur needs to learn: you are going to suffer adversity and setbacks. There is no escaping them. But your success depends on how you handle those setbacks. If you can push through, keep your spirits, your determination, and your courage up, and if you can learn from the experience, you'll come out much stronger than you were before.

Running a business is not for the faint of heart. Adversity can hurt. Your mistakes can be humiliating. When you find yourself in that place—when a new product fails, when your partner quits, when you're denied a loan, when a competitor steals one of your best customers— you cannot take it as a sign from the universe that you should give up. Every success story has these dark chapters. If you want to keep your business alive, you *have* to press ahead, overcoming the situation at hand. However, *this* was adversity at an entirely new level.

I have come to think of everything that happened, from our founding in 1973 to that period in the early 2000s, as a kind of game, a warm-up for all that was to come. It was my accidental business period: Love and Quiches Lite. The adversity brought on by 9/11 pushed us to become something new, different, and better. It served to show me that I *could* do it, that *we* could do it. On some level, it was like a magnified version of that six-thousand-case order for our delicious Pecan Brownie Pie in the late seventies—it catapulted the business up to a new level and catapulted *me* into what would be the rest of my life.

We'd found ourselves in absolutely the wrong place when 9/11 struck, but it helped us realize that we needed to completely overhaul our business model. And we sought a lot of outside advice to make sure our path would be all up from here. From that point forward, we slowly gained ground that we have never relinquished. The changes we went through in the early 2000s were transformational, and we ended up bigger and stronger. (More on how we did it in the next two chapters.)

As a business owner, it's part of your job to prepare for the future, but we're all subject to forces we can't control, whether it's an unthinkably tragic terrorist attack or a sudden economic downturn. The test of your business is in how you respond to those forces when they come—and they *will* come.

As I've described in previous chapters, Love and Quiches has been profoundly affected by several major recessions since its inception. And most people don't even remember the one early in the decade—in March 2001, statistically ending in November of that year—because of the tragic events surrounding 9/11. But we were still battling the effects of that early recession when the unthinkable occurred.

In addition, the commodities debacle of 2007 was particularly harmful to *my* industry: the prices of our most basic ingredients— eggs, soybean oil, butter, flour, cream cheese—skyrocketed, sometimes doubling or even tripling. It was more than we had ever paid since our founding. We could not, of course, raise our prices to match, since our customer base fought us tooth and nail. When those items began to moderate, we then experienced the same escalations in the prices of sugar, chocolate, and nuts. And we use a *lot* of sugar, chocolate, and nuts! These, too, eventually moderated, but they never fell back to prior levels. Other commodities will soon escalate, and so it goes.

Coupled with the Great Recession and the ensuing global financial meltdown, times were, and remain, challenging to say the least. We all now are still at battle with the lingering aftereffects. This is the new reality; the cycles are never ending.

And so it will be with your business, whether you are selling web designs or artisanal cheeses. The first key to success is staying determined and positive during the hard times so that you can emerge, newly strengthened, on the other side.

Chapter 10

From Overstuffed to Lean and Mean

Success is not final, failure is not fatal;
it is the courage to continue that counts.
—Sir Winston Churchill

After 9/11, we steeled ourselves to keep calm, not to panic. We all knew that going forward every step would be important, and as an organization, we were ready to act. We knew transformational changes were needed, and we were prepared to face them head-on.

Every business owner, especially in the manufacturing sector, has to learn how to construct an organization that adheres, above all, to principles of efficiency, or your chances of turning a profit—or surviving in the long run—are slim indeed. Growth is a wonderful thing, but it merely exacerbates problems if you aren't ready. Our time to *get* ready was upon us. At the heart of our reinvention was our move from an overstuffed, overstaffed operation to a lean and mean one. We went from having an unnecessary glut of inventory to operating more efficiently than ever before, and it saved Love and Quiches.

Our first steps in the "lean and mean" transformation were to lay off some workers—hard to do, but necessary—and to hire our first CFO. Our director of operations from out West (the one who had pumped us full of more inventory than we could possibly use) was shown the door. We planned our withdrawal from our unneeded space across the street. We trimmed all discretionary spending; if we didn't need to do it or buy it, we let it go.

It was during this period that we contracted our first consultants, who brought to the table two extremely important developments. First, we adopted a "just in time" (JIT) business model, which completely changed how we had been operating since 1980, the year we had moved into our facility at Freeport. Second, we instituted a "pipeline" approach to our sales efforts.

One word of caution about consultants before we talk about these two developments. When hiring consultants, define very clear parameters when it comes to the scope of the project, the time line, *and* the cost. Otherwise, before you realize it, the costs can easily spiral out of control and eat up all the improvements the consultants suggest. In our first time using consultants, we were too innocent, and although they brought a lot to the table, the experience was very costly and we had difficulty ending it. Since then we have been careful. We *also* have found that it is never a good idea to hire a consultant into a permanent position. Usually, consultants have a very specific area in which their expertise lies, causing them to *lack* flexibility. If we have learned one thing *really* well, it is how to change course, to be flexible, and people who can't be flexible don't work well as permanent parts of our organization.

Despite these caveats, it remains true that consultants can bring fresh eyes and expertise to a situation or a process. Sometimes we kept doing things merely because we had always done them that way. Every company—small businesses as well as giants—suffers this same weakness at some point, and consultants can be a good way to help an organization move beyond it.

Learning to Be Lean

In simple terms, JIT means that we keep very tight reins on our inventory, both raw and finished. Theoretically, when we receive an order, we order the ingredients, produce the product, and ship it out as quickly as possible. As a result, we contain our inventory and carrying costs and increase our cash flow. Cash is king. We only bring in supplies for our purchase orders in hand. We turn over our finished inventory every two weeks and are assured that what we produce is already on its way out the door, with no excess or potentially obsolete inventory of either type.

This may seem like a gross oversimplification of our path forward, and a business of our size is, of course, extremely complicated. But the JIT method is now ingrained in our organization and serves as the synchronizing rhythm for all departments.

We have had other very fruitful consultancies since the first one in 2002. Shortly after that first experience, we received a grant from the New York State Department of Economic Development to help us learn lean manufacturing. Lean manufacturing is also known as the Toyota method because that company first developed it. Its key element is called *continuous improvement.* We changed *everything*: how we did things, where we did things, nothing out of place, and bringing the work to the worker, not the other way around. This new business model transformed us forever; it is the nuts and bolts of how we generate our revenue and profits.

The grant picked up a large part of the cost of hiring consultants to help with the process of educating us.

The consultants we hired taught *all* of Love and Quiches' employees, from the top down: I participated, as did the line workers, the porters, and everybody in between. Since we still had the building across the street at the time, our "teachers" set up their "classroom" there to minimize disruption to the day-to-day running of the business.

The consultants set up a simulated clock factory as the model we would follow. It's not as strange as it might seem: all manufacturing processes have much the same elements in common, whether you're making clocks or cheesecakes. We were divided into teams to produce these clocks, which were made of paper, plastic, clips, and other simple parts. Rudimentary as they were, the finished clocks actually worked!

We followed the consultants' procedures from orders coming in to gathering supplies, manufacturing, packaging, and shipping. During each session we were timed and made to start over again and again; with each repetition we recognized more and more efficiencies and shortcuts to help speed the process without sacrificing quality. More often than not, our efficiencies and shortcuts even improved the quality of the product. We got faster and faster, again without sacrificing quality, with each team competing to beat the other with process improvements and completion times. It was absolutely amazing!

There was a second part to the project. This time the teams participated in a virtual order for carrot cake (no actual cake, just the process) from taking the order to shipping it out the door. So many things that we had been doing the hard way became glaringly obvious. We started to institute changes even while the learning process was still under way.

The most obvious lesson was the great advantage that teamwork, team building, and mutual respect can bring to an organization. We reorganized our work centers, brought the supplies *to* the line workers to avoid downtime and cross traffic, and maximized *value added* (in layman's terms, *productive*) activities. We have never lost these principles; as human nature inevitably dictates, however, when we see some practices slipping, we reboot and retrain. This is ongoing.

Today we more or less measure *all* activities in actual minutes, product by product, but the groundwork was set during that six-week lean manufacturing consultancy as we were beginning to recover from the effects of 9/11. And we all had a great time to boot!

This is not to say that you need to hire consultants to benefit from lean manufacturing and just-in-time processes. There are plenty of great books on this subject (see my favorites in Recipes for the Mind). As you continue to build your organization—whether you teach yourself about lean operations by reading such books or you decide to spend money on bringing in lean consultants—you must focus on reducing waste and increasing efficiency. Bring on people who have experience with these methods, and work consistently at keeping the dynamic going.

Prioritizing Pipeline

The purpose of any business, first and foremost, is the pursuit of profit, and all the changes we made after 9/11 going forward would assure that we stayed on that path. We are survivors, and each change to the company strengthened us.

Our first round of post-9/11 consulting also taught us the importance of pipeline. At the end of the day, everything depends upon the orders in hand. Everybody waits for the phone to ring, the faxes to come over, the electronic orders to be emailed because no matter how carefully and detailed the sales budgeting process may be, no one has a crystal ball. Unexpected changes—from a hurricane down south to a change in management or ownership of a very large account—can affect gross sales. Adjustments can be made to produce goods more efficiently and with less waste, and equipment can be kept running smoothly with less downtime. Yet the sales numbers inform it all.

So many things compete for your attention when you're running a business, but it's imperative that you not lose track of your pipeline. We now keep our pipeline filled, making sure enough new prospects are waiting in the wings while we work on closing current new customers and bids. A robust pipeline doesn't mean everything is going to fall in your lap, so we track our *potentials*, our *in-process*, our *decision pending*, our *closed*, our *lost opportunities*, and *why* the opportunities were lost. We have gotten rather good at it, and each salesperson is required to update a Pipeline Report weekly.

So, even though it's the bottom line that counts, the top line has to be healthy too. No matter how efficient the operation is with all its parts, if the phone doesn't ring, you have nothing. With few exceptions, after 9/11 we managed to hold on to all of our customers, and we rebuilt together.

———

By 2003 we *knew* that although there was a lot of work ahead, we would be okay. Thanks to the improvements we had made on efficiency and pipeline, we were going to make it through. In September of that year, we were invited to a franchisee conference by our big Middle East customer—the one who'd just happened by our NRA booth in Chicago about ten years before—and Andrew and I flew to Dubai to attend. The temperature in Dubai at that time of year never falls below 100 degrees—even at night; it's a fabulous city, but hot! Our hosts did everything just right, top drawer. Attendees were assigned places for all of the meetings, and all of the vendors were rotated to assure that they got to interact and sit with all of the franchisees at least once. There I was, a Jewish female business owner from New York among a sea of Middle Eastern men, quite a few of them dressed in flowing robes and headdresses, but I was treated as if I were one of them. Andrew blended in much better than I did! At the closing banquet, much to our amazement, Love and Quiches was honored as Vendor of the Year for the region. They recognized us for coming through the 9/11 tragedy with no lapses in our quality or service levels. I will never forget that evening.

9/11 set in motion what became a decade of change and improvements for Love and Quiches. By examining every aspect of our business and going from overstuffed to lean, we created a strategy that has allowed us to survive, thrive, and grow in any economic climate. First were the short-term survival strategies while we developed our new forward vision. We changed or refined our policies and procedures, instituted cost-savings initiatives, and didn't forget to count the paper clips. We revolutionized our manufacturing procedures, developed quicker changeover times between products, staggered lunch breaks to keep the lines moving, scheduled all-chocolate days on the production floor, and so on. When it comes to improving efficiency, if you can think of it, do it!

After years of intense work, we've come out with a clear vision of where we are going and how we are going to get there. Even if lean operations and building our pipeline were our top priorities and ruled everything that came after those changes, our focus after 9/11 went toward the goal of becoming an organization that had a strong control of all its complex parts so that we could produce our excellent, high-quality quiches and desserts with efficiency and, above all, at a profit.

Chapter 11

The Next Level

*All you have to do is look straight and see the road, and when
you see it, don't sit looking at it—walk.*
—Ayn Rand

Through every new development in the relatively short history of Love and Quiches, one common theme always held firm: we were constantly moving to the next level. No matter what we encountered, we were always upping our game, building our organization, and preparing for future growth. If your company is going to truly thrive, you must be ready to constantly revolutionize your operations—sometimes in ways you never foresaw—and take the business to the next level.

In the years following 9/11, we continued our habit of forward momentum and took some giant steps. The sense of urgency created by that crisis and, later in the decade, by the financial crisis and the Great Recession became a significant lever for change for us to once again move to the next level—and to keep doing so even through the present day.

Building a Rock-Solid Organization

Even before those tragic events, as we crossed over into the twenty-first century, it had become apparent that too many decisions were still being made at the top, and we knew this had to change. We had learned to be lean, but an equally crucial achievement was the building of our organization from the bottom up with strong, high-performance teams and equally strong directors and middle managers. We needed to further develop an organization that could support the demand we had created.

One of the rewards of successfully growing an organization is seeing it develop from humble beginnings—perhaps just you and some part-time help—into a real fleshed-out and well-organized team. After the early years, when we hired our first rudimentary team, I was no longer alone. As our organization grew, more and more of us had the same goals at stake. We were all climbing the mountain together, solving and overcoming each obstacle. Now there are a lot of us, and each of us is skilled in his or her particular area. All the parts have come together, and, finally, we have more of a dance than a struggle to the top. But we *do* need to keep climbing. There is no other way to do it.

You all now know that I was singularly unprepared for opening a business, and a woman in manufacturing was a rarity back when I started. Thus the process of building an organization around myself was exceedingly difficult and seemed unattainable from where I started. But once I got into the rhythm, each step naturally flowed from the one preceding it. I built something, *did* something, and everything happened from there.

If I could do it, there is hope for others like me. (There are also a lot more resources to call upon now, a great advantage compared to when I started out.) Whether you're talking about a small company or a middle-market one like mine, running it still involves the same twelve- to fifteen-hour workdays, the same hard decisions, the hiring, firing, and all the rest. If you have the backbone *and* a great idea, think it over *very* well and then, maybe, go for it.

So, as the years passed, we continued the process of, as Jim Collins says in *Good to Great*, "getting the right people on the bus," and we continued tackling our *constraints*. I learned from the late Eliyahu M. Goldratt's *The Goal* that a single constraint (bottleneck) can hamper the *entire* process. Having the right people, attacking and smoothing out our bottlenecks, keeping the sales coming, and never compromising on quality: all of these moved us closer to achieving our goals and sustaining that achievement today.

We think like the big manufacturing guys do. Our business has all of the same parts that General Electric must administer to succeed; each department needs to be held accountable for both performance and budget. At Love and Quiches, beneath the executive team at the top, eight main departments support the structure, each with its own director:

1. Finance and Administration

2. Operations (which includes all aspects of production)

3. Purchasing and Logistics (which includes customer service)

4. Sales and Marketing

5. Research and Development

6. Quality Assurance and Food Safety

7. Human Resources

8. Engineering

All of these departments are inextricably linked in the process of commercialization and bringing our products to market. Beneath this group of directors, there are middle management, team leaders, line leaders, and so on down the line, so that everybody knows where they stand.

We differ in one major way from the big manufacturing giants, though: we have never been confined by our business plan and its details, and we have always kept it fluid. Effective planning is essential, but your plans should not confine you to the point that they limit your ability to change direction, to be flexible when times change. Our flexibility has always been one of our strongest points—yet when it comes to the departmental structure that helps to support that flexibility, we've come a long way.

As a private family business, we have fewer layers of management in the decision-making process, which gives us an advantage over some of our larger competitors. We also know more than we did in prior decades, and that knowledge has given us our willingness to adjust to new realities. We can react more quickly to seize an opportunity; we can change course when necessary with a less jarring nudge. This flexibility allows us to move with the times, to read the market, which can change with amazing speed, *or* to deal with inevitable setbacks. We can also hold our employees' feet to the fire more gently and without engendering panic. No one here has to be constantly watching his or her back.

We know the strengths, weaknesses, and capabilities of each of our eight teams. We think of all of these teams as cogs in a wheel. Our team members have a keen sense that each part is highly dependent upon the others and that one weak link can bring it all to a grinding halt. We do not want that to happen. It is all about implementing a good strategy and recruiting good talent; with those two things, a lot can happen. These teams of people form the meat and potatoes of what we do; it is they that deliver the results.

As part of the process of improving our overall structure, we have become more collaborative. Here's an example: we come up with new products to give our sales teams more ammunition. But, as is often the case, sales teams need to be controlled so that they don't try to throw "upside-down widgets" our way. So before greenlighting product development, we always run new projects up through operations, purchasing, and engineering, which helps to ensure that our sales teams understand the constraints on what they can sell and reasonably expect the other departments to produce. As a private company we can act quickly while remaining coordinated internally, which helps us compete with the giants. Our customers like that.

Still Next-Leveling . . .

It seems that the process of next-leveling is never quite done for Love and Quiches. Each time I think we are there, there's always a new summit to mount. So it is for any company. Often, refusing to take on that next challenge leads to stagnation and a slow but steady decline. That's never been our mindset.

Because of our commitment to momentum and constant improvement, we have recently taken some bold steps. To start, we have hired some savvy, computer-literate supervisors and mechanics with firsthand experience, and our workers appreciate the more focused direction they are receiving. This process was initiated by our next-level chief operating officer (COO), who originally came to us from one of the industry giants. (Obviously this is another benefit of next-leveling; experienced employees bring their expertise with them when they come to you.)

To complement that initiative, he has begun what we have all dubbed "L&Q U"—Love and Quiches University. He constantly reminds our production workers: "First, we are going to train you, and then we are going to train you, and then train you yet again. And after that, we are going to train you and then train you even more." The training area in our employee lounge is cordoned off with what resembles shower curtains when in use, and staff affectionately call it the "Shower Room." There is almost always a training session going on in there. Training likewise takes place on the production floor, and we have called upon our equipment suppliers to send in technicians to

retrain everybody on the use of our machinery. There is *always* something new to learn. And to increase the effectiveness of our work, our
aim is to give everyone the skills they need to find and implement their
own solutions. Our policy of educational training is good for them *and*
for the company.

Our COO describes all of these improvements variously as *moving
around quite a few parts on the board, breaking the glass house, remov-
ing the clutter,* and *getting rid of the noise.* He uses these buzzwords
quite a bit—one of my favorites is "prior planning prevents poor
performance"—but in doing so he has energized a lot of people, and
they are all on board and loving it. I find myself repeating the buzzwords as well. It's contagious.

He leads by example: "If you touch it, you can understand it; if
you understand it, then you can change it." By doing it himself first—
taking training courses he's established, adopting processes he wants
the rest of us to adopt—he makes sure he gets his hands around any
change before making it.

To guide our operations, we are now using the five basic principles of sound business practices. All standard operating procedures
are designed around these five principles: Safety, Quality, Productivity,
Communication, and Training. All the good results come from these
five keys.

We also recently went live with a new and robust enterprise resource
planning (ERP) business management software system that integrates
everything in one place: accounting, inventory control (both raw and
finished), labor, purchasing, sales, marketing costs, traceability, and just
about everything else we do. It was very costly and took over a year to
put in place, but we *survived* pushing the button and are pleased, so
far, that the new system has provided us with much more accurate and
finite information. Even better, it has delivered us from so much that
had been recorded manually.

I admit that I am among the least computer literate of all of us,
but I know a *lot* about this business and its details. One can learn

quite a bit in forty years' time. So before going live, I sat for countless hours with various staff organizing the data required, helping to
cheerlead the grueling tasks and to point out what data needed to be
cleaned up before being entered: garbage in, garbage out. As long as
the information going *in* is good—and we devote a lot of training
to making sure that it is—we can then use the information coming
out to make more informed pricing decisions, production planning,
and—most importantly—accurate strategic planning to keep moving
the company forward. We can now make these decisions using up-to-
the-moment information.

We measure all movement: pounds per employee per hour, per shift,
per week, per month. We have industrial engineers on the floor with
stopwatches who look for ways to do things with greater efficiency and
with fewer non-value-added movements. They are also tasked with
finding ways to reduce errors. Even taking the fatigue factor (yes, that
too) into account, we have found ways to do things more efficiently
with fewer people and with better results and quality. This is where I
step back and let it happen.

One of the main functions of these engineers is to identify ways to
mesh functions and divide areas of responsibility in order to avoid duplication of effort. (Jill and I did that on a rudimentary level forty years ago
when she became the inside person, and I stayed outside with sales and
delivery.) If you can save labor, you can reduce costs, and that will allow
you to offer better pricing and compete more strongly for that new piece
of business. Conversely, cross-training is equally vital to any business so
that no function will ever go *uncovered*. Seeing to it that employees are
cross-trained is one of our hard-and-fast rules for several reasons: One,
when team members take off for a holiday or a vacation, they don't have
to worry that their desk isn't being covered. Two, we are not left high and
dry if the team member gets hit by the proverbial bus. And three, no one
employee can ever have us over a barrel.

We use these same methods to measure and reduce waste. If
you want to know where all your profits are going, just look in the

dumpster. One of my most important pieces of advice is to take the waste factor into consideration when offering pricing to prospective customers. Otherwise, all your new business could end up low margin or break even or possibly result in a loss. It is very difficult to catch up on low-margin business once you accept it, and it may not be possible to catch up at all.

Never estimate any of your costs. By whatever method, make *sure* you know your material costs, labor costs, marketing costs, shipping costs, and all the rest for your particular business. We measure everything: throughput, output, materials as a percentage of sales, waste, sales per samples, sales per trade show, and so on. And *everything* gets shopped. By virtue of this, we know where we stand financially, and with that knowledge, we are able to make realistic projections in line with our resources.

I have been hammering home over and over that by far the most important thing I have *ever* learned is this: the purpose of business is the pursuit of profit, not glory. Profit is the engine that keeps us going. Since we constantly review our financials, we implement changes when we see the need, and we do not accept unprofitable business as we once did.

Our measurements don't end on the production floor. We carefully analyze our customer base by channel: restaurant chains, retail, airline, military, convenience stores, and so on. This analysis helps us see where we need to concentrate, and with the information now available from our new software, we are able to better analyze our profitability product by product and channel by channel. We also see which products can more easily cross over to more than one channel, and we push those products heavily.

Product rationalization is an important process in our sales analysis by channel. We now have *hundreds* of products across our customer base. It may be the same chocolate cake in ten different sizes, case packs, and varied decorations, but each one is considered a *different* product in our business. Each one must stand on its own, and if there is not enough volume to support a particular version, *out* it goes, even if it means having to disappoint a current customer. (We always offer a similar version that's more widely bought across more channels and gently suggest that it was their idea!) *Every* reduction, even if it's a very small one, is a victory for operations.

The yearly budgeting process begins during the last quarter of each year in advance of the year to come. For the first twenty years or so, all we did was get out there and sell. Now our sales force must estimate their sales customer by customer, taking attrition into account and also deciding what amount of new business they will bring on. They must do this not only yearly but monthly. Our salespeople are held accountable for bringing in the numbers they decide on. Then, based on those projections, each of the other departments—from operations to R&D to engineering—needs to formulate its own budgets, and senior management holds them equally accountable for keeping their spending within those numbers. Each department follows a similar path: all expenditures, from uniforms to capital expenditures and everything in between, are carefully planned. On occasion, adjustments must be made to account for events beyond our control or for new initiatives, but these are shared decisions. We track our progress, follow up, and revise as needed.

The old adage "You can't manage what you can't measure" cuts both ways: we have to *manage* the business, not just *measure* it. Once we have our detailed financial results, our measurements, we share them with management, and we make sure management understands the role their jobs play in affecting these numbers. Coming up with solutions for affecting these numbers empowers them. We also perform an ongoing analysis of *budget vs. actual*. To do this, we need metrics for everything that's important to the whole. All results are tracked and measured from all angles, but to achieve focus and results, it's vital to measure *key* metrics, not everything and anything. These rules apply to almost any business, especially to brick-and-mortar ones.

We have also instituted an overall company initiative to identify improvement opportunities. We no longer have problems; we have *opportunities* instead. We invite participation and input in identifying such opportunities at all levels, and we've put incentive bonus plans in place for positive results. These incentives encourage teamwork on all levels. But good ideas are nothing if they don't move from innovation to execution, so we make sure to act, not just to plan. In this competitive environment, *we are dancing as fast as we can*; a medium-sized company can do well in any economic climate if all the parts are running well.

There is no question that we needed to learn to spend money to make money. So we did. We have just spent millions of dollars in capital improvements, particularly high-speed online equipment for cutting and packaging our products as they make their way out the door. We are striving to finally move completely away from *Push* (pushing product through the plant through obstacles) to *Pull* (pulling product smoothly forward through efficient automation). Every new piece of equipment costs a fortune, but we are doing it one step at a time, and the return on investment is often immediate.

It has taken forty years, but another important step we took with *total* agreement was to form a board of advisors. We invited key industry and business leaders from outside to serve as an advisory board in order to help us make our growth plans become reality. Our board is made up of four outside members, as well as our executive team, and we meet for a full day quarterly (or more often if something needing immediate attention comes up). In addition to their vast industry knowledge and experience, our four board advisors offer a perspective unencumbered by the emotions of being involved with the business day-to-day. (They also have extensive contacts, a plus for sure.) A board of advisors gets paid for each day they sit, plus travel expenses, so the decision to form one should not be taken lightly. We needed to have reached a certain level before it even occurred to us, but now the process is indispensable. As we review our progress, the outside members tell it to us like it is, which can be pretty intense. And *then* we go out for a great dinner just like old friends!

With all of these positive initiatives, I feel as if Love and Quiches has finally positioned itself to weather the storms that, inevitably, are still to come. I still worry—it is part of my job description and I do it *very* well—but I don't have to do it quite as much as I used to.

Where do we go from here? The walls are crowding in on us again. We need more office space, more state-of-the-art high-speed equipment and space for it on the production floor, more warehouse space, more frozen storage, more of *everything*. The planning stages for addressing those needs have already been set in motion and some steps already taken. We have a five-year plan in place to accomplish all of this, and I have total faith in our ability to do it. Our progress forward through the decades has been a bit more painful than we would have wished, but that pain just made the victories that much sweeter.

As your business takes form and grows, you're going to find yourself facing new realities over and over. You'll outgrow facilities, go head to head against new competitors, and face the challenge of building teams within the organization. The answer to these opportunities is this: always be willing to take your company to the next level. If you don't keep moving forward in a competitive business, you may find yourself moving in the wrong direction. Get comfortable with revolutionizing and evolving because the more of it you do, the stronger your business will be.

Chapter 12

Company Culture

A single twig breaks, but the bundle of twigs is strong.
—Tecumseh

All of us who are running businesses today compete in an exceedingly fast new world. To succeed in this environment, we have to develop a company culture that can keep pace with that world. The heart of our business is its culture, one that is cohesive and well nurtured. Without this mission, a company is likely to end up directionless, stagnant, and fractured. At Love and Quiches, we've worked hard to build a culture that unifies our people and enlists all of them in maintaining our agility, supplying us with new ideas and new thinking, and keeping our customers loyal. Our *people* are the most important component of our operation, as they must be in yours.

Our company mission provides critical direction. To reach its goals, every business should have a mission statement that focuses on culture.

Our brand promise is: "To Always Deliver Ultimate Taste, Quality, Innovation & Value to Our Customers Across the Globe." It has taken a thousand baby steps to get there, but now our entire organization is critical to that effort.

Building Team Spirit

In one form or another, we have always taken steps to come together as a team, even if in the earlier years it was merely Team Building 101. We've never been just a collection of people doing their jobs. We've always strived to be a real team, one that's made up of people who fit the culture of the company. The strength of our teams and their teamwork informs our success.

Ever since we started hiring, we have employed some *very* smart people—if not always formally educated ones—who helped move the organization forward. These include a production worker who became one of our best quality assurance directors; a line worker who is now our operations director; a truck driver who became our IT manager (and who then, as mentioned earlier, moved on to a top position with the New York Jets); and of course Don, our first driver, who ended up running the back of the house. Then there was Karen, who started as a receptionist thirty years ago and recently retired in a position very close to running the company.

There were a lot more. If we saw that they had it in them, we gave them the chance. We sent many of them to school and provided other formal training. We promote within the company cautiously, though, keeping in mind the Peter Principle: elevating workers to the point of incompetency is not good for them or for the company. (On the other side of the coin, we *never* single out an employee for public humiliation, no matter how grievous the error.)

We keep track of many of the Love and Quiches alumni, and we have watched them all grow up and start families. They are constantly stopping in to say hello, even now, decades later—a real testament to the culture of this place.

In spite of the rosy picture I have been painting here, things were rarely perfect or easy. No matter how great your team spirit is, there will always be some problems between employees; it is a business, after all, not a love affair. As we grew, employees started to offer their input, which we encouraged, but as is often the case, not everyone saw things in exactly the same way. So I often honed my newfound leadership skills by moderating differences of opinion between employees. It was all part of the job. And, inevitably, there is some jockeying for position. I am relieved that today we deal with these issues on a much more formalized basis through our more structured human resources department.

Whether your company has an HR department or isn't quite big enough for that yet, promoting collaboration is the key to keeping your team culturally vibrant. Some companies promote healthy competition between departments and teams, but to my way of thinking, *too* much competition isn't very healthy. As I mentioned in the previous chapter, collaboration is a far better way to go, and that is the type of team interaction we strongly promote.

In our company, we maintain detailed job descriptions; everybody knows exactly what is expected of them, and it follows that they know exactly where they stand. Nobody has to waste time looking over his or her shoulder, as is often the case in larger corporations. We all know that, sink or swim, we are in this together, and we can get a lot more done this way. Along one wall in our employee lounge, for instance, we have an organizational chart that turns the traditional format on its head. The top line includes all of the line leaders; the next line lists the supervisors they answer to, then the managers, the directors, on down to the executive team at the bottom. It's just one of the many ways in which we show our people that it doesn't matter where you are on the org chart; each person is a vital part of our team's success.

Of course, providing plenty of opportunities for your employees to bond and have fun together is a great way to develop culture and increase collaboration. Since the beginning, we've always thrown parties for our crew. In 2008, however, we made a joint decision with middle management to scale back our many extravagances. The yearly events in the park were just too distracting and time-consuming to plan when we needed to concentrate on the very survival of the business. Each step we take is commensurate with the economic climate we find ourselves in, whatever year, whatever time. And because of our long tradition of blowouts, this step was not an easy one to take. But major decisions like these were no longer made just at the top, and we decided, together, that this needed doing.

We didn't cut the fun out entirely, and coming together to celebrate remains an important part of our culture. We still hold quarterly fiestas in the employee lounge, where we bring in delicious and varied catered food, and top management does the serving. We still have music and dancing, and we do it several times on each fiesta day so that each shift can have its party. We all dance, mix, and match, but some of the Latin dance songs seem *never* to end, and my feet pay the price. During these fiestas we are a family; when there is work to be done, we are a team.

Through all the years, some of them difficult, we have managed to maintain our esprit de corps. This was demonstrated vividly by the amazing behavior of all 250-plus of us in the aftermath of Hurricane Sandy, which fell on Halloween in 2012. All of Long Island was decimated by the storm, and our Freeport facility suffered extensive damage. *Everybody* on our staff showed up, wanting to know what they could do to help. Once our electricity was restored—which was within two days, since our village has its own power company, unique for Long Island— everybody pitched in no matter their position in the company, hands and knees on the ground, whatever it took, and we were up and running within seventy-two hours. They were magnificent.

Culture and Hiring

At Love and Quiches, our culture thrives on having the very best team members seated on our bus. That means that we don't want to hire good people—we want the *great* people. We have taken off the rose-colored glasses, and we realize that weak links affect the whole, and can inhibit our overall success. As a result, we devote a lot of our energy to building our teams and making sure our hires are both a good fit culturally and in line with what we need to accomplish. We promote from within or recruit from outside to get the best people on board. And of course it is not only getting the *right people* on the bus; it is also putting them in the *right seat*.

As you may have noted throughout the book, we have always been rather color and gender blind in our hiring policy, and this diversity turned out to be fundamental to our processes. We learned that innovation can come from *anywhere*, and we throw a wide net to get it.

It is a great skill to know how to hire right the first time. Love at first sight will never do, nor will a gut feeling that this or that person is the answer to all your prayers. That never works, and only rarely does hiring someone from a competitor work well. If you think back to some of my stories, we made some colossal mistakes—more painful because they were so very costly.

But as the years passed, our hiring practices have evolved. Besides using some of the free or nominal-cost online services, we don't hesitate to use a search agency for important hires; they have access to a wider range of candidates than we do and prescreen them before offering them up to be interviewed. After that, it is up to us to make the right decisions. We look for people with a good track record and problem-solving skills.

And we no longer make all hiring decisions at the top. When we are evaluating a candidate, we now have them meet and speak with a few people within the team they will be joining to make sure the cultural fit is there. Afterward, the department director selects the optimal candidate.

Our constant learning never stops. We now use the STAR job interview technique to evaluate the candidate's problem-solving skills. The questions in this process are designed by behavioral psychologists: We ask every candidate to describe a *difficult situation* they found themselves in, the *path* they took to resolve the issues, the specific *actions* they implemented, and the *end result*. Many large companies use this process, and if it is good enough for Sara Lee, it is good enough for us. Of course, each candidate's past experience and qualifications are also key to the hiring process. In particular we take a hard look at the candidate's employment history because we've found that a person who changes jobs constantly (called a "jumper"), even if he or she claims to have been looking for the right place to finally pursue a career, is not a good bet.

Although there are two schools of thought on the subject, we have never discouraged nepotism. We have employed married couples, children, siblings, and so on, without any issues. But employees who are dating one another present a trickier situation, particularly if there comes a bitter or volatile breakup. It is hard to control these liaisons, yet I do not believe in interfering in people's lives as long as it doesn't affect performance on the job. I know some larger corporations have unbending rules in this regard, but we never have. (Remember, we even held a wedding right on the production floor in the early days!)

Culture and Customer Service

Building a strong culture makes everyone's time at work more enjoyable, and just as importantly, your company's cultural values affect how your customers will be treated and thus how they see you. If most of your people have "9 to 5" syndrome and fly out the door as early as possible, your level of service will drop. But if your people are invested and committed, your customers are going to get truly great service.

You may recall that one of my first lessons in what customer service truly means was when I was just starting out, and Gertrude of Gertrude's, one of the top "in" restaurants at the time, made me get up in the middle of the night to drive to the city and bring her four Chocolate Mixed Nut Pies. I did it because even back then, I knew I needed to answer when my customers called. It was a mere $20 sale, but she did me a great favor. One of my next lessons in customer service was changing to ten-inch straight-sided pans for my cheesecakes instead of forcing my then current nine-inch pie-shaped versions down the throats of my customer base because that was the only size pan I had at the time.

In short, I learned early on to do whatever it takes to keep customers happy, and that became a cornerstone of the Love and Quiches culture. There were plenty of initial lapses in customer service that were both stressful and harmful, but I was learning a whole new business language and didn't know any better. The company finally reached a level of reliable customer service in the mini-factory in the late 1970s.

It is not enough to have a high-quality product; the service and spirit behind it have to be high quality, too. Our employees are taught that the image conveyed to our customers and the industry in general is what, at the end of the day, pays our salaries. There are plenty of other choices out there, and our products alone don't tell the entire story. We must give customers and prospects myriad reasons to choose *us* over our competitors, including polite demeanor on the phone *or* by email, responsiveness to their needs, flexibility (within reason) to emergency requests, on-time delivery, and good fulfillment rates.

Our company culture trickles down throughout the organization, both the front and the back of the house, and it is management's responsibility as part of the training to convey the image we want to show to the outside world. In particular, we want a *consistent* image. Manners count, and we have a dress code (informal, but neat; no jeans), both for ourselves and because we have frequent visitors. And this consistent image extends way beyond our customers; we must show the same professionalism to our vendors, truckers, freight forwarders, and agencies, as well as to anybody else we deal with in the course of conducting business. We then both provide good service and get good service in return.

So at the end of the day, as a supplier, our most important strategy is to engender in our expanding customer base the confidence that we can flawlessly meet their needs for service, quality, and innovation in order to help *them* distinguish themselves from their competition and *us* to distinguish ourselves from *ours*. We partner with our customers and participate in their dessert development and planning processes, even halfway across the world. But more importantly, we try to strategically balance the needs of the company with the needs of our customers.

On occasion, we see the other side of this coin. When a customer is *too* demanding (and this does happen, but thankfully not too often), it can become demoralizing and disruptive to the teams and the organization as a whole. Then a decision has to be made to walk away for the good of the whole.

High-Impact Meetings

Every company has meetings, but not everyone realizes that how meetings are handled is a vital component of the company's culture. Meetings are where people come together; they're how we keep it all running smoothly. If your meetings are long, boring, and full of patronizing behavior, company culture is going to suffer. On the other hand, if you do meetings right, you can give your team's morale and effectiveness a huge boost.

At Love and Quiches, we communicate a lot; we meet a lot. We hold daily huddles, weekly management meetings, weekly executive meetings, weekly cap-ex meetings, team-building meetings, and ongoing training meetings. We also have monthly town hall meetings during which we share news about our plans and our progress, as well as discuss any issues. We do not talk down to or patronize our employees at these meetings; we need them. I urge you not to listen to those who complain that when there are so many meetings nobody can get anything done. Meetings are important; businesses need to communicate to make sure everyone is marching in the same direction and to avoid working at cross purposes. Differences of opinion, conflicts, and conflict resolution are prime reasons for meetings; do not avoid them.

But once a decision is made, the team needs to implement it—even those who do not quite agree.

Effective meetings are one of the most essential ingredients of a successful company. Meetings are where decisions are made and agendas are set, and good meeting behavior is important to avoid descending into chaos. We learned some of this the hard way, and as a result, we have decided to hang a sign on the door to the conference room: "No Cell Phones or Egos."

Here are my suggestions for meeting protocol, my rules of the road:

- Make sure to start and end on time, with a $1 fine in the pizza kitty for every minute late.

- Think about having a meeting standing up if it promises to be a short one.

- Have an agenda. Time cannot be replenished.

- Have someone take notes, or set up a white board/flip chart on which to record decisions and action items. Note how these action items will be implemented and the person responsible for that implementation, along with time lines and an end date.

- Discuss the progress being made on all of the action items at the next meeting.

- Don't allow multiple idea discussions. Focus on the topic at hand.

- Don't allow any interruptions when a person is talking.

- Don't tolerate any side conversations.

- Don't tolerate any personal attacks. Never! And treat each other with respect and dignity.

Keeping People Motivated

Your company culture depends on a group of employees who are motivated to do their best work. So how do you keep them invested? At the end of the day, money talks, but so does recognition, and we devote equal measure to ensuring both motivators. Our employees understand that their best job security is the success of the company and vice versa. We need each other, and we all know it.

We hold State of the Company meetings in which we inform *all* of our employees, from our porters to our managers, of our progress, and during which we express our appreciation for their good work. Our transparency is appreciated by our employees and keeps them engaged. We share financials with some levels within the hierarchy. We also recognize and reward longevity with gift cards, announce Employees of the Month from each department, raffle off TVs and other prizes when production goals are met, and so on. But when necessary, we do *not* hesitate to discuss any issues that need addressing so that we can all participate in the solution.

Our employees share in our profits based on performance—a great motivator. And everybody who works here knows that we *always* look to promote from within before going outside. So all of us have skin in the game and the same goals at stake. We treat our employees as partners; we show them respect, and that goes a *very* long way.

Management by walking around is making a comeback, but I never stopped. I wander around in the back a few times each week, greeting employees and identifying issues. Our production workers look forward to top management spending time with them. To my production workers, I am "Miss Susan," while Irwin is known as "Poppy." This is how we do it. This is the Love and Quiches philosophy in the short form.

We have chosen to remain a private business, a family business with the second generation in place. This is key to the future of Love & Quiches Gourmet (our new name as of 2013, which you will learn about in chapter 14, "Marketing and Branding"). I have my partners—my husband, son, and daughter—at the top with me, as well as a few other essential executives.

I think being a family business provides a comfort level to the organization as a whole and encourages our teams to participate fully as we move forward. The process of improvement never stops; we are never good enough. Innovation can emerge from anywhere within the organization, and our employees are empowered to improve our company systems and products. We tap into those abilities across the entire organization, salute good work, and understand that mistakes will be made, which is fine as long as they are recognized and corrected as quickly as possible.

But each and every employee's performance is also crucial to our future. Our cake pans need to be clean and ready for the next day's production, and what we will bake depends on the orders we've received, which need to be scheduled properly so that they can ship on time. (And with hundreds of products, this is no easy task.) We need orders, so our sales force must be out there making it happen; our marketing department needs to help them by spreading the word; our R&D chefs need to keep the new products coming; our quality assurance department needs to make sure everything is perfect; our CFO needs to be "Chief Bean Counter." And that is only the start.

From the top, we try to generate a hunger for needed changes and initiatives rather than imposing them. We try to share the decision-making process, which means sharing the risks and the rewards. Real leaders don't have all the answers, and that is how it should be. We need people better than we are in their particular areas to become a great company. At the top, we need to be visionaries. We need to set the direction in line with our resources while at the same time inviting the input of everybody below. And this implies some risk. As leaders, we guide our employees to overcome the fear of that risk, the fear of change that creates barriers to moving the organization forward. And just as I had to overcome such barriers without any help, the strength of our numbers now helps us to overcome these fears together and keeps the dynamic going. We need creative ideas to tackle the barriers, which further means we need our people to generate those ideas. Fortunately, the employees of Love and Quiches have always been and still are a passionate group, and the ideas keep coming!

Chapter 13

Constant Learning

You have to know where the dots are to be able to connect them.
—Paraphrased from Steve Jobs

When I started my business in 1973, I was a blank slate. My story was written one quiche at a time, and in the very early days, Jill and I learned primarily by making mistakes. Learning from your errors is indeed important, but you can't stop there. As soon as I bought Jill out, I knew that the time had come for me to learn as much as I could about running a business and about my industry, and I knew I had to do this rather quickly. That process of gathering as much relevant knowledge as I could has never ended. All along my path with Love and Quiches, I met more and more people from whom I could learn, and I began to create outside support systems to which I could go for advice.

In any industry, markets are constantly changing and evolving, and you must likewise constantly watch for and react to those changes, offering new products, new price points, new packaging. This process of constant learning ensures that you will not fall behind. I have learned that the only way to stay ahead of the game in an ever-shifting (if not completely transforming) world is to take in knowledge from wherever I can get it.

For an entrepreneur or business owner, the sources of this continuing education are truly endless, and insights can materialize in places you'd never expect. It's a process of constant learning—from mentors, from networks, from the competition, from customers and suppliers, and from industry counterparts. Some of my most reliable sources of learning have helped keep both my company *and* me at the top of our game.

Learning from Mentors

Finding a mentor is a good thing; finding a mentor who grows into a sponsor, someone who can offer concrete support (such as helping you find that job, or funding, or putting you together with a likely partner for a new business venture) is even better. I have had many throughout my career.

You might recall from the beginning of my story that my first mentor was Marvin Paige. I was introduced to him through a friend while I was still hawking frozen quiches from my home kitchen to local accounts on Long Island. When Marvin set up my first appointment in the big city at O'Neals' Baloon, *that* was the beginning of the rest of my life. That was the catalyst; I was off and running.

I adored Marvin. He knew a lot of people, and he always had time for his friends. He spent his entire career in foodservice, owning several restaurants that were all very hot for a while. Before I met him in the 1960s, he was a partner in what was arguably one of the first theme restaurants, the Tin Lizzie, and he later opened a restaurant called Claire's in New York on Seventh Avenue and 18th Street; it was in the Chelsea area and catered to the gay crowd. The food was delicious, and we went there often. He opened another Claire's in Key West, and he later developed another concept, Hamburger Harry's.

From the early days on, Marvin would speak with me for countless hours, teaching me all about the restaurant scene in New York City. One of the best pieces of wisdom I got from Marvin was this: "Watch the pennies, and the dollars will take care of themselves." It was a vital lesson that changed the way I ran my business. I was in the city at least three days a week on sales calls, and I often set aside time to stop in wherever he was at the time to get off my feet and chat for a half hour. Irwin and I would often meet Marvin for dinner with whomever he was married to at the time. We remained friends for decades until his premature death a few years ago. Ironically, given how good his advice always was, Marvin was a poor businessperson, and he ended up running all those previously mentioned restaurants into the ground. Nevertheless, I learned to always listen to what he said, not imitate what he did; the former was gold from the start. Meeting him truly changed everything.

Although none of them matched Marvin's influence on my career and business, there were other mentors in my life, including Jack Harris, my equipment dealer; restaurateur Stuart Levin; and two of the executive chefs at airlines Love and Quiches supplied. I picked mentors up from across the industry, wherever I could get them. If you find someone who's open to mentoring you, even on a limited basis, jump at the opportunity. You never know who the Marvin of your business will be. My daughter, Joan, now serving as our executive VP of sales and marketing, is following in my footsteps and has more than a few mentors she looks to for advice. And now she's doing what all of us who receive mentoring must eventually do—mentor others in return.

Learning from Your Network

For any entrepreneur, a strong, well-cultivated network is a vital source of informal business education. New relationships are forged, old ones are cemented, and opportunities are identified at trade shows, conferences, luncheons, dinners, and on and on. Each time I met somebody, I listened and learned something.

And today, of course, tremendously powerful and instant social networking is possible over the Internet.

Whatever method you use to do it, networking can ease the transition from employee—where you may have had lots of camaraderie in a larger company setting—to entrepreneur, which is a very lonely place at first. Whenever you can, network with other people who are in the same boat. Today, you have so many options for doing so. A good way to start out is to join networking organizations related to your field. The help offered there will be invaluable and may just make the difference between success and failure. These organizations connect people and support them by creating a community that fosters their ideas, provides necessary tools, and encourages them to keep going to reach their potential.

For me, that meant joining networking groups in the foodservice industry such as the Women's Foodservice Forum. I was active in the organization for quite a while, and I am still invited to be a panelist on occasion, but Joan is the one who remains very active there. She is the quintessential networker, a perfect poster child for it all. I also joined broader groups like the National Association of Women Business Owners, which has members from every field. Andrew's years as a very active member in the Young Presidents' Organization has provided him with invaluable contacts and resources with thousands of members all over the world, several of which serve on our advisory board.

Another fantastic networking resource available to people starting out in my industry today are incubator kitchens, wherein aspiring entrepreneurs hoping to start a food business can rent space in already-licensed facilities. These facilities also provide classes in business basics—as well as mentoring, advice, networking, and moral support—while the aspirants are trying to figure out whether they have something. What's more, they provide it all without the need for substantial financial outlays.

There are plenty of places to seek advice and help both locally and nationally that didn't exist when I started out forty years ago. You will find that your chosen field is peopled with knowing, generous, sophisticated, and (mostly) loyal participants. Take advantage of that fact by networking regularly, with the goal of learning from anyone you can.

At the end of the day, of course, networking does more than support your constant learning—it also keeps the company in the public eye. Today, Love and Quiches is still learning plenty from the organizations we belong to and the events we attend, but doing so also ensures that we remain front and center.

Learning from Customers

Selling is an art, and if you watch and listen carefully, your customers can help make your business successful. Pay attention to what your customers tell you; listen to their feedback. They are another valuable source of constant learning.

I learned early on that I had an innate ability to sell, and over the years I learned to read the needs and personality of the person or organization I was targeting when I cold canvassed. I asked each and every potential customer what *they* needed in the way of products and service. That included not only the product but also the price per portion, shape of portion, packaging, ease of use in the kitchen, shelf life, and other factors.

I did my research: I checked out every prospect's menus, and menus from similar venues before each appointment. I went in knowing which products would fit; I knew what to suggest. Now we have a cadre of sales professionals who service our customer base, and we partner with these customers to fulfill their needs exactly without sacrificing our own. Our vice president of R&D often travels to customer headquarters to work side by side with *their* executive chefs to develop products in line with their current needs. Our test kitchen gets many of its freshest ideas from finding out what our customers want and need; after all, we wouldn't want our customers to become bored with our offerings.

Customers want to be assured that we can fulfill their needs as authoritatively and decisively as we can, which gives us yet another reason to stay as informed as possible. They want assurance that we care that they buy from us, that we continually develop our knowledge base, and that we remain aware of the latest trends in the industry.

The other side of the coin is that we make sure our sales staff learn how to get to the *decision makers*, that they present our product to the person who has the power to say "yes" to the sale. We keep good records of our sales staff's activities and the results of every sales call; the "no" this time around may be a "yes" the next time we contact the customer—existing or potential. (We also have learned that, on occasion, a potential buyer will hand our proposal and product samples to our competitors for duplication and a competitive bid. It happens, and there is nothing that we can do about it unless there is a signed *non-disclosure agreement*. If the project we're pitching has a lot of R&D effort behind it, we do not proceed without such an agreement.)

In most cases, if you are a loyal supplier, the loyalty will be returned. We have been servicing some customers for decades. Sometimes, for whatever reason, customers are lost; you must accept that nothing lasts forever. But usually you will be given the right of last refusal.

Learning from the Competition

As I pointed out in Part I of this book, the difficult economy of the early 1990s "did in" many of the smaller dessert companies—and as we all now know, those years were a mere warm-up for the coming decade. So now we have fewer competitors, but the friendly fighting between us is fierce. It took a while, but we now see that there is enough business to go around if we stay calm and focus on what we do best. There is room for all of us, and the stronger the competition, the better our situation is because strong competition pushes us to do everything that much better.

No matter what industry you're in, you stand to learn a lot from what the competition is doing. We make a habit of constantly watching our competitors: We look at their booths during trade shows just as they look at ours. We monitor their press, view their websites regularly, and mine the industry gossip (while minding our manners and watching our professionalism). We always keep them in our sights, look for gaps in their offerings, and fill them quickly. We are committed to the R&D process of gathering technical and market intelligence and seeing how it may benefit the company, and because we have remained private, we can quickly react to what we learn.

We strive to stand somewhat apart. There needs to be a point of difference in our products so that we can distinguish our offerings from those of our competition, as you should distinguish your offerings from those you compete with in the marketplace. Love and Quiches and our competitors all make cakes, brownies, cheesecakes, and other similar products, so the distinguishing factor may be price structure, pack size, packaging, or something else such as level of service or consulting abilities. Above all, we try to win over the market by the superb taste of our products.

––––––––

Love and Quiches started with just an idea, yet it turned out to be a very good one. We observed a need for more varied and finer food in establishments that lacked the facilities and staff to produce such foods but had a clientele who wanted them. We had identified our market. We knew there was a need for our products and services, but if Love and Quiches was going to survive, we would have to constantly seek advice and information, and we would have to use that knowledge to enable us to deliver on our promise. As the decades passed, we did just that.

I have always asked a lot of questions, and I advise you to do so as well. The key, however, is to *listen* to the answers before deciding whether they are right or wrong for your business. You will hear a lot of hard truths, but don't dismiss them out of hand just because the answer is not what you wanted to hear. Remember why you asked the question in the first place. I realize how hard it is to take advice when you feel that your goals are slipping through your fingers, but the advice just may be the key to helping get you back on track.

Yet sometimes it will be your gut that has the right answer. My banker (the one we nicknamed "Black Jack Fagan" when we moved to Freeport in 1980 and became first-time borrowers facing 22 percent interest rates) asked me a few times, "Why don't you just cut your losses, close the business, and call it a day?" He was so sure that we would fail, but that is one piece of advice I am glad I never took.

So, if you think you have a good idea for a new business, or if you have already started your business or service, get as much advice and help as possible from wherever you can: family, friends, professionals in the field, your accountant, trade organizations, the SBA, regional economic development government agencies, the Internet (used properly and carefully—more on this in chapter 15, "You Can't Taste a Cheesecake over the Internet"). I have gathered principles of sound business practices along the way (available in Recipes for Success), and I urge you to use these resources to help you come up with your own business plan. This includes what you hope to achieve in the first year, the second, the fifth, and beyond, as well as what you will need in the way of resources (for rent, equipment, marketing expenses, employees, and the like) in order to get there. My business plan outlined what we needed to do to generate revenue and profits, but it always remained flexible and fluid so that we could move with our markets.

Not every business needs to reach for the moon, and a successful business can be just one shop, one restaurant, one bakery, one regional area as a local supplier, and so on. That said, Love and Quiches has grown and keeps growing. As we get bigger—as our customer base grows and our team of employees expands—the learning curve steepens. We realize that even now, forty years into the life of the business, we have plenty to learn, and we'll take that knowledge from wherever we can get it.

Chapter 14

Marketing and Branding

Authentic brands don't emerge from marketing cubicles or advertising agencies. They emanate from everything the company does.
—*Howard Schultz*

No matter how good your product is, it cannot entirely speak for itself. As an entrepreneur or small business owner, you're absolutely going to have to put effort into crafting a compelling identity for your company and telling people why your product is their best option. In the forty years I've run my business, I've learned some clear lessons about marketing and branding, and I've learned them in my usual manner: by trial and error.

Marketing is a huge job, and I recommend that you hire a PR or a marketing firm if your funds and the size of the company allow it. Doing it yourself works only if you are very, very talented. If your PR people are good, they will have great contacts and access to print press, radio interviews, and maybe even TV appearances, and they will also be able to help tailor your social media campaign. They will constantly pitch your company to their (hopefully) huge arsenal of contacts. In addition, a *marketing* company—which can be hired on a project-by-project basis—may have design capabilities and other services way beyond your company's expertise, especially when it comes to web design.

If you're not ready for outside agencies, do the very best you can. That's what *I* did until recent years, and as I look back over it all, I find that I haven't done too badly. There are plenty of low-cost ways to market your business: social media, networking events, public speaking, homegrown news releases (you never know), blogging, cold calls, building a database, and the telephone. Of course, we now have talented marketing people on staff who direct our strategy for promoting Love and Quiches to the world.

No discussion of marketing and branding these days is complete without mention of the incredible power of the Internet and social media, where our message can be broadcast worldwide with the tap of a button. Love and Quiches makes use of *every* tool in the online arena, including Twitter, Facebook, LinkedIn, email blasts, my blog, and all the other usual suspects. But I also have my reservations about these tools, as well as about what can happen when individuals and businesses rely too much on them. I've saved that discussion for the next chapter.

For now, it's more important to talk about the fundamentals. You must have an understanding of how marketing and branding works, and here are some of the concepts I've found to be of most importance.

Build a Powerful Brand

Every thriving company has a strong brand: an identity that tells its customers what they can expect when they do business with the company. Your brand is your reputation, and it's the most powerful way to communicate your worth to consumers and partners. If you're able to craft a brand that's distinctive, that resonates with your customer base, and that instantly communicates what you're all about to everyone who sees it, you're well positioned for success.

At Love and Quiches, we've had a complex branding journey. As a company that now sells primarily desserts, our name doesn't quite tell the story or define who we are. Yes, we started out with quiches, but our primary products and growth have been in the dessert arena ever since that first pecan pie we sold forty years ago at the request of one of my first quiche customers. To date we have flown hundreds of millions of portions of our delicious brownies, blondies, and oatmeal chewies on airlines all over the world with our name printed right on the top of the package.

By the time the dessert segment of our business became dominant, it was too late to change the name. "Love and Quiches" was an established brand in the business-to-business arena, and we decided that it would be too harmful to change it and lose the reputation and recognition we'd built behind it. Instead, we decided to trademark the name "Susan's Sweet Talk" in the mid-1980s and to tout it on packaging and in marketing materials as the "sweet goods division" of Love and Quiches. But, as described, we struggled for ten years to get our market to recognize the name. In 1995 we finally gave up the ghost and changed the name to simply "Love and Quiches Desserts." It's a contradiction in terms by any measure, but we had used it for almost twenty years. Yes, we were stuck with the name, but at the end of the day, it had served us well. Most people comment that they love the name. (We *do* face a challenge in the business-to-consumer arena, where we are not yet an established retail presence, but we're working on it.)

Despite the "quiches" in our name, we constantly look for ways to strengthen our brand. One of these is to let graphics tell the story of who we are. Our retail packages show our mouthwatering cakes and other desserts, which makes the oxymoronic nature of the name less apparent. We have tons of fan mail—from handwritten notes back *before* the computer age to the many emails we still get today—praising our dessert products and asking where the sender can purchase them. *No one*, so far, has chastised us for causing confusion or asked why we're called "Love and Quiches" when we do desserts. It goes to show how effectively you can communicate your brand through strong graphics and a consistent product alone!

Branding is ongoing, and to remain au courant we update our brand as needed, making changes that reflect the evolution of the business without fundamentally altering our name and image. We have just completed our fourth rebrand since our founding. In part, this has involved restyling and modernizing our logo in line with current marketing wisdom. We are losing the old-fashioned lady (which I originally got from a children's coloring book) and using more chic, of-the-moment colors. Now we are in the corresponding process of redoing our stationery, business cards, packaging, printed film, truck graphics, cake boxes, the overhead sign at our building entrance, trade show graphics, point-of-sale material, and a thousand other little details. All the while, naturally, a complete overhaul of our website is on the agenda, too. From now on, we will be known as "Love & Quiches Gourmet," with the tagline "Desserts from the Heart." The battle raged for months on the exact wording, but we all finally agreed, and we love it.

We also work on other aspects of our brand, including our trademarked "Gourmet Grab and Go" line of prewrapped snacks and the phrase "Dessert Partner to the Industry," which connotes one of our premier services.

As you can surmise, we will *never* be done branding ourselves. Our name, our high-end products, the images we use, and our reputation for good service are all part of the brand, and we pay close attention to each, making sure that our message is *very* clear. When you define who you are, what your company has to offer, and you deliver on that promise, you're on your way to having a great brand.

Find Your Niche and Serve It Well

Of primary importance is to identify the *market* for the product or service being offered. The most fabulous upside-down widget is utterly useless unless someone can be persuaded to pay for it. First, research if there is a need; then, research whether that need is already being filled. Last, determine whether the product or service you're offering will be a little better or sold at a better price.

I now live in Manhattan, and we spend a lot more time walking around than we do in cabs, so I've noticed on our many walks that a new cupcake store seems to be opening up practically every week. There's one every few blocks, *they all look the same,* and some are from the same companies. To me, these stores never seem to have enough customers in them no matter what time of day it is. It is almost as if they are competing with themselves. Of course, some of them will be here in years to come, but I am giving this example because I fear many of them will fail. Again, to distinguish your company from that of your competition, you must learn what they are doing and then create a *point of difference* in the product or service you're offering. You need to distinguish your product or service to market it effectively.

What I did, purely by accident, was create a need. While I didn't invent the quiche, what I *did* do was start the trend that popularized it as an alternative to the hamburger, available to the middle market rather than served only in fine French restaurants. And there are millions upon millions of people in the middle market nationwide. Just think of the chain restaurants, pubs, convenience stores, catering halls, hotels, cafés, supermarkets, and on and on, all of which offer quiche. We have plenty of competition now, but *my* company was first. Desserts came later, but quiche has become a staple in the American diet. And *we* did that; we made our mark.

We target our marketing messages specifically, gearing the message to each individual channel. We do business in quite a few different areas—restaurants (our sweet spot, and we put a lot of muscle into it), airlines, convenience stores, military feeding, export, and retail—and we treat each area as its own niche, ensuring that we meet that specific customer's needs as best we can. There is no point in offering a prewrapped brownie to an upscale restaurant chain, no matter how delicious it is, nor does it make any sense to offer an elegant Espresso Mousse Cake to a convenience store chain located in gas stations where they have no way of serving it and would have to sell it for $5.99 a portion if they *could* serve it. So we tailor the message, the samples, the presentation of the particular product, the PowerPoint slides, and the pricing on a channel-by-channel basis. This saves time both for the target and the company, and it will more likely lead to a sale—which is our reason for making the call in the first place.

We exhibit in four or five major trade shows a year, some of which are visited by tens of thousands of buyers. That is a *lot* of potential customers, but we choose those shows carefully, as exhibiting can become rather costly. We can gather enough leads at these shows to keep us busy all year. Sometimes all you need is one good hit to make all the expense worthwhile.

In addition, members of our sales staff and our executive chef attend a few much smaller, more casual, and targeted conferences each year. These niche events, where you can often find some of your best opportunities, are very effective. For instance, our staff meet and exchange ideas with other suppliers in the industry—and sometimes with our competitors—and they are able to talk one on one with targeted accounts to pursue sales opportunities or new menu items for existing customers. These conferences don't come cheaply either, but they in no way require the extensive funds, planning, or personnel that major shows demand.

But Really, It's All About Quality

When we first started exhibiting at the NRA in Chicago, there was an exhibitor from Texas who was a direct competitor. The proprietor was a woman about my age who spent more time marketing herself than her goods. Dressed like a hippie, although this was already the early 1980s, she wore long, colorful skirts and a big straw hat (despite it being an indoor event). She also would have gone barefoot if they had let her! But however strongly she marketed herself—I definitely remember *her*—either her products or her service was probably not so good because her company disappeared quickly without leaving a trace. The lesson here is that you need to deliver the goods, not yourself. She caught my attention, and she might have caught others' attention for about a minute, but that wasn't long enough to build a brand or a company of value.

We have become a brand, and our customers know what to expect and what we can do for them—so they seek us out. We learned early on that we could not be everything to all people. We are bakers, and we have always done what we do best. Knowing who we are has always helped to clarify our image and keep our message consistent.

No matter how many products we offer, from exotic bread pudding to praline tarts to mango cheesecake—and we do offer a wide array of these unique desserts—most people go for the comfort of familiarity. We still primarily sell cheesecake, chocolate cake, carrot cake, and brownies. We answer people's desire for this familiarity, and that keeps them coming back.

Our sales force represents us and are our face out in the field, so they must be company rather than ego driven. We train them well so that they never communicate any mixed messages. We provide them with the tools and ammunition to bring the sales home.

But our quality, consistency, and service always speak the loudest. Ours is a *very* busy test kitchen, as are our operations, quality, warehouse, and customer service teams.

Giving Back

For the past several years, we have felt rather strongly about several causes, and so we've introduced programs to contribute what we can. We factor in the value of these efforts while we're planning our marketing campaigns—as do most other companies—and we broadcast each program for not quite selfless reasons. But more fundamentally, we are happy to participate and to give back.

In 2009 Love and Quiches launched its ongoing Cakes for Kids program in partnership with the Long Island–based nonprofit Island Harvest through their network of distribution centers. The program distributes birthday cakes monthly to disadvantaged children all over the island. Monthly birthday parties are held, and the donated cakes are served in recognition of the children's special day. At Love and Quiches we think birthday parties should be a part of everyone's childhood, and we are happy to help make that happen. From time to time, we travel to some of the schools and day-care centers to serve the children ourselves, and it brings a smile to see the children's lit-up faces with frosting all around their mouths.

More recently, our charitable activities expanded to include the Wounded Warrior Project administered by the R&DA Military Assistance Project. We support our fallen heroes by donating a portion of the company's profits each year. And as a vendor to the military, we are also honored to supply our brave servicemen and women in the field with a taste of home for dessert.

Not to forget the Salvation Army, which adores us, and will send a truck on a moment's notice to pick up any unneeded inventory or overruns.

Our charitable activities have been met with tremendous approval both from our employees and our customers. Logos for both programs have been added to our Gourmet Grab and Go snack product line, as well as on our corrugated packaging and some of our brochures.

———

When all is said and done, it is our customers that provide the fuel for our success. The focus of our marketing efforts is to keep them informed of positive company developments and thus build customer loyalty and retention. Your best customers are the ones that stay with you.

Nevertheless, our most important ammunition is the quality of our products—we *never compromise*. Excellence first, marketing later. We never falter in staying on top of our game in marketing and branding our products, though. Fortunately for us, the trend toward upscale, high-quality desserts is growing across all channels—even fast food—and that further helps to fuel our growth. We are lucky to be in the food business. People always have to eat—and that's a good thing!

Chapter 15

You Can't Taste a Cheesecake over the Internet

You are what you share.
—Charles Leadbeater

The web and social media have brought us some great things, but in many cases they have also caused the death of relationship selling. Communication becomes clipped, quick, and less personal; relationships become shallower; the experience of the product becomes less tangible. But this is not the case in the food business, which is still a taste-before-you-buy kind of business. Our sales team members are all road warriors. They meet people in person and have them try real samples of our products. No matter how crisp the image or enticing the description, the experience of tasting—savoring—one of our scrumptious cakes or pies could never be re-created on a screen. Just about everything else is done digitally—from the PowerPoint presentations to the pricing spreadsheets to the final contract—but it is the taste that seals the deal. And *that* is our advantage.

I draw a distinction between the computer age, which began in the 1980s, and the digital age represented by social media. The first is a triumph. The second concerns me more than a little. What hath the digital age wrought? I am not exactly a Luddite. I love my laptop, my e-reader, my iPhone, my iPad. I can find things on the Internet with just a few touches on the keyboard. I can stream movies, record my favorite programs, download music onto my iPod (on which I now have more than three thousand songs, or nine days' worth!).

What I *am* worried about is this: I fear society is unraveling on the Internet; that so many people so depend on all the devices we have, that we are becoming more *isolated* than *connected* as entrepreneurs, as business owners, and simply as people. The closer the world gets to our fingertips, the further away it moves from our real selves. I use all these connections as tools, but I am not consumed by them as so many of my fellow human beings are, especially the younger ones. Of course, from my vantage point, almost everybody qualifies as a younger one.

As I walk down the street, I notice that *everybody* is looking down and texting as they walk, or they are listening to something through a pair of ubiquitous earbuds, oblivious to the world around them. On the Long Island Railroad (the train on which I commute to the office), *everybody* is reading email, playing games, or doing something on a device. On the subway platform where there is no connectivity (although that is rapidly changing), everybody is *still* staring down at their devices. It seems as though people—too many of them—are uncomfortable just thinking or being alone within themselves, as if they're afraid they will miss something if they turn off the electronic gadgets.

People share *everything*! Even couples do, which is trickier unless the pair sets up some rules, a kind of social media prenup, if you will. Does the world really need to know what we ate for breakfast? Facebook has been storing everything its eight-hundred million users have been sharing about themselves for years. Is this what social media was originally intended to do? Maybe so, or maybe it just evolved that way because we have been *willing* to let it happen. I think we surely need more self-censorship.

What has happened to privacy? Public feuding on Twitter is a new blood sport. Politicians, too, use it as a platform upon which to bicker or as a weapon with which to humiliate opponents rather than as a platform from which to express ideas. I once read an article—can't remember where—in which the writer, a psychiatrist, was quoted as saying social media was intended "not really to communicate some bone of contention; it's to humiliate the person in front of the whole world. Social media in general, and Twitter in particular, is the coward's way of expressing yourself." Has everybody forgotten that phones are available for us to use if we need to fight privately, or that we can fight in person?

I am by no means an expert, but I am intensely interested in the subject of social media, and I have noticed more and more articles being written about it all, some of them quite alarming. The writers of these articles are not just addressing social media, but technology in general. The title of an article in the magazine section of the *New York Times* one recent Sunday says it all: "Just One More Game . . . How time-wasting video games escaped the arcade, jumped into our pockets, and took over our lives." Another *Times* article I clipped was titled "The Flight from Conversation." In it the author contended that "the little devices that we carry around are so powerful that they change not only what we do, but who we are." It went on to say that "we expect more from technology and less from one another"; that "technologies provide the illusion of companionship without the demands of relationship"; and that "when people are alone even for a few minutes, they fidget and reach for a device. Here connection works like a symptom, not a cure." In the same article, a sixteen-year-old is quoted as saying, "Someday, but certainly not now, I'd like to learn how to have a conversation."

It all moves into the workplace. People are isolated even in an office without walls. Coworkers sitting at adjacent desks or cubicles email one another. I think that as more and more devices, software programs, and apps are added to workers' arsenals, efficiency will eventually suffer and technology will overwhelm us. Don't forget that we are all mere humans, and we will need new rules of the road and best practices for using all this wonderful technology to help rather than hinder us.

I admit there is a great deal I don't understand, but my instincts tell me that this brave new world with all of its advantages is no cakewalk. When the technology becomes the most important thing in our lives, it is time to rethink the human connection. We need to put in some balance.

Nevertheless, I have been forced onto the bandwagon. Now I have both a Facebook and a LinkedIn account; my marketing team *insisted*, and I am, as ever, nothing if not a team player. I was also bullied into starting my blog, where I have chronicled the history of Love and Quiches and where I comment on "of the moment" subjects. The marketing team's reasoning was that my blogging would help add to the visibility of our company, and I hope it has done just that. I admit that I have come to enjoy doing it. Then, by natural progression, came my book. (And of course I wrote this book on the computer using the two-finger method because I never learned to type. I couldn't have done it without the computer, since I rewrote it over and over and then over yet again.)

So here I am, a reluctant participant, with hundreds—approaching thousands—of Facebook friends and LinkedIn connections, and with invitations to connect coming faster than I can field them. These invitations keep coming, so I suppose that people must know me after forty years in the industry—or more likely, all the sharp and social media–savvy people that work at Love and Quiches have helped raise my profile. I have accepted that personal anonymity, which would be my choice *if* I had a choice, isn't a good thing for building a business. So I vigorously continue this process of gathering "friends" and "connections" even though I am not a believer.

Our public relations team is tutoring me on how to "engage." They also gave me marching orders to post comments at least twice a week, which is not too hard to do because I always have a lot to say. What *is* a problem is that the best time to comment (or so I am told) is on Wednesday and Sunday evenings, the later the better, just when I would rather be watching *Masterpiece Theatre* on PBS, or *The Good Wife*, or *The Mentalist*, or *Shameless*, or *Mad Men*, or reruns of *The Sopranos*. I guess the whole world is online late at night instead of relaxing, winding down, reading a good book, or going to sleep.

I do not yet use Twitter, and this may be where I draw the line if my team presses me to tweet. I read an article recently titled "Where Have All the Neurotics Gone: They're everywhere. But now we call it Tweeting." You can actually *buy* followers on Twitter or *buy* positive book reviews for a fee—*not* my idea of fair play. Then there is Yelp, where a thoroughly unqualified reviewer can kill a restaurant if he or she did not like the meal, and the terrible review is there for the whole world to see. I am trying to come to terms with all of this because this is the way it will remain, with much more to come.

Please do not misunderstand—I would *never* want to go back. All of the tools available today are vital to any business, from a start-up to the middle market and to the giants of industry and business. They are vital to government, education, writers, professionals, and all the rest of us. We use them both to keep our company front and center and to keep ourselves instantly informed about vital developments within our industry. As I discussed in more detail earlier in this book, Love and Quiches' software systems are vital to our day-to-day operations, information streams, and forecasting, and our website helps us broadcast our products and capabilities all over the world.

Businesses, especially new ones, need to use the tools available to help them advance. Crowdsourcing can help new businesses raise seed money and seek advice; e-commerce systems can help both young and established businesses sell some of their products online. Plenty of websites exist—particularly Smart Brief (www.smartbrief.com), which offers an excellent best practices series—where entrepreneurs can seek sound business and leadership advice. These sources provide helpful advice on such topics as preserving sanity, time management, procrastination, burnout, leadership skills, business planning, *and* the effects of answering email at 2:30 a.m. Some of the articles may seem silly—like "Leadership Lessons from Outer Space"—but the majority will be *right on*. Still other places offer up-to-the-minute industry news and vital information. Just be careful not to visit so many of these free informational sites and request so many of their newsletters that your inbox becomes unmanageable.

No matter how useful the Internet and social media can be to advance your business plan and to market your product, from my experience the successful entrepreneur should never let these tools supplant personal connections, relationship selling, and living in the real world. No business can survive without strong customer relationships, without engaging face to face somewhere down the line, and without meaningful interaction; this is especially true in the food business. People buy from people.

Social media and the digital world have *value* and are here to stay—get used to it. Whether you love them or hate them, you cannot ignore them. But they will never become my primary means of communication. The human connection is much too important and precious to me to let that happen. I still believe in the art of conversation. I guess I was born too soon.

The advantages that today's technological advances afford us are endless, and I wouldn't want it any other way. But we need to find a way to effectively use the one without losing sight of the so very vital other.

Me vs. a Futurist: A Short Digression

I occasionally attend the Women's Foodservice Forum's yearly conference to catch up with friends in the industry, and I always really enjoy myself when I do because it is wonderful to see so many (as many as 2,600) young—and not so young—women gathered for a few days to network and help each other advance their careers.

Because of my position as chairwoman and founder of Love and Quiches, I was invited to some of the smaller, more private events at the 2013 conference. During a luncheon for some of the higher-level participants, the speaker was a well-known author and consultant whom I consider a futurist. His vision of the world we will be living in, in the not-too-distant future, was really scary. He began by telling us that medical advances will be so vast that humans will live 140 years or more and will all have our own personal robots to help us cope. We will not need human interaction; our robots will take care of us and keep us company, which will allow us to remain in our homes.

He then said that each of us, both young and old, will have his or her own genie, maybe sitting on our shoulders or imbedded under our skin, to serve as our taskmaster and conscience. The genie will store our statistics, recite our up-to-the-minute blood pressure and cholesterol counts, and slap our hands when we reach for the french fries.

The vision went on (and here he was prescient): We will all wear glasses that will give us our calendar reminders, the weather report, our email messages, the ability to make purchases from anywhere in the world, and so on. This technology, though just getting off the ground, is already available to consumers and is picking up steam. Our connections will become more and more virtual as people become more and more dependent on their countless devices. And this by *choice*.

He also said that higher education will *all* be virtual. There will no longer be a Harvard or a Princeton or any other university as we now know it. Online education is growing by leaps and bounds, but for higher education to cease to exist altogether as we know it today—no more sitting in a classroom, every single college campus disappearing altogether—is more than I care to contemplate.

This speaker was *so* definitive and persuasive in his arguments that you could hear a pin drop. But I was not convinced. I'm not sure where

I got the courage, but I raised my hand in the Q&A that followed his talk. I asked him, "What about the human connection?"

In not so many words, he said we won't need any, that the technological advances will be so vast that they alone would be enough for us to live fruitful lives.

I hope we have all bargained for a lot more than this. This brave new world doesn't sound like much fun to me. Whatever the future brings, I'm confident in one thing: human connection will always remain important. I encourage you to embrace the Internet and social media; both are powerful tools for telling the world about your business and connecting with customers, partners, and mentors. You *will* need a media presence to build *any* business; get started on establishing it.

But at the same time, don't discount the lasting power of having deeper conversations, of meeting face to face, of letting people experience your product or service in the real world. With so many of your competitors increasingly putting a digital buffer between themselves and everyone else, give yourself an edge by welcoming in-person communication and human warmth.

Chapter 16

A Global Perspective

One's destination is never a place, but a new way of seeing things.
—Henry Miller

My very favorite thing to do is eat in restaurants all over the world. Over the years, seeing, tasting, and touching the food of the far corners of the globe became an obsession for me and a significant part of what we at Love and Quiches are all about. This was especially so as our export business took on a major role in our growth and future planning. For me, travel is a way of broadening my horizons, and I recommend that any entrepreneur or business owner who is able to, to travel the globe. It's amazing how new sights, sounds, tastes, and smells stimulate your mind and show you new possibilities.

Even my childhood memories of travel seem to be linked to the food I ate, saw, or learned about. One of the first such events occurred when I was thirteen years old: while on a cross-country teen tour, we were treated to an elegant lunch at Chateau Lake Louise in Banff, Canada, and we were served a delicate and cool fruit soup as a starter. Soup made from fruit? Soup that wasn't hot? I found it incredible! Later, as young marrieds before Bonne Femme began, Irwin and I went on a whirlwind tour of Europe—five countries in ten days!— that included many wonderful food-related memories. In Paris I broke some kosher taboos, eating simple ham sandwiches on well-buttered bread (positively divine) and lobster at the legendary Maxim's de Paris for a gazillion dollars! In Rome we learned that all Italian food was not always red. In Lisbon we were served a small portion of scrambled eggs topped with fresh tomato sauce as a starter for *every* meal, accompanied by beautiful and haunting Fado music and, often, dancing. And in Madrid I exercised my newly acquired taste for pork, dining on whole roasted suckling pig at the storied Casa Botin, founded in 1725. On another pre–Love and Quiches trip, a Caribbean cruise on the *France*, I learned to eat Beluga caviar by the carload—no accompaniments, just the caviar *neat*! I was obsessed with the stuff.

After we had been in business for ten years, I found that I could get away for a week or two without everything collapsing around me. So began Irwin's and my more serious and purposeful travel around the world. In any place we found ourselves, we always hit the streets and visited as many bakeries, gourmet shops, open markets, covered markets, small local grocery shops, food bazaars, and supermarkets as we could. We looked for *anything* baked, *everything* sweet. We were amazed to learn that in every corner of the globe, the very same size racks and bun pans serve as a universal baking "language." Our best finds were often far off the beaten path, and everything we learned about local tastes and customs helped Love and Quiches as the company transitioned to more sales worldwide. Each experience contributed a part to what I brought home to my business—perhaps a color, a flavor, an unfamiliar fruit, or a unique presentation—things that helped us in subtle ways to become what we are today.

Sometimes, on our way to South America or China or Europe or Russia, we have been served our own desserts on the flight, which has always made me feel *very* good. On a Delta flight, I once asked the stewardess what we were being served, and she replied, "It's an apple something or other." It was actually our lovely Swiss Apple Custard Tart, and I was disappointed with her description but I didn't correct her. Other times we've noticed little hoards of our brownie, blondie, or oatmeal chewie snacks put aside for the pilot and crew, even when they were not being served on the flight.

Taste Sensations

We have taken a major trip once a year since our serious travel began. Admittedly, our first few trips were a little less adventurous, and we confined ourselves to Europe. But the food was another story. We once flew into Paris during Christmastime, rented a car, and immediately headed north to the Champagne region and Reims, our destination the lovely Château de Fère in Fère-en-Tardenois. The inn is located on the grounds of a thirteenth-century ruin. Our dinner was exquisite, but the table settings were quite intimidating: a dozen or more forks, spoons, and knives in shapes we had never seen before. We ended that meal quite a bit more educated than we were when we had gone in.

Now, as seasoned travelers, we can adjust our inner time clocks with ease, but on that early trip, by the next morning, we had no idea where we were or whether it was day or night! At noon the proprietress entered our room and shook us awake, knowing we wanted to be on our way. We drove down the Rhône River, stopping in many little villages along the way and always asking the innkeeper for suggestions on where to eat, going from three-star restaurant to three-star restaurant, some that are now gone—like Alain Chapel, a culinary landmark in Mionnay, whose chef-owner was credited as being one of the originators of nouvelle cuisine—and others that are still there, like Oustau de Baumanière in Les Baux-de-Provence. More fun were the simple unknown places we happened upon for a meal at random—genuine French comfort food. On that trip, we ended up on the Riviera for New Year's Eve, where we celebrated at Le Relais de Mougins. The owner, André Surmain, was the founder of Lutèce, one of the original haute cuisine restaurants in New York, and he was so happy to see New Yorkers at that time of year that he spent the whole evening at our table.

At first, Irwin and I never intended to visit all of the earth's seven continents, but we've nearly done just that. (We still need to visit Australia to eat fresh-picked kiwis and to sample Foster's beer from down under.) We would study an illustrated world atlas and collect brochures from travel agencies as we planned our various tours to South America, Africa, Asia (Central, Southeast, and the Far East), Europe, and North America. No distance was too daunting, and as we all know, the language of foodies is universal, so being English-speaking tourists was no barrier. Each country—whether it was behind the Iron Curtain, as during our visits to Poland and Hungary, or embroiled in political disputes, as in Egypt—offered so much richness in its culture, history, architecture, and of course, cuisine! If you'd like to read some humorous episodes from our many trips abroad, I've collected them at the end of the book in Recipes for the Soul.

———

Why have I told you these stories about our trips? To bring home the fact that in order to broaden your reach in whatever business you're in, you need to broaden your horizons and learn what's happening in other parts of the world that you may not have thought possible. For me it was travel both in this country and abroad. Not only did we broaden our culinary horizons, but further honed leadership and organizational skills as we met and traded ideas and secrets with chefs and food manufacturers from all over the globe. And as a New Yorker through and through, I have always immersed myself in everything culinary that this phenomenal international city has to offer. I've seen every market, every bakery, and every food hall (a growing phenomenon here), and I've tasted every cuisine.

In my case, I needed to broaden my taste buds so that we could build a better chocolate cake—and *that* I think we have done. Ironically, I have found the world over that people *love* American desserts. Even in places where they hate us, they love our chocolate cakes, our cheesecakes, our brownies. They can't get enough of them, and that has been a good thing for Love & Quiches Gourmet.

Chapter 17

Family Matters

It's not personal, it's business.
—from The Godfather

I started my journey at Love and Quiches with one partner, Jill, and am ending it with another, my family, who joined me, one by one, as the business grew. We have segued into a family business slowly: my husband joined the organization in 1980, my son in 1992, and my daughter in 1996. It has been quite a story from the time I started delivering quiches out of the trunk of my car. Andrew and Joan have gone from being children who helped their mother crack eggs in the kitchen to becoming major players in our ever-growing company. Love and Quiches has already celebrated its fortieth year in business, and we plan on celebrating our fiftieth and then our sixtieth as well. There is just so far into the future we need to look. I like to deal with the somewhat more immediate future; nobody has a crystal ball.

Jill's and my original partnership lasted just a bit longer than one year, but our friendship is strong even today. Yet I started with a decent support system; Jill did not. Jill's family didn't think she should put in the time, whereas my husband *always* supported me and cheered me on whenever I needed cheering. Irwin has been my rock, my advisor, and the behind-the-scenes pillar of wisdom at Love and Quiches. And he's funny—he has kept me laughing since the day I met him. I need the laughter; this is a rough business. He is also one of the smartest people I have ever known, and he has proved it over and over during the almost sixty years we've known each other (we've been married for more than fifty of them). He has always had the numbers cold while everybody else, to this day, is madly calculating on their devices or counting on their fingers.

The Home Front

When I started my business, my parents, at first, couldn't understand what I was thinking; it didn't fit the pattern. I was just a girl. Even when I was a child, they never taught me to ride a bike and they neglected to get me braces for my teeth. I taught *myself* to ride at the embarrassing age of twelve, and I decided to fix my teeth at forty! By then my father practically begged me to let him pay my orthodontics bill because he felt so guilty, but I wouldn't let him. By then I had a stubborn streak that hadn't been there during my formative years but that I surely needed as the business grew. As I mentioned earlier, my father finally became so enthusiastic about Love and Quiches that for a while he showed up almost every day.

My in-laws, the world's most neglectful parents (Irwin grew up wild and undisciplined and often on his own), morphed into the world's most *incredible* grandparents, and I really needed that support. They were of immense help: always there for anything I needed, no questions asked, and I surely needed them for all the car pools I would otherwise have missed. If not for them I would never have been able to pursue my business and to work the hours needed to make it all happen. They took my children *everywhere* for me—to the dentist, to their lessons. Irwin's parents did anything else I needed, too, including waiting at my house all day for a repairman if something was broken.

Andrew and Joan were extremely close to both sets of grandparents.

It is obvious that no one can be in two places at once, so for any entrepreneur with small children, it is crucial to have a support network of spouse, family members, friends, or (if you can afford it) good child care as you pursue your dream.

———————

Long before I started my business, Irwin and I always exposed our children—even as toddlers—to fine foods both at home and in restaurants. So, much as it was during my own childhood, it has always been all about the food for our children also. When they were still very young and I was just developing my own passion for fine foods and cooking, Irwin and I spent a lot of time with Andrew and Joan. We loved to take them out to dine in fine restaurants on occasion. Even at three, Joan would look up after we read her the menu and order such dishes as Lobster Newburg. Then she would eat the whole serving with relish. Andrew at that young age was not quite as adventurous, but he got the exposure nevertheless. Eating well as they became teenagers and beyond has always been in our blood as a family, part of our DNA.

After I bought Jill out, I was working nonstop, but Irwin and I still saw to it that homework got done, dinner was ready (thanks to Bridget), and we *always* ate together. We made sure that both Andrew and Joan participated in at least some activities besides school: dancing lessons, piano lessons, and the like. (This was still the era before most parents started to obsessively overschedule and push their children in so many directions.) Another family thing we never gave up were occasional trips into the city to visit museums and attend the theater.

Andrew and Joan are close in age, and they were always good friends as young children and teenagers. They remain so now as adults and business partners. They managed to survive their childhoods even though, since I was so busy working, I wasn't always there for them. I admit that I left them, in some ways, to semi-drag themselves up. Although they never caused me too much grief, inevitably a bit of rebellion set in, like the time Andrew walked in with an earring in his ear, not at all common in those days, and it turned out that Joan had done the piercing! And they tell me *now* about all the wild house parties they had while we weren't home. We had no clue!

Bringing Skills to the Table

Andrew's and Joan's eventually joining the business had been a natural progression, a given. They both had always known they would, and they both brought considerable skills to the table. With the second generation on board by the end of the 1990s, Love and Quiches was officially a family affair with a succession plan in place. So far so good.

Andrew was a bit like his father growing up; he ran wild. We became quite used to his phone calls that started with "You won't believe this, but . . ." He would tell us, for example, that he'd just mowed down a row of rare Japanese maples while teaching his friend Michael how to drive and ended up with the car in the duck pond. Of course his friend was only sixteen at the time and didn't yet have even a learner's permit. He was also constantly in trouble in school until he was a senior in high school, at which point he was invited into a special alternative program where the students designed their own curriculum. I am grateful his advisors recognized his abilities, and this started his transformation. As he put it, "I have too much respect for my brain to continue screwing up," and from then on we knew he was going to be fine.

Andrew attended Michigan State University and graduated with a business degree in hotel and restaurant administration. During college, he did a summer at the École Hôtelière in Lausanne, Switzerland, a world-renowned hospitality and culinary school, where he caught the cooking bug at a much earlier age than I did. Then he changed course and attended law school. After practicing primarily labor and real estate law for eight years, he brought his negotiating skills with him and joined Love and Quiches. The experience he garnered during those years of practicing law has meant he's brought a great deal to the table here. Andrew is heavily involved in managing operations and financial planning, while still spending time selling and promoting the company.

Andrew is the visionary who sees Love and Quiches becoming potentially much bigger than it is now. But he has learned—as I have a thousand times over—that it doesn't just *happen*. So he tempers his enthusiasm with practicality: how we can best get from here to there, and what we need to do this.

Joan, as a child, was Miss Personality. These skills stayed with her and are intrinsic to her present role in the organization. Before she came to work for us full time, she did some local sales, on and off, while we were still doing store-door deliveries. After graduating from Boston University with a degree in marketing, she worked for MGM for a while; then came marriage and children. Her first husband, Frank, worked for us in sales. There was a divorce, and, democratic organization that we are, he stayed and Joan left. It was several more years before it was time for Frank to move on, and she rejoined the company, this time for good.

In the intervening years, Joan took me as a role model in order to figure out how to be entrepreneurial while staying home to raise a one- and a three-year-old. She got her yoga certification and became a personal trainer. Meanwhile, *her* children were getting a bit older, and eventually she returned to Love and Quiches to make use of her marketing degree to help promote our twenty-fifth anniversary. Joan continued in sales, and now she manages our entire sales department while performing many marketing functions. She can really *sell*, and she runs her department with an iron hand. She has completely revamped our sales reporting and all its complex parts. She even got our export reps on board with reporting—if *no* New Business Data Form, *no* samples. Joan is the communicator, and she has taken my place—which I gratefully relinquished—from a networking and mentoring perspective.

Today, we all hold equal positions on the executive committee at the top with a few of our other key employees. Even so, on rare occasions I still allow myself to throw my weight around and get two votes. But I have learned that I *can* be outvoted, and I am okay with that. We have managed, for the most part, to work it all out. We are fortunate in that we not only love each other, more importantly, we actually *like* each other, which is very helpful when we are fiercely going head to head, which happens very often in a business as complex as ours. We have to try *very* hard to coexist effectively in the office.

All in the Family . . . Business, That Is!

No business is easy. We've had our share of battles, and some of them have been rather explosive. But we find a way past them. I might add that it is always a good idea to have a third neutral party in the room as a referee of the combatants. This is *very* good advice.

The people you spend your life with greatly influence your path. We are a close-knit family who find ourselves in business together, a difficult proposition in any circumstance, and we have had to find a way to live with it. Family businesses come with their own unique set of challenges. *We will ourselves to keep the personal out of it, to focus on the end game.* It was a process and took quite a while; we are still at it.

The sacrifices I have made have allowed my children to follow their own destiny, to put their stamp on Love & Quiches Gourmet and the direction the company will take going forward. So my husband and I have learned to step back, to let go, to allow the organization and its high-performance teams to do their jobs without being micromanaged.

In any organization—whether private or not, whether operating during periods of a difficult economy or vibrant growth—there *will* be disagreements, both among the family members and among others in the organization at all levels. *Clearly defined areas of responsibility and job functions help keep this to a minimum, especially when it comes to family members.* Communication, mutual respect, and coordination are key. And *not* just for the four of us.

As we all know, change is inevitable as the needs of our target markets evolve, and we realize that as a family-run private business we have the advantage of flexibility, with fewer layers at the top for important decisions. This is yet another example of setting aside the personal and moving quickly to seize an opportunity. Our employees appreciate this distinction. Our longevity depends upon keeping both our customers and our employees happy.

Sometimes, as our personnel numbers expanded, the togetherness grew a little too literal as the office space correspondingly got smaller and smaller. I still have the corner office, but now Irwin and I share it, sitting opposite one another across a partners desk. And it is not only us; sometimes, I am embarrassed to admit, if visitors need some private office time, we must seat them in a chair opposite the bathrooms with their laptops in their laps! More office space is on the agenda.

The statistics are disheartening for family-owned businesses; only about a third survive beyond the founding generation, and only 12 percent make it into the third. *This* family business will try to beat those odds. We have a willingness to change and remain relevant that has been demonstrated throughout this book. Family members have to earn their positions both now and for future generations, and we are open to seek outside help when needed.

Forming our formal board of advisors, discussed earlier, was an important move for us. Because family businesses tend to make emotional decisions, we knew that the time had come to seek crucial input from outsiders, each of whom brings their business experience and *unemotional* advice to the table.

We have always done a lot together as a family, and we still do.

We can't seem to get away from each other. And even though we work together—often *more* than enough for family members—we *also* spend a fair amount of time out of the office during holidays, at the beach, while out for a meal, and so on. Away from the office, we try to refrain from discussing business as much as possible. Realistically, especially during this digital age, this isn't always possible; sometimes issues or decisions cannot wait, especially in a business of our size. We understand that and accept it, but if it *can* wait until Monday, we certainly let it do so.

Whatever the hardships of working with family might be, I've found those hardships outweighed by the gratification of being close to my husband, my children, and now my six grandchildren.

I think a fit end to this chapter is a poem my granddaughter Sari—now fourteen and always creative—wrote when she was eleven:

> Sugar dust and flour spots,
> Rest upon our big, gray pots,
> A hair net to keep our tresses attached,
> And white chef gear just to match,
> The smell of brownies in the air,
> And chocolate cake with devotion and care,
> Blondie crumbs on our glove,
> And our pretty quiche,
> That's made with love,
> Love and Quiches is the place that's best,
> Because we're better than the rest,
> So eat our brownies,
> Treats and more,
> Then like us you'll be sweet,
> Just down to the core.

—Sari Axelrod, age 11

Chapter 18

A Look in the Mirror

Most people live and die with their music still unplayed.
They never dare to try.
—Mary Kay Ash

There was absolutely nothing in my upbringing to prepare me for the fact that I would eventually find myself in a leadership position and that people would wait and want to hear what I had to say or what I thought. As you all now know, building my business from just one quiche to where we are today was not what was supposed to happen, given where I came from and the playlist that was set out for me. Nevertheless, here I find myself; I have met and exceeded goals that I never knew would be mine. It is ironic that I ended up in the dessert business, considering that my real passion for cooking and food hadn't initially been for baking at all. It shows how random these things can be. An opportunity presents itself, and you either go with it or you don't. I chose to go with it.

The only personal role model I had was my beautiful friend Phyllis. She died much too young, but Phyllis always knew what she wanted and went after it. She decided against having children (she happily used mine instead) when that option was frowned upon, and she had been on track to become superintendent of schools in a large district on Long Island. We were very close friends who could discuss anything and everything without passing judgment, yet we always had fun together.

There was an entire genre of male chauvinist pop songs in the 1950s and 1960s. Phyllis's and my favorite was "Wives and Lovers," sung by Frank Sinatra, in which he advises the little woman to fix her makeup, comb her hair, and take nothing for granted just because she has a ring on her finger; that girls in the office will go after her man; no curlers or he'll be gone; always run into his arms the moment he comes home; and other equally hilarious and sexist advice!

Every time we heard that song, we would *howl* with laughter while our husbands looked on, perplexed. I must have known even then that this would not be my role for too much longer. And I know Phyllis would have *loved* to learn about this book.

Although I started out not quite as a "lady who lunches," I was nevertheless one who attended charity luncheons, wore wide-brimmed hats, and dressed to kill at these events. That was my milieu. For most women of my generation, marriage and then children was a given, automatic. In that era, female entrepreneurs were a fairly uncommon phenomenon. There was Estée Lauder, of course, but that was a *very* long shot.

But then I blindly plunged into this business, surprising even myself. I wasn't the *only* woman who worked. Many women were real estate brokers, owned clothing shops, worked in the arts, or were teachers, nurses, and so forth. Manufacturing, however, was largely a man's game. On my level, I was a pioneer, albeit an inadvertent one. On the rare occasion when I found a half hour to run out and meet a friend for a quick lunch, people used to stare and point at me, but I never cared. My community of acquaintances may have been a bit critical, maybe even a little jealous. But my close friends were *always* my cheerleading department, encouraging me to keep going in spite of the obstacles in my path.

At the start of this narrative, I admitted that my single credential was that I loved to cook and had a passion for anything and everything connected to food: not a very promising background for entering the highly competitive manufacturing arena. I had had no exposure to the corporate or business world. As the business grew and became more corporate, and our customer base became more corporate, I had to learn to navigate that world as if I was born into it.

I didn't know any better—but once I got started, I *did* know that I had this tiger by the tail and wasn't going to let go. *I could do this!* After that, everything I learned about business I learned by doing. Mine is a story about learning on the job, about developing a fierce determination to try my luck at something new—and get lucky in the process. I am still learning.

There is no such thing as a straight line to the top. I would not take no for an answer, yet I recognized that I was in for a long and often bumpy ride. My friend Jack, the equipment dealer who in the early days sold me my freezers and became one of my mentors, asked me more than once if I thought I could take it. Of course I would answer "yes!" to which he always replied, "But, can you *really* take it?" I painfully learned over and over again during the following decades what he had meant and was trying to tell me.

My path in business has been full of twists and turns. I liken it to my cooking style. When I cook, I just keep making adjustments: a little more wine or stock or olive oil . . . salt, pepper, herbs, and so on until the flavor is just right. I use my instincts here just as I have learned to do in business: what ingredients to add and how much vs. what to do next and when. It's a skill learned from experience that has served me well. My advice is not to be afraid to veer a little to the left or to the right. Use my cooking as a metaphor for your career path; take the road to wherever it leads you. Dare to be a little bit different.

Through it all, I have *never* lost my passion. On some level, each phase of our development—both the good *and* the bad, as well as planning how to overcome the latter—has been filled with excitement.

Creating Balance

One would think my life has been all about food pretty much 24/7, but there *has* been some balance. Everyone needs some balance in his or her life. I played a lot of tennis—advanced *singles* tennis—and always loved it, except that I am now paying the price: my knees hurt, my shoulders hurt, and so do my wrists. When it became apparent that it was all over, I gave it up. I was sure that I would die if I had to give up my tennis, but I didn't die. I'm still here, just like Love and Quiches. These days I walk *a lot*. I keep it moving all the time.

My next grand passion, almost up there with food, is reading. We own and have read so many books that we ran out of shelves to keep them on, especially since we now live in an apartment. I am grateful for my e-reader, although at first I was sure that I could never get used to not feeling the comforting heft of a real book in my hands. When traveling, we used to carry a separate bag with us containing thirty pounds of books. Now I can walk around with a hundred books downloaded onto my Kindle. I also make sure to read the *New York Times* cover to cover every day; however, I am constantly a day behind. I can *never* seem to catch up on that day, but I never miss a page. Theater and the movies come next in my list of passions; I drag Irwin to see at least one every weekend, and sometimes two. As a New Yorker, I have a lot of choices. And I never, ever tire of dining out. Turning off the pressure in these ways renews me.

As the decades flew by, I developed a new persona. I became unafraid of my own style; I never again followed trends. If I like something, I will wear it for twenty years. I never wear platform shoes, and I only wear one color, black, because it's easier. Irwin says I dress like a widow. I don't shop unless I absolutely have to, and I never shop in a department store (too complicated). But food is another story. I don't mind shopping for hours to find the perfect melon or cheese. Food is still first on the list.

Climbing That Mountain

I have had a recurring dream for decades, and the theme is always the same: trying to get from one place to another. I can't quite get there, or if I do, I arrive with the parts not quite in the right place. It may be as simple as forgetting my dress shoes when attending a wedding and not being able to go back for them because there isn't enough time, or because there's too much traffic because of a baseball game, or a concert, or the president being in town. Sometimes the raincoat is inevitably in the wrong place during a storm.

Most of the time, however, the obstacle in my dream is *much* more dramatic: mountains, floods, torrential rains, mudslides, a bridge that is out. No matter how hard I try, I cannot quite get from one side of the chasm to the other. Or perhaps I don't have the correct address for the place I am trying to reach and there is no turning back to get it. I find myself hopelessly off course.

They're not quite nightmares, but they're unsettling nevertheless. And so it goes.

Building a business from scratch, from just an idea, is much the same. For me it has been a forty-year climb to get to a plateau high on the mountain, a place where I could stand without fear of falling. Along the way there have been hundreds of obstacles thrown in my path: recessions, competition, commodity spikes, blunders, flat tires, you name it. But I kept climbing because I had no other choice. It was too late to back down; there was too much baggage; I had bet the farm.

As I freely admitted in the prologue, my business didn't come with an instruction manual. There was no "how to" book. If there was one, I had no idea how to get my hands on it. Many years later, I learned that the US Small Business Administration had several helpful booklets about starting a business that had always been readily available. By the time I learned about these, I didn't need them anymore, but I'm sure they are still out there, no doubt online and updated to the present day. There are also myriad new business management books both online and in bookstores, and of course there are all the networking sources, local economic development organizations, crowdsourcing sites, and other help mentioned throughout this narrative. I suggest you look for and utilize any of them that can be of help; it would put you way ahead of me right out of the gate and save you a lot of grief.

As Love and Quiches' reputation has grown, I have been invited many times to speak at industry conferences in order to share my experiences and knowledge on various subjects, including sales, marketing, building an organization, product development, and the like. During the question-and-answer period, I have always found that when all the hands shoot up, all anybody *ever* wants to know is *how I got started!* I hope I have demonstrated just that in this book.

It is difficult to know how it feels to walk in somebody else's shoes, but I'd like to offer some of the advice that I only wish I could have had while starting out. I now know the food business very well, inside out and upside down, but these principles apply to almost any business endeavor. When the job market is difficult, starting your own business may seem an easier path, but it is a dangerous game, and being very careful as you take your first steps is of the utmost importance. To start a business it of course takes a good idea, but after that it takes guts, vision, a sense of humor, a tremendous capacity for work, and an ability to let go of doubts and the fear of failing.

Let me get this out of the way: There is no glass ceiling when you own your own business, and you can't be fired, either. But when you fall, it is on a sword of your own making. Even during boom times, most new businesses fail. Plan B careers are extremely difficult. There are no guarantees, and undeniably there's just as much or more stress as there is in corporate jobs. Don't be afraid of Plan C: to go back to the corporate world or your old job (if you can get it back) if you have given it a shot and failed. Even today, less than 2 percent of woman-owned firms pass the $1 million mark (although, happily, that number is growing). So most small businesses are *small*. Given that, I guess I have done a pretty good job.

I accepted at the outset that there would be low pay—in *my* case, no pay—long hours, no benefits, and on and on. As you know, I had no expectations, and we were lucky to have just enough money to get by. I didn't *expect* to have a career at all; but the thing is, I *could* and I *did*.

If you want to do the same, first gather your resources, and be careful not to risk more than you can afford to lose in case the enterprise fails. I took those kinds of risks more than once, and I am not ashamed to admit that it wasn't any fun. So do what I *say*, not what I have sometimes done.

During every one of my speaking engagements, I have found that everybody is also hoping to hear, during the questioning, that building a business involves nice, neat, and orderly growth. It simply doesn't happen that way. The pressures never end. Building a business is a 24/7 proposition, and it is very painful. People are also hoping to hear how glamorous it all is, but again, it simply doesn't happen that way. I'm not saying that there is *never* any glory or that there are *never* any victories, because there are plenty of both in a successful business, even in the beginning when you take your first small steps and make your first sales.

What I *am* saying is that it hurts and you have to prepare for the pain. I once heard Richard Melman, founder of the Lettuce Entertain You restaurant group in Chicago, liken building a business to running a marathon: You cannot reach the end without experiencing pain. He called himself the "King of Pain," and I think it's fair to call myself the "Queen of Pain."

Business life is not immutable. Things change with lightning speed, and my organization—both my people and me—had to learn to prepare to change with the tide or be left behind. I had to teach myself to stop wishing that nothing would ever go wrong, because things inevitably will. There will always be problems: problems between employees, problems with customers, with suppliers, with products, with ingredients, ad infinitum. There will be competition and money worries, and there will be downturns in the economy, and on and on.

As soon as I bought my original partner out in early 1975, I found that my real education was just beginning. I developed ambition overnight. I would see a plan through and *nothing* would stop me, but the resources and management skills needed to see me through the start-up years were all in short supply.

I quickly became mindful that the food business is extremely competitive, highly capital intensive, and difficult. Ours is a perishable product with a shelf life that begins ticking the moment we produce it, as well as a thousand other obstacles that I could list and that I've talked about throughout this book.

I needed good instincts and good "antennae" to anticipate the challenges and battles ahead of me. I had to learn to overcome the fear of failure and keep moving on, and I had to accept inevitable truths. I had to *will* myself to develop certain invaluable skills, all learned on the job, that I have used throughout my decades-long career.

Some things are in the hands of the economy. Things will always shift beneath you, and you need to develop the skills to adapt and the fortitude to persevere.

I have learned to:

- Recognize an opportunity and go with it

- Take measured risks

- Learn from my many mistakes

- Innovate, try something different

- Remain motivated and motivate others

- Develop a sixth sense for things that may need correcting

- Never take anything for granted, no matter how good we get

- Learn early the strategic use of the word "no"

- Choose courage over fear, and play outside my comfort zone

- Keep calm and deal with the chaos; things happen and we must be ready

- Concentrate on the good, not on the bad stuff; build on what is right

- Not ignore my weaknesses, but tap into and build on my strengths

- Prepare for the inevitable setbacks, many simply beyond my control

- Make a decision, and once made, never look back; the best leadership skill of all

For me, these were *all* newly learned skills, honed the hard way: one by one. I have learned to cope, not to show my pain, to encourage people to move forward, to keep focused on the end game, and to celebrate the victories. It's kept me busy for forty years, and I have never been bored.

Being a Woman Is a Good Thing

I have never really allowed gender to affect how I have conducted myself during my career as a business owner, but in many ways I suppose my gender has helped the growth of my business. I have won quite a few awards that I may not have won otherwise, all of which has brought attention to Love and Quiches. So that has always been a good thing.

I have been honored by *Long Island Business News* as one of the Top 50 Most Influential Women in Business on Long Island so many

SUSAN AXELROD
Love and Quiches Desserts

Hall of Fame
2009 HONOREE

Sixth Annual
WOMEN OF THE YEAR AWARDS

presented by

NEW YORK UNIVERSITY
CENTER FOR FOOD AND HOTEL MANAGEMENT

Love & Quiches' Axelrod Elected Woman of the Year

Susan Axelrod, president and founder of Love & ...hes, Freeport, N.Y., has ... voted Regional Small ...ness Woman of the Year in ...ufacturing by the ...en's Foodservice Institu-...f New York University and ...Small Business Adminis-...ion.

The 5th Annual
Woman of
Distinction
Awards
1998

Susan Axelrod

Axelrod started her frozen food business nine years ago. What she began as a cottage ...

times that I was finally inducted into their Hall of Fame, along with some other woman business owners in the region, in 2009. There have been many other awards throughout the years, many of these because of my gender.

Year after year, in conjunction with Women's History Month each March, I am kept busy with all sorts of events, and I am happy to tell my story in the hope of encouraging others to take the leap.

One of my best stories came rather early in the game, in the early eighties. I was invited to Chicago to conduct an all-day seminar preceding the monthly meeting of the Purchasing Managers Association, as well as to be the speaker at the meeting itself. It still remains a powerful association, and I was probably invited because of our excellent relationship with one of our major distributors—and *also* because I was a woman who started a business from scratch against the odds. Throughout the years, my motivation for seeking this kind of recognition has *always* been to promote my company, not my ego. I have always been much too busy for ego.

One more important advantage that has served us well is our certification as a Minority Woman Business Enterprise. Because larger corporations and public companies, airlines, chain restaurants, buying groups, the military, and so on are required to do a certain percentage of their business with minority companies, our status is a tremendous boon.

As I've said, in spite of all this, we operate in a rather color- and gender-blind way, and I am hopeful that my employees respect me for my ideas and leadership rather than for unimportant distinctions.

Only *once* was I subjected to truly blatant discrimination. Early on there was a powerful buying group called North American. For those unfamiliar, "buying groups" are organizations of otherwise unaffiliated companies that pool their buying power to gain an advantage in terms of price and marketing dollars. The vendors favored by these buying groups then have a "hunting" license and an advantage over their competitors with similar products.

Eventually, a distributor invited Love and Quiches to present our line, and we were able to secure a showing. We flew out to Chicago at the crack of dawn because we were told that we had a 9 a.m. slot. In practice, we sat there all day, and we were not invited in until 5 p.m. We could not get anybody to taste even one thing, nor were we asked any questions. *We were invisible.*

We left quite dejected, but the next day dejection turned to outrage when the distributor who had invited us to present our line contacted us. He told us that the minute we had left the room he had been asked by *everybody* present if I was his girlfriend. *He* was angrier than I was.

By standing back, not leaning in, I was able not to let my anger distract me—and this was not the worst thing that happened to me *by far*. Besides, most of the companies involved were sold and absorbed into even larger companies, and North American no longer exists as a buying group. We have established programs with several other buying groups as the years have passed, and we have had the last laugh after all.

The Feminist Conversation

Fifty years ago the culture of the day was such that women who worked were thought to be killing time while searching for a husband, and a wife who pursued a career was considered to be maladjusted, someone who would damage both her marriage and her children. It was in this context that Betty Friedan predicted in her book *The Feminine Mystique* that if American women would embark on lifelong careers, they would be happier, their marriages would be happier, and their children would be better off. Friedan was not a well-known journalist when she proposed the book to her publisher, W. W. Norton, as a treatise on the plight of the American housewife, and it took four years for the book finally to go to press in 1963. Friedan blasted what she considered the suffocating vision and mythology of the "happy housewife," and the book was an instant hit. In many ways, it inaugurated the "mommy wars" of that period and after, in which working women and stay-at-home moms resented one another. Through the years the book has been praised, denigrated, dismissed, you name it.

Of course a lot has changed since 1963, especially the notion that a woman's sole reason for being is to be married or to have children. In many ways, though, I think Ms. Friedan has been proved right, although it has taken decades.

The Feminine Mystique was considered to have started "*second-wave feminism,*" according to Lisa M. Fine, who just published an annotated scholarly edition of the book through Norton. (Don't forget the suffragettes here in America who preceded Betty Friedan.) From today's vantage point, the book may seem more like a symbolic totem. Not everybody was a housewife or lived in suburbia. In the 1950s there *was* a small but growing number of women with notable careers. Consider Margaret Thatcher, for instance, who started her career as a food scientist specializing in cake icings, and we all know how far she took working outside the home.

Still, the book galvanized women. Friedan *started* the conversation.

Then, roughly ten years later, the first issue of *Ms.* magazine was published, founded by Gloria Steinem, a feminist, journalist, and social activist; and a whole new initiative and push for feminist equality was born. Betty Friedan and Ms. Steinem never got along, and Ms. Friedan once famously refused to shake Gloria's hand. *Ms.* has just celebrated its fortieth anniversary and has been owned and published since 2001 by the Feminist Majority Foundation. Ms. Steinem has gone on to co-found the Women's Media Center in 2005, and continues her involvement in politics, media affairs, lecturing, and publishing books.

This period was also when the story of Love and Quiches began. I started my accidental business in my home kitchen in that year, even before the founding of the National Association of Women Business Owners in 1975. Back in the beginning, during the sixties, I was living Ms. Friedan's suburban housewife model. But I wasn't unhappy; I was developing my grand passion for everything culinary and honing my cooking (but not baking) skills. *Then* came the offer to teach some courses for a local charity—and get paid for it.

That was it! The time had come to jump in, and I have never looked back. Yet I have never been very active in the women's movement. I was always too busy doing what I had to do, putting one foot in front of the other, fighting myriad challenges, then picking myself up and moving on until, finally, I succeeded. My contribution has been to share my story as it all unfolded.

Now there is a new movement on the horizon, with Sheryl Sandberg, the COO of Facebook, publishing her book, *Lean In: Women, Work, and the Will to Lead,* which talks about women in the workplace. Ms. Sandberg reread Ms. Friedan's book, and she wants to start her own revolution: a new conversation, a new movement, but this time centered in the workplace.

Ms. Sandberg has been criticized for accusing women of just not trying hard enough, when most women simply have not had the advantages that she has had. Hers is a loftier perch than most of us sit on; that is, those who are more earthbound and who struggle with the more mundane issues of balancing family, careers, and the search for new ways to break through the glass ceiling that definitely still exists. As of January 2014, there were still only twenty-three female chief executives of the current Fortune 500 companies. And so on down the line.

Ms. Sandberg may be trying to promulgate the idea that women can have it both ways, easily balancing family and career. A new discussion of this is always welcome. Nevertheless, in my opinion the "mommy wars" are over. Everybody is now free to choose their own path.

Who I Am and How I Got There

Feminism, as I have said, has never played a role in our organization. I was merely a pioneer who found myself in the manufacturing sector, a brutally competitive arena.

I was more of a bull in a china shop than anything else in my home business, trying to figure out what I wanted to do and to be. I took it from there to where we are today through the series of moves described throughout my narrative: from my garage to a small storefront, from there to a small factory, and ultimately to our present home where we have, during our thirty years here, grown the business from local to international supplier with major customers worldwide.

I beat the odds. I started supplying quiches to a variety of establishments that had no way of preparing quiche from scratch, as well as quiches that could also be served *any* time from breakfast through late night. I had settled on a versatile product that served as the catalyst for the growth of my business. And I had the perfect marketplace to hone my skills. The metropolitan tri-state region (New York, New Jersey, and lower Connecticut) provided me with thousands of potential customers: there were pubs, restaurants, hotels, gourmet shops, etc. almost everywhere I looked. My idea turned out to be a very good one. I *created* the need for what we sold. I had found my market, and I was off and running.

I built the business slowly, one quiche at a time. With drive and focus, I learned what business is. I made lists and sweated the small stuff, all of which adds up to the whole. To this day I find that keeping lists and ticking them off helps to keep me organized. I still keep my "to do" lists on index cards just as I have since starting my business forty years ago. It works for me. Pen to paper helps me get my head around what I need to do. I still give myself *deadlines*. That was my trick, whether it was for my grocery list or for following up on customer leads: I wouldn't stop until I got it all done.

Without this focus, I don't think Love and Quiches would be where it is today. Thank goodness that what I started and spearheaded for the first twenty years has been gradually taken over—I gratefully concede—by a cadre of people as organized as I have been. More talented, too.

I got help wherever I could find it. I never stopped seeking advice from my mentors, my customers, my suppliers, my professionals, my industry contacts and friends, and later from my employees, consultants, the SBA, and various NY state and local economic development agencies. In the early years, I took my many embarrassments and small failures in stride, and I would not allow myself to be sidetracked. I was stubborn, and I would not allow my optimism to falter. Small though it was, I slavishly adhered to my budget; early on we had no reserves and could not afford any errors that may have proved fatal. I remained patient, and little by little the dollars started to build and we were on our way.

One step at a time I developed the knowledge and skills I needed to run a business and become a leader, all by just living it, by doing it. And as the organization and the volume grew, so did I.

My Thoughts on Leadership

Do not forget that when you are a boss, the workday never ends. I used to say I would kill simply to have a *job* because the stress of business ownership was so high, but I eventually learned to live with it and to cope. I accepted that I could not have it all: perfect wife, perfect mother, perfect leader, perfect executive.

I have been in business for a long time, and I have had plenty of time to hone my skills in becoming an effective leader. I often look back on my business life and replay scenes, trying to view them from an outside perspective. I see mistakes, I see poor choices, but I cannot change them. They are done, so I have just kept going.

Many of the answers lie within. It is always good to seek advice from mentors, colleagues, and other industry leaders, but true leaders intuit what is best for their particular business, and that is a skill that *can* be learned. I was not born a leader. *I had to learn how to do it.*

A great business idea is only half the battle; you must be an effective leader to move it forward.

First and foremost, I had to believe in myself. I have been responsible for the livelihoods of so many, and I still bear that burden. But as we grew, I hope that I have shown my organization both passion and *patience*. I gratefully acknowledge that all I did was *start* the thing. Our organization is bigger than any one of us. Together we have a shared sense of purpose that creates in us a willingness both to weather difficult times and to go for the gold.

Some people think it is best to lead from the back of the bus, and some think it is best to lead the charge from up front. I'm still pondering this, but I think it may be a combination of the two. A good leader defers to the experience and expertise of others. I would certainly have achieved *nothing* without this very strong organization, built slowly with the help of my family and others who share top positions at Love and Quiches. Our management teams, as I have demonstrated throughout, were built through a combination of promoting from within and bringing in outside talent when needed. They are a passionate group, very diverse, and together we make up an organic whole.

Here, Now

As Love and Quiches gained its position in the industry, I became known as "The Quiche Lady." I was a poster child for the era, a 1970s pioneer who built a bakery manufacturing business out of thin air. To my great surprise, on some level I am considered an industry icon that has helped forge a path for those who came after me. I have chosen this life, have achieved a measure of success, and if I have inspired others, that is one more element that has made it all worth it.

As chairwoman and founder, my most important role now is to know when to do less, to be a very good listener, to ask what I can do to help make my teams more effective, and to inspire them to push beyond their comfort zones (the story of my life). I ask a lot of questions, but I let them come up with the answers and solutions and execute them. My hope is that I am respected and not feared.

Real leaders know they don't have all the answers, and so it is my staff that have made me a good leader. They make me look good. By handing off many of the day-to-day responsibilities, as it should be, I am often there with my hands behind my back, but I am there. Our company is like a living and breathing organism, and, as its founder, I am part of its lifeblood. But now, happily, I am just one part of the whole. Perfect!

Where Will We Go from Here?

If your actions inspire others to dream more, learn more, do more,
and become more, you are a leader.
—John Quincy Adams

Here I am at the end of the chronicle of my accidental business. I have described my journey from my home kitchen to today, and my hope is that my story has entertained, informed, and inspired. Given a thousand chances, I would never have guessed that a simple idea—just one quiche—would start me on the road to where I find myself today.

I've told my personal story, the Love and Quiches story, drawing on my experiences during the past forty years as we grew from home kitchen to local business to international supplier. I learned so much during each stage of our development, and my hope is that other budding entrepreneurs and business owners will find wisdom and rules of the road to take away from my stories too.

Although for decades we have flown hundreds of millions of our brownies all over the world with our name on them and although we've recently developed a Gourmet Grab and Go line of prewrapped snack products with our brand, Love & Quiches Gourmet is, nevertheless, an important "behind the scenes" supplier. We are not a household name yet, but we are an integral and well-recognized member of the foodservice community. We make our customers look good by supplying *them* with superb products, products that are on trend and of the moment. If our products are presented as their own, that makes us happy; that is our game; that is what we do.

Our growth as a business continues to benefit from the fact that high-quality desserts are growing in popularity and demand in every conceivable channel, including the fast-food industry. This is an exciting time for us with new opportunities to explore.

As I have demonstrated, our road forward has not been an easy one. First, we had to overcome my utter lack of preparation for business ownership. Over the years, we weathered a flawed business model, economic recessions, 9/11, key account loss, and other storms, many of which were well beyond our control. Each time, we picked ourselves up, dusted ourselves off, and moved on, myself a little smarter, Love and Quiches that much stronger. We are still here, and we are now in a position to overcome almost any obstacle placed in our path. We can use even a bad economy to fuel our growth.

We have learned to focus on what we are good at, and we do it well. People will always have to eat, and if we operate smartly, a good share of all that can be ours. Our eyes are laser focused on the prize. We stay on message, and our market knows they can depend upon us. We are now well into the new century, a well-oiled machine that is ready for the future. Our organization has developed a sense of urgency to see what comes next. Our focus will be on sales growth, improving processes, increased efficiencies, cost reduction, *and* the bottom line. We will build only what we can *sustain*; if we aim for a star, it will be a *reachable* one.

We are still evolving and improving. Our walls are once again stretching to their limits, and we have just taken an additional twenty thousand square feet of warehouse space around the corner. We can grow another 20 percent or so in this facility, and then, perhaps, we will be in a position to move to our dream facility—the next leg of our journey—so stay tuned.

By owning my own business, the weight of responsibility on me to my family, my organization, and my customers is always there. Like breathing. It will *always* be there, but the burden has lightened as the years have passed and Love & Quiches Gourmet has grown. The responsibility is now shared by all of the talented people who work here and help run the company. I can step back quite a bit without worrying and let the others bask in the victories.

Business ownership has allowed me in many ways to control my own destiny in spite of the many roadblocks thrown in my path. The many years of grating cheese, rolling dough, schlepping samples, scrubbing floors, suffering burns all up and down my arms, knocking on doors, and on and on, has toughened me. And I needed toughening to fight my way to the position we enjoy today. The scars have faded, but the lessons are still there.

Little by little, one step and some leaps at a time, we took a lesson from each and every foible, from each mistake and heartbreak that kept moving us to where we are today. Every business has its own story, but I truly believe that we would not be where we are today without what had come before—every bit of it.

Along the way, I have strived to become a good and effective leader. At the same time, I've provided encouragement to others who have a good idea, ambition, and a dream. In being able to inspire and motivate others to succeed and keep moving the company forward, I have achieved my most important accomplishment.

And I've had fun doing it. It has been a great ride. If I had to do it all over again, all the pain and the glory, would I make that choice? In a heartbeat, I would.

Acknowledgments

Just as I never, in a thousand years, thought I could start a business in my home with just one quiche and bring it to where it is today, it was even less likely that I would write a book, so I have a lot of people to thank who helped me all along the way.

First, Aaron Hierholzer, my talented editor at Greenleaf Book Group, who worked with me 24/7 for months on end as I wrote this book, and then rewrote it, over and over, until we got it right. Thank you, also, to all the other talented people at Greenleaf who contributed greatly to the final product: Neil Gonzalez, Justin Branch, Linda O'Doughda, to name just a few among the Greenleaf team who touched it.

There are so many others:

My dear friend Jill Krueger, who was my partner at the beginning of Love and Quiches.

My parents and my in-laws, all gone, who each played a part—especially my father, who I know would have gotten a real kick out of how far I have come.

The late Phyllis Wilens Zaphiris, my friend and cheerleader who, in my opinion, coined the phrase "You Go, Girl."

The late James Gilliam, aka "Jimmy the Baker," who you have read about on these pages and whose contributions were invaluable.

A special thanks to all the talented and dedicated people who have worked at Love and Quiches across the decades and essentially "wrote" this book for me. So many of them are still here.

I especially want to recognize Michael Goldstein and Toni Salvato, our R&D specialists, for all of their hard work in verifying the favorites I share in Recipes from the Heart.

Thank you to JoAnn DeTurris, who jumped right into the end game and saved my sanity.

My children, Andrew and Joan, who started by cracking eggs every day after school and now share in running the company.

My husband of fifty-three years and partner, Irwin: my best friend, sounding board, and stealth editor, who contributed more than he realizes to the final version.

And just a note of thanks to all my Fire Island friends who kept Irwin company, and who somehow cheered me on while I was in the house tethered to my computer working on the book . . . while they were all outside relaxing or sunning themselves on the beach.

Coda

Recipes for Success:

My Accidental Business Primer

When I started writing this book, I never meant for it to be a definitive "how to" business book. Rather, I attempted to show through my stories how my business was built one step at a time, as well as how I have lived it, together with all the dedicated people who have been part of the Love and Quiches community across the decades.

These "recipes" are meant to capture the principles and practices that have guided us as the Love and Quiches story unfolded, and they are the essence of our philosophy and ethics. These and so many more tenets help us to stay healthy, viable, and on message. We have survived. We have thrived. We are still standing, with more to come.

- **Businesses exist to make a profit,** not to fill up the day. The best ideas are nothing unless you can persuade someone to pay for them.

- Every new business must **start with a sound business plan**. This includes a good idea, a target market, what you hope to accomplish, and *everything* (rent, staff, resources, supplies, equipment—ad infinitum) needed to get through the period until a positive cash flow can be created.

- **A business plan *must* remain flexible.** Never stop seeking knowledge about your particular industry. Markets are *constantly* developing and evolving, and you must change with them to remain cutting edge.

- **Take one step at a time**. Growth does not solve problems; it merely amplifies them if you are not ready. There is always a process; be patient.

- **Invest in solid professional advice.** In addition, seek advice from your suppliers, customers, mentors, sponsors, and industry counterparts. Later on, utilize consultants, but choose them carefully.

- **A strong banking relationship is vital**, unless funds are unlimited. Your available capital will limit your participation in the marketplace; respect those limits.

- **Be aware of *all* your costs, and price your products or services properly** (but in line with your competition). We keep what works well and rationalize out those products (or services) that do not generate enough sales or profit. The top line is important, but it is the bottom line that counts.

- **Offering products with price points at more than one level will enable you to reach more potential customers.** Small changes (such as weight, decoration, or pack size) within a single product can greatly multiply the product's reach with no impact on operations.

- **Most businesses fall within the 80/20 rule.** Because 80 percent of volume is done with only 20 percent of customers, treat these customers well.

- **Develop high-performance teams.** Across the decades, this has been our greatest achievement; our human capital is our most valuable asset.

- **Hire people better than you are and treat them as valued insiders.** We foster a culture of mutual respect and honesty, and we understand that our success is a team effort. We share detailed financial results with management, and we offer participation as goals are achieved.

- **Create an orderly hierarchy.** In this way, each employee knows exactly where he or she stands. Strong leadership and management can lead workers in achieving goals.

- **Empower leaders within the company, but don't tell them how to lead.** There is no one-size-fits-all management technique. We provide direction and goal setting, clearly communicated, from the top, but our department heads and managers run the meat and potatoes with complete authority. Learn to trust—to let go.

- **Train constantly.** We do this for all employees over and over yet again. Cross-training is vital so that no job ever goes uncovered.

- **Communicate, communicate, communicate.** Everybody needs to be on the same page so that everybody will march in the same direction and not be at cross-purposes. Frequent communication will also avoid duplication of effort.

- **Run effective meetings.** Mutual respect and no elephants in the room are the order of the day.

- **As a small business, you cannot be all things to all people.** Focus on what you are good at and do it as well as you can. Your customers will come to rely on that. Above all, quality first. Never compromise on that.

- **Clarify your image so your target market knows *exactly* what your business is all about.** Use *all* the tools available, from your website to your point-of-sale materials to customer service to one-on-one selling, to get the message across.

- **Networking works.** Participate in all applicable social media outlets, trade organizations, trade shows, conferences, speaking engagements, and so on in order to increase your connections across the board and broaden your ability to grab on to opportunity when it crosses your path. Find a mentor, and then mentor others in return.

- **Watch the competition with a very practiced eye.** Strong competition will push you to be better; there is enough business for everyone if you remain aware, focused, and calm.

- Businesses do not create jobs; customers do. **Satisfy your customers' needs at all times.** Provide your market with high-quality and innovative products, excellent and consistent service, competitive pricing, and appreciation for their business. And *always* deliver on your promises. If you do, that loyalty will be returned.

- **Balance the needs of the customer with the needs of the company.** Do not allow any one customer to account for more than 5 percent of sales.

- **Learn the strategic use of the word *no*.** If the fit isn't there, if you cannot make a profit, walk away.

- **Strategize by business segment, channel, and class of customer.** Our sales, marketing, and R&D departments work hand in hand in the process of tailoring our business to different segments, gathering technical and market intelligence. (We *never* put all our eggs in one basket.)

- **Never stop taking it to the next level.** We are never good enough, and improvement is a constant.

- **Establish a standard operating procedure for *everything*** so that nothing is ever left to chance.

- **You cannot manage what you can't measure.** We measure *everything*. Our strong accounting practices get us the information we need to make smart projections and strategic decisions for sales, marketing, labor needs, capital expenditures, and so on. On a current basis, we know where we are, so that we can plan smartly for the future.

- **Capture the power of the Internet, but be wary, too.** The world has become a much smaller place, and we can reach every corner of the globe with just the touch of a mouse to market our businesses, but carefully vet any advice or help you may seek. In many respects, the Internet is still the Wild West. Also, never let quick Internet exchanges replace meaningful communication with customers.

- **If you're running a business with family, keep the personal out of the office.** Business is never easy, and the family dynamic makes it that much more difficult. It is vital to pick your battles and leave family drama at home, where it belongs, while you stick to the business of business.

- **Seek new perspectives.** For us, it was travel as our business grew; for any business owner or entrepreneur, it is crucial to expand your horizons in order to see what is going on around you to help bring new ideas to the table and to help you formulate the path forward.

- **Success is never a straight line to the top.** Each failure has been a learning tool, a clarifying moment. Our failures have made us better, since we don't often make the same mistakes.

- **Learn from your successes so that you can repeat them.** We never take anything for granted and are always aware and on the alert.

———

One last word: sometimes, **just do it!** When opportunity knocks, open the door and let it in.

Recipes for the Mind:

A Few Favorite Books

I 've always been an avid reader; from the time I was quite young, I can't remember when I wasn't in the middle of reading *something*. Once I started Love and Quiches, reading fiction and memoirs became my escape and business books my learning tools. Here are a few of my favorites.

Business Books

There are certain classic books and some new ones on subjects as diverse as manufacturing, leadership, management, influence, marketing, social media, inspiration, best practices, and so many more. Every businessperson, entrepreneur, or member of the corporate community should read at least some of them. I enlisted the Love and Quiches team in this effort, and together we think the following list covers a lot of important ground:

- *The Art of War* by Sun Tzu; written over two-thousand years ago by a Chinese warrior-philosopher, it remains a profoundly influential treatise on military, business, and legal strategy in the world today.

- *Outliers* by Malcolm Gladwell; examines high levels of success with examples drawn from subjects as diverse as Bill Gates, the Beatles, and Canadian ice hockey players.

- *Death by Meeting* by Patrick Lencioni; focuses on a cure for the painful problem of modern business: bad meetings and their toll on a company's success.

- *The Goal: A Process of Ongoing Improvement* (second revision 1992) by the late Eliyahu M. Goldratt; a management-oriented "novel" that demonstrates the theory of constraints (bottlenecks) and how to alleviate them.

- *Good to Great* by Jim Collins; examines why some companies make the leap to great and others don't, proposing that greatness is a matter of conscious choice and discipline.

- *Swim with the Sharks without Being Eaten Alive* by Harvey Mackay; how to out sell, out manage, out motivate, and out negotiate. Mackay spells out his path to success.

- *The 7 Habits of Highly Effective People* by Stephen Covey; a business self-help book from 1989 that proposes a paradigm shift in how we interact with people in a business environment, as well as the habits we can cultivate in order to effect that change.

- *Who Moved My Cheese?* by Spencer Johnson; a story featuring two mice and two "littlepeople" who look for cheese in different ways. This book is about change and how to embrace it.

- *The New Rules of Marketing and PR* by David Meerman Scott; the bible for all aspects of successful marketing today.

- *The 10 Laws of Enduring Success* by Maria Bartiromo; beautifully written and concise, it is partly inspirational and partly solid advice on how to conduct yourself in business and career building today.

Additionally, there's the **US Small Business Administration website**: www.sba.gov. There you will find a wealth of practical information about starting a business in addition to resources and contacts.

Women in Business

- *The Feminine Mystique* by Betty Friedan; for historical perspective and for starting the conversation.

- *Lean In: Women, Work, and the Will to Lead* by Sheryl Sandberg; having it all from the top of the food chain.

- *Wonder Women: Sex, Power, and the Quest for Perfection* by Debora Spar; proposes "satisficing," which supposes that sometimes second best is a good place to be. A very good read.

- *Women, Work, and the Art of Savoir Faire* by Mireille Guiliano; a very personal story about being the highest-ranking woman at Veuve Clicquot since Madame Clicquot (who died in 1866).

Memoirs

Here are three great reads that are all about food and keeping on subject:

- *Blood, Bones & Butter* by Gabrielle Hamilton

- *The Sharper Your Knife, the Less You Cry* by Kathleen Flinn

- *Kitchen Confidential: Adventures in the Culinary Underbelly* by Anthony Bourdain

- *Yes, Chef: A Memoir* by Marcus Samuelsson

Novels

I read memoirs and biographies and have enjoyed some fantastic reads in these genres, yet my most favorite books have been fiction, an escape into another world. I have always chosen from a vast array of authors; some of my selections may be from past decades, some more current. But, to me, they are all timeless and unforgettable. So, just at random, I have loved:

- *The Poisonwood Bible* by Barbara Kingsolver

- *A Fine Balance* by Rohinton Mistry

- *The Alexandria Quartet* by Lawrence Durrell

- *The Cairo Trilogy* (*Palace Walk*, *Palace of Desire*, and *Sugar Street*) by Naguib Mahfouz

- *Angle of Repose* by Wallace Stegner

- *Postcards* by Annie Proulx

- *Love in the Time of Cholera* by Gabriel García Márquez

- *Geek Love* by Katherine Dunn

- *Cutting for Stone* by Abraham Verghese

- ***Let the Great World Spin*** by Colum McCann

- ***The Sweet Hereafter*** by Russell Banks

- ***March*** by Geraldine Brooks

- ***The Beet Queen*** by Louise Erdrich

- ***The Beans of Egypt, Maine*** by Carolyn Chute

- ***What's Bred in the Bone*** by Robertson Davies

- ***Paris Trout*** by Pete Dexter

- ***Dinner at the Homesick Restaurant*** by Anne Tyler

- ***Cambridge*** by Caryl Phillips

- ***The Guernsey Literary and Potato Peel Pie Society*** by Mary Ann Shaffer and Annie Barrows

- ***Martin Dressler: The Tale of an American Dreamer*** by Steven Millhauser (1996 Pulitzer Prize)

- ***The Known World*** by Edward P. Jones

- ***Half Broke Horses: A True-Life Novel*** by Jeannette Walls

Last, in case you have not read anything by John Updike, William Faulkner, John Steinbeck, E. L. Doctorow, or Pearl S. Buck, I urge you to do so now.

This should keep you busy. I could go on and on; I have, most probably, read thousands of books. But it is too late to count them all.

———

I simply must recommend one **film** "above all" both for the *appetite* and for the *soul*—***Babette's Feast***. This is a Danish drama from 1987, based on a story by Isak Dinesen (Karen Blixen), which won the Academy Award for Best Foreign Language Film. (It's available on DVD.) Magnificent!

Recipes for the Soul:

Travel Abroad

Some of my fondest memories of traveling around the globe include the following:

- Driving through the Cotswolds in the early eighties while visiting my daughter, Joan, who was doing a college semester in London. We stayed at an exquisite country inn and were served a marvelous dinner, but the featured dessert was a Rice Krispies Pie (no kidding!).

- During a Greek Island cruise, we had a spectacular lunch with some new friends from what was then Rhodesia whom we had met on board. The restaurant was situated near

Istanbul alongside the Black Sea. We had delicious grilled fish and shrimp, crisp vegetables, salads, tomatoes, and the like. We were already finished with our dessert, literally dripping with honey and crushed nuts, check in hand, when we saw the waitstaff serving the largest and most beautiful lobsters we had ever seen. We all nodded to each other briefly and started our meal all over again.

- Returning to Rome for the fourth time, we went back to a classic restaurant—Ristorante Passetto, which we had once visited on our first whirlwind tour as young marrieds—to savor their fettuccini with white truffles, one of the dishes I had replicated fairly well while I was still throwing my storied dinner parties. The maître d', a true professional, greeted Irwin, twenty years later, with "long time no see!"

- Trying to recall our most favorite foods in Italy is useless because there is no such thing as bad food in Italy; we have eaten our way from below the boot in Sicily to the lake region up top, marveling with each visit about the cheeses—especially those in Sardinia, the best of which they do not export—the pastas, the gelato, the pastries (especially the macaroons in Sicily), the breads, the Florentine beef, the seafood in Venice.

- For over-the-top decadence, I would point out Dubai in the United Arab Emirates, where all the hotels, restaurants, and food markets are quite remarkable; an ever-changing mirage surrounded by desert. The philosophy here is *more is better*. There is no cuisine that cannot be found, and you can buy a $3 million necklace in the mall right alongside a souvenir shop. I always seek out the Gulf or Middle Eastern (especially Lebanese) restaurants while there on business.

Behind the Iron Curtain

We traveled more than once behind the Iron Curtain before it fell, and certain foods still stand out—vividly—in my recollections. In Budapest, a beautiful city, I ordered a dish of foie gras and was served three huge globes of it fanned out atop a mountain of sinfully rich mashed potatoes, so creamy they were unctuous. All of this was smothered with yet another mountain of supremely crisp tendrils of fried onion, somehow all standing at attention. This was tall food before there even was a Gotham Bar and Grill in Greenwich Village in New York City. Then, while we were in Warsaw, our waiter tried to sell us black market caviar that he had hidden under his apron. In Prague, which was known as the Paris of Eastern Europe, there were already what were then called *free* (private) *restaurants*, and we enjoyed many sophisticated meals while there.

The first night we arrived in Moscow from Warsaw, we arrived at the hotel rather late in the evening and had missed dinner. Irwin followed his instincts, and we found a bustling restaurant (at midnight!) tucked behind all the banquet rooms on the second floor. We were the only outsiders there and had a great steak dinner, albeit *very* well done, the only way you could have it . . . Our waiter was already quite drunk, and he wanted to know where Irwin's gun was—he thought all New Yorkers had a gun! This was a great dose of local color.

We hit the streets, seeking out the places where Muscovites shopped and ate. In the food shops, we found that there was absolutely no variety. There would be lemons one day and oranges the next, cucumbers one day and lettuce the next. But for foreigners and diplomats living and working there, there were other markets, closed to the ordinary citizen, that were crammed with every fruit, vegetable, meat, and delectable foodstuff imaginable. The contrasts were startling.

Eating American in Moscow before the fall of the Iron Curtain.

On to Leningrad, long before it was renamed Saint Petersburg, where we found everything freer and more plentiful, including the food. There we had afternoon coffee at the Literary Café, a far better precursor to Starbucks, and where Pushkin spent his afternoons.

France vs. Italy

If I had to vote, Italy would most probably win out over France—but only just—as my favorite place to eat simply because pasta is my favorite food. But French food is very serious business indeed. In my opinion, it is far more classical and formal, even the bistro food. Just as we have done in Italy, we've been to France many times and have eaten our way through it from top to bottom. In Paris itself, we have had our share of three-star meals, one being at Guy Savoy, where I still remember my ethereal appetizer of caviar and truffles floating on very soft and creamy egg yolks and butter. We also had a meal at the original Le Bernadin in Paris, then an up-and-coming restaurant opened by Chef Gilbert Le Coze and his sister, Maguey, who hailed from Brittany, until they decided to move their successful bistro to New York after winning two Michelin stars. We had met Chef Gilbert during our meal there thanks to our dining companion who knew him; the chef had confided to us his dream of owning a restaurant in New

York. His dream came true. He died young quite a few years ago, but Maguey has run it with her new chef ever since, and Le Bernadin has remained one of the finest restaurants in the United States ever since it opened in 1986.

Paris has always been on top of my list as the best walking city of all. We have been up and down *every* street, seen *every* neighborhood with its own particular flavor, *every* food hall, *every* bakery (which exist in countless numbers; the bread, in my opinion, is the best in the world). Paris has always had quite a few permanent open air market streets peppered throughout the city, and we have seen them all. These are groups of many shops offering a dazzling array of fresh fruits and vegetables, meats, fish, cheeses, chocolates, pastries, *croissants* to kill for, and countless other delicacies. These markets are a way of life for all Parisians.

Keeping It Moving

I always do my research before setting out on a trip—we never allow ourselves to be confined to the typical tourist routes—and that is how we have always been able to stumble upon things that more truly define the city, village, or town that we find ourselves in.

In Santiago, Chile, for example, at the end of a cruise around South America, we went *with* our taxi driver for lunch at the Central Market, where there were many food stalls. The three of us ate together. We let him do the ordering, and we had, among other things, a Chilean specialty of razor clams with cheese—don't say "no" until you've tasted it. Despite the common perception that pairing seafood and cheese is a mistake, I have found during my travels that doing precisely that has rewarded me with some of my favorite dishes, and I often combine the two when I cook.

There are so many other memorable food moments, from the Indonesian *Rijsttafel*—the Dutch word for "rice table"—that we ate three days in a row in Amsterdam, to an astounding brunch at the Arab-run American Colony Hotel in East Jerusalem, to an exotic *nouvelle cuisine* dinner at an Athens restaurant called Spondi (sadly marred by an American couple who sat stony-faced and scrolling through their BlackBerrys the entire meal).

Irwin and I enjoying Rijsttafel in Amsterdam.

Our Asian Odyssey in China

We visited China in 1996, when it was still fairly difficult to navigate between cities independently, especially if you wanted to cover a lot of ground, which we did. We joined a small tour group of eighteen people.

We first spent a few days in Hong Kong on our own, and as usual, we hit the streets and the food markets—and flower markets and bird markets—both on the Hong Kong Island and the Kowloon sides. Although there is always a mix in any city of the old and the new, Hong Kong exudes money; you can almost smell it. We had high tea served in the exquisite lobby of the landmark Peninsula

Hotel, the *grande dame* of the city. I have never quite seen more beautiful, more confident and important-looking, more glamorous, more well-dressed people than we did here—even the children, of which there were quite a few.

In mainland China, each city that we visited had a mood and flavor of its own. The must-see places are unforgettable: the Great Wall, where we saw, halfway up, what must have been some *very* high-level people picnicking, complete with table, china, and silver settings, servants in formal clothing, and champagne; the Forbidden City in Beijing with its nine hundred buildings and thousands of rooms, which was the Chinese Imperial Palace and seat of government for five hundred years beginning in the early 1400s; the Terracotta Army in Xian (thousands of them) sculpted to be buried within the mausoleum of the first emperor of China, Qin Shi Huang, in the third century BC.

It was in Xian that we had a special dumpling dinner, served ritualistically and made up of exactly twenty courses followed by one more fairly plain one that we were expected to be too full to eat, or else our hosts would be sadly disappointed that they had failed us. Many of the dumplings were fashioned in the shape of what the filling contained: a little duck, shrimp, fish, eggplant, and so on, each more delicious than the one before it.

We spent one night in Chongqing, where we had the pleasure of visiting one of the most fantastic and vast covered markets that we have ever seen, rivaling Mumbai, Istanbul, Paris, Santiago, or any place else. There were snakes, pigs, goats, and myriad varieties of live poultry; there were spices, exotic fruits both fresh and dried, fish and seafood, vegetables, candies, filled buns and sweets, baskets, clothing, and on and on. We were put up at a slightly seedy Marriott—another surprise—but the dining room served very traditional Chinese cuisine, and we had another fabulous meal. We all had learned by then not to question too closely what we were being served.

Once we got under way on the Yangtze River "cruise ship"—and I use the term loosely, since we noticed more than once that they washed the dishes off the back of the boat in the not-too-clean river water—we were rewarded with truly majestic and mountainous scenery as we stopped in small towns and cities along the way until we finally reached Shanghai.

This city had color and then some. We spent one of the days walking for hours and hours and found our way to the Bund, an area along the river embankment in the center of the city. There are lots of older buildings here, and building height restrictions are enforced to keep the flavor of the area. In the American Hotel, which was not American but, instead, a small, elegant, and old-fashioned place, we had a lovely lunch overlooking the water and all the activity below.

Beijing, in contrast, was much more gray and formidable, but we had the best Peking duck that we have ever tasted: tender meat, crisp squares of skin from which *all* the fat had been rendered, and all the accompaniments. We insisted they bring us the carcasses—much to the waiter's surprise, since I'm sure they had planned to use it for the next day's stock—and we gnawed on them until the table was *completely* strewn with the bones!

I remember China more for its noodles than its rice, and for many of the meals the noodles were stretched and cut for us right before our eyes—long, thin, chewy, and sensuous. Unforgettable.

The Cashew Factory in India

Wherever we traveled, we always sought out the wholesale markets, wholesale bakeries, and such—in other words, those businesses, both large and small, that serviced the same type of establishments that we did at home in the United States: restaurants, hotels, caterers, retail shops, cafés, and all the rest. We've found that any place, anywhere, there are *always* bakeries.

In Central America we happened upon a local bakery supplier on the top of Monte Verde in Costa Rica whose owner claimed to have been baking there forever. It had the same kind of Hobart mixers that we did and the same kind of racks, pans, and rotary ovens, however ancient, that we did.

In South America we stopped in Ushuaia, in Argentina, which is regarded as the southernmost city in the world. There we found and were given a tour by the very friendly proprietor of a wholesale bakery located on all five floors of a perilously narrow building. There were just very steep staircases, up and down which hundred-pound bags of flour and all the other ingredients were constantly being transported. We were enveloped in the clouds of flour and sugar dust that permeated the whole building. This bakery serviced almost every food establishment in the whole city, and it was a bee-hive of efficient activity. They were turning out a lot of goods, all of them top quality.

But by far the most fascinating and jaw-dropping tour we have ever had was of a cashew processing plant in New Mangalore, near that port in India. It all happened quite serendipitously. We just happened to mention to our guide that we were in the food manufacturing business, and our guide said she belonged to a Symphony Society whose director, a Mr. D'Souza, owned one of the largest cashew processing plants in the world; she insisted we stop by to meet him if he was in his office. He was.

He welcomed us very graciously, and we first spent an hour comparing notes about our businesses. He described the cashew industry around the world for us, with India having the lion's share. Then he offered us a drink before our tour of the plant. (To digress: while in India, it is very important to drink *nothing* unless it comes in an unopened bottle. You risk getting *very* sick.) We politely said we weren't thirsty. He nodded and then called in his general manager, and our tour began.

The facility was very large, and we were first brought into a vast room, as large as a football field, with several hundred women all lined up in rows, sitting on the floor with piles of shells on one side of them and the pile of nutmeats on the other side. *On the floor!* This was quintessential handwork, and their hands moved so quickly that one could hardly follow the movements. Then the nutmeats were transported in wheelbarrows to the oven rooms and transferred onto trays for roasting. The ovens were so thickly blackened and so ancient that they took my breath away. When the manager pulled out a tray (the same ubiquitous and universal bun trays) to show us the roasting process, some of the nuts got away and fell to the floor; he blithely gathered them up and put them back on the trays. Then he smiled and simply popped them back into the oven.

By now I was thinking that I would never eat another cashew nut as long as I lived, but as we moved through the rooms and the processes, the areas became cleaner and cleaner, as did the equipment, until we finally found ourselves surrounded by glisteningly clean walls and stainless steel tables and equipment for the final sorting, quality checks, and packaging. During the processing steps, nothing goes to waste. The shells are burned for fuel, the skins are used to produce color dyes, and subquality nuts are sold somewhere to someone. It was fascinating. The tour took more than two hours.

We were escorted back to Mr. D'Souza's office. "So *now* you must be thirsty?" he inquired. After such hospitality, we would never dream of insulting our host. "Yes, we are," I answered, fully prepared to die if necessary. But on the tray shortly brought in were only bottles of lemon soda pop and a bottle opener. I had underestimated our elegant host! The soda was tooth-shatteringly sweet, but we drank every drop! As it happened, he also owned the soda bottling plant as well as other businesses in the region: cars, electronics, and others. These are the kind of experiences that aren't easily forgotten.

The lovely ladies of the cashew factory in India.

On that same trip, which was on a small cruise ship with only a hundred passengers, we had started out in Singapore and continued on to Malaysia, with stops in Penang and Kuala Lumpur, then to Phuket in Thailand, then on to India, with stops in Cochin—a fishing port with the most unusual boats whose nets resembled vast yet exquisitely delicate spider webs—New Mangalore, home of the cashews, Goa, a Christian enclave and a market town, and finally Bombay, now called Mumbai. We ate our way through these places, albeit carefully, and we came away with a thirst for more exotic travel *and* a great passion for mangoes!

India, Second Time Around

Of all the countries we have visited, India, with all its beauty, smells, colors, contrasts, and both poverty and riches, remains my favorite. In spite of the poverty, there is a sense of both peacefulness and vibrancy among the populace that's like no other place in the world.

Our next trip to India, in 2006, began in Mumbai, and we traveled through inland Rajasthan, visited the Taj Mahal, and ended in Delhi.

The chaotic food markets and bazaars in Mumbai are a feast for the eyes, especially the Crawford Market, built in 1869, a vast marketplace with a startling array of fruit, vegetables, meats, poultry, spices, cheeses, chocolates, and on and on. Runners, mostly barefoot, carry and deliver purchases packed in huge baskets balanced on their heads.

On this trip there were six of us: a couple from Maryland, with whom we have formed a friends-for-life relationship, and never-to-be-forgotten Mary, almost ninety, who was traveling with her niece. This was a strenuous trip, and Mary admitted: "I very simply lied through my teeth when I filled out the form that I was fit for any eventuality. I very much wanted to see the Taj Mahal before I died." We left Mary behind quite often, which she was happy with as long as she had her martinis to keep her company with each meal, even breakfast.

Rajasthan was a sensual whirl of colors, odors, lushness, and emotions. It was simply gorgeous, with stunning scenery, and because we wanted to see it all, we drove through the countryside from city to city rather than flying as originally planned. As usual, we ate our way through the region. We were a bad influence on our traveling companions, but the food was terrific. I became a tikka masala aficionado, but didn't try any street food, a hard and fast rule with me in certain countries.

We visited Jodhpur, the Blue City, because of the color the Brahmins use to paint their houses; Jaipur, the Pink City, painted pink for Prince Albert when he visited India in the late 1800s; Udaipur, the city of lakes, the Venice of India; and many small villages and farms along the way, which were almost the best of all. There are food stalls, camel carts, cows, elephants, and monkeys all over the place, even in the cities. We walked along sidewalk shops that overflowed with luscious foodstuffs, pottery, and fabrics.

Rajasthan is going green, and at one "organic" farm we visited along the way, one of the main crops very closely resembled opium. They cooked it up and invited us to all partake of a spoonful. I couldn't get myself to do it, but everybody else did!

On this trip, we stayed at almost embarrassingly decadent and opulent hotels, perhaps more beautiful than anywhere else in the world. Most of them are housed in actual converted palaces, no replicas here, and with service to match.

In Agra, the Oberoi Amarvilas resort was the best of all, and our visit to the Taj Mahal just before dawn was haunting. It was a *very* long walk. Mary stepped up to the plate and made that walk with us; this was, after all, why she came. Delhi was much like Mumbai. It was much more buttoned up, but had the same great food. (Our farewell dinner on this trip was, by the way, Chinese food: Cantonese, Peking duck, and all the other usual suspects.)

On to Singapore, Bangkok, and Vietnam

Our next trip, in 2009, began in Singapore, where we were to meet a customer and a personal friend. Singapore is pristine and new; all the old neighborhoods have been razed and replaced with new neighborhoods *made* to look old. It is an independent city-state that was part of the British Empire until a little over fifty years ago, and you can see the British influence in the architecture and at world-famous Raffles Hotel.

We spent one of the days touring all the food markets and bakeries with our friend. The supermarkets are all quite modern and there seems to be a bakery on every street with very elegant and elaborate cakes and pastries of the type found in major cities the world over. They love chocolate! Singapore is a great target for Love and Quiches.

There are elegant bakeries all over the world.

Our next stop was colorful Bangkok. Our dinner that evening holds a place way up there. I admit that elegant dining in a beautiful setting is among my favorite pastimes. We booked a table at Le Normandie, considered by many to be the finest French restaurant in Asia, on the top floor of the exquisite old-world Oriental Hotel. We were seated at the window and enjoyed wonderful views of the river and promenade below with our perfect and quite memorable dinner, and with a price tag to match!

Vietnam was the main focus of this trip, and Ho Chi Minh City (Saigon) was our best stop. Saigon is a bustling port city with a fragrant profusion of fruit, flowers, and foodstuffs everywhere we turned. There were open markets where meats and fish were also spilling into the streets with no particular emphasis on refrigeration, but where everything looked fresh and appetizing. There were also many bakeries with displays of quite elaborately constructed cakes, similar to the displays we had found in other larger Asian cities. The bread here looked particularly good, possibly because Vietnam was originally part of French Indochina. Wherever we have traveled throughout Asia, our overall impression is of an overabundance of food.

The beautiful cakes of Saigon—a feast for the eyes.

In Halong Bay, Hai Phong, we took a boat trip in a fabulous old wooden boat where we were entertained by small floating rafts spilling over with produce: floating grocery stores from which children climbed up to our windows hawking their wares. It was very touristy and we loved it.

Egypt, Between Conflagrations, During the Arab Spring

We took a holiday in Egypt, way up there on our bucket list, which we had planned long before the Arab Spring and all the calamitous events taking place all across the Middle East. We took this trip in spite of almost everybody we know asking us if we had lost our minds.

Actually, we watched Khadafi meet his end on CNN while in Cairo, which in a way was quite surreal, since Libya was right next door.

Our experience was brilliant. We were a very small group of six plus an Egyptologist, along with an armed guard! We visited Cairo, and during a Nile cruise, we stopped in Abu Simbel, Aswan, Esna, Luxor, and Dendera. Egypt's history spans thousands of years, and the antiquities we saw were exquisite and awe inspiring.

We arrived in Cairo a day early, as is our practice, so that we could spend some time touring the city with an eye toward seeing as much as we could about our favorite subject: the food. We hired Azza as our private guide that first day, and we visited a small and ancient bakery with ovens even blacker than in the cashew factory in India; saw a typical local supermarket; and walked through a vast *souk* where the locals did most of their daily shopping. In Cairo almost all of the food is displayed right on the sidewalks: neat piles, gorgeous fruits and vegetables—especially the tomatoes, which taste like pure sugar—along with the spices, the fish, and the meat. There was simply *no* refrigeration whatsoever. Wherever we looked there was food being displayed, all over the city, everywhere. There were small herds of sheep near each butcher shop with hanging meat up front: tomorrow's dinner for sure. We saw very few European-style bakeries of the kind we encountered in India and Vietnam, but workers were constantly carrying huge trays of fresh warm *pita* and *lavash* breads to various destinations all over the city.

Cairo is by far the dirtiest city we have ever seen during our travels. Debris is everywhere! In India, by contrast, garbage is an industry and nothing is wasted: There are even vast piles of *neat* garbage, with all the scraps of fabric, food, metals, and so on sorted to be sold or otherwise used.

The food was excellent everywhere we went. We had two memorable and typical Egyptian meals while in Cairo. One was at a restaurant named Abou el Cid, an atmospheric and elegant place where there was a hookah at every table, all placed low to the ground with couches for seating. They offered a specialty called *haman*, rice-stuffed whole pigeon, but I opted for the grilled quail instead, and we shared many other typical Egyptian dishes that the waiter suggested along with tons of the ubiquitous hot, fresh pita bread. Another typical local meal we had was at a famous place called Andrea, where they have their own pita oven and bring out fresh hot ones every few minutes. Their specialties are spit-roasted chicken and myriad Middle Eastern salads and hors d'oeuvres. They showered us with so much food, and we shared it all with the thousand flies that visited the outdoor patio where we were seated.

Our Nile River cruise ship was a luxurious yacht with accommodations for thirty-six passengers, but there were only the six of us and a staff of forty-five, down from fifty-eight.

I toured the kitchen, and the chef did a cooking demonstration for the few of us who were there. I noticed during the tour that the double convection oven, a major space saver, was the exact one that I had in my garage when I started out almost forty years ago. It was a newer model, of course, but essentially the same, and it made me smile.

The best word I can use to describe the Nile is *lush*. It was unbelievably verdant on both sides for at least ten miles, with sugar cane, corn, and many other crops and vegetables as far as the eye could see.

Back in Cairo we did a lot of walking through the ancient thoroughfares of the old city and wandered around in the Khan El-Kahlili market, Cairo's vast street market, with its tourist traps as well as its aromatic spice shops and food stalls where all the locals shop daily.

For us, nothing is more intrinsic to a place than its food, which conveys its true essence. But in Egypt the antiquities may have surpassed anything else.

Western Harbors of Europe

In 2012 we traveled the western coast of Europe from the Normandy region (to see the World War II landing beaches) in France all the way down to Lisbon, with a great stop in Cork, Ireland. All a bit closer to home.

In London we had dinner in *the* hot restaurant of the moment, Dinner by Heston Blumenthal. They serve classic English fare, sourcing some of their dishes from cookbooks that date as far back as the thirteenth to fifteenth centuries. It was Irwin's birthday, and we decided beforehand to forget there were such things as calories. We most often head for the most "in" restaurants in any city we find ourselves in, but lately we seem to notice we are almost always the oldest people in the room. I guess this is because older people usually take the easy way out and eat in their hotels. Not us.

We started with something called Meat Fruit: chicken liver parfait in a preserved mandarin orange shell with grilled bread. It was silky smooth and ethereal, and I am sure it had as much butter and cream in it as liver because I used to do the same thing when I would cook for my friends way back in the early seventies. Then we shared a Bone-in-Rib with mushroom ketchup and triple cooked chips from *The Cook and Housewife's Manual* by Mistress Meg Dods, dating from 1830. I commented to the waiter that the "chips" were the best I had ever tasted, and he revealed that this was because they were cooked in beef fat. Uh oh! But it was worth it because they made any other fries totally irrelevant. I am sure they used another of my old methods of gently but constantly shaking the potatoes while frying them; this allows them to absorb a lot more oil and become super crisp, as well as super deadly.

Although the restaurant offered such things as Quaking Pudding from *The Accomplisht Cooke* by Robert May (1660) and Tarte of Strawberries from the *Book of Cookrye Very necessary for all such as Delight therin* by A. W. (1591), we resisted dessert. They brought us a plateful of cookies anyway.

By the time we got back to our hotel, we were so full that we were almost ready to go back home to New York.

In Cork, Ireland, in defiance of its reputation, it was brilliantly sunny. Here we saw bakery after bakery. Wherever we turned, it seemed there was at least one or two on every block. All the offerings were a bit more homespun, less elegant and jewel-like than you would find, for example, in Paris. But they were hand finished, overstuffed, and luscious looking—and there were lots of quiches, to my great delight.

From Cork, we crossed the sea to the Continent. We were traveling by small ship for this trip, a great way to cover a lot of ground without having to pack and unpack over and over. The first thing I did once we arrived on the ship was to introduce myself to the chef, a thirty-one year old guy from Belgium. His kitchen was small and incredibly clean, and absolutely *everything* he made was from scratch: all the stocks, breads, pastries, sauces, stews, and so on. We got very used to having just-out-of-the-oven scones with clotted cream and jam every afternoon.

Bordeaux is wine country, and we visited Chateau Giscours for a tour of the winery, a lesson on wine making, a tasting, and an elegant dinner. We traveled to get there through mile upon mile of vineyards, where we noticed the soil was sandy and dry so that the vines had to *struggle* for the roots to go deep. At Giscours all the grapes are picked by hand and then x-rayed to identify any fruit that's less than perfect. After pressing, fresh-cracked egg whites used to be used to clarify the juice, and the yolks were used to make special cookies sold all over the city (they still are). Now the use of fresh eggs has been outlawed, so powdered whites are used instead. Next, the juices are aged in stainless steel tanks to complete the fermenting process before being sealed into the oak barrels for two years and then bottled. Each barrel gets candled to gauge the sediment on the bottom. Wines at Giscours are all estate bottled. Sulfites are introduced *only* because they are used to clean the barrels of bacteria between uses.

The barrels are used for only four years. After that, they are sold to the port makers in Portugal who use them for forty years, and then the port makers sell them to the whiskey makers who use them for another forty years, and then they get sold to us as *antiques* to use as planters and the like.

Wines continue to age in the bottle. The 2010 wines were released in 2012; the 2011 wines in 2013, and so on. Fine wines should be allowed to age for *at least* another seven or eight years in the bottle before drinking. So those of us who may order a 2008 or 2009 wine thinking that it's a fine thing to do are actually philistines . . .

Many of the steps we saw in the process were strikingly similar to our practices at Love and Quiches. There was the same careful sorting of the best grapes (or in our case, raw ingredients), the quality-assurance steps, the x-rays, and the tasting room with spittoons (just as we taste and spit in our test kitchen—if we didn't, we would all weigh three hundred pounds by now!)

Many, actually most, wineries have been bought up by larger companies, and the family-owned winery is almost a thing of the past. Irwin and I felt a great affinity to this place, probably because it remains in private hands.

Later that night on the drive back to our ship, like a mirage in the middle of nowhere, we saw a well-lit McDonald's, with lines around the corner. I didn't know whether to laugh or cry.

Finally, we went to Lisbon, where, despite its reputation, there were excellent restaurants and pastry shops *everywhere* we turned and where we visited the Confeitaria Nacional, the oldest confectionary in Lisbon, founded in 1829 and still remaining in the founder's family five generations later. There we feasted on the ubiquitous *pasteis de nata*, delicious custard tarts in flaky pastry, also served and displayed *everywhere*, in every shop. Well worth the calories.

And then we were done. Time to go home.

Recipes from the Heart:

A Few Favorite Recipes

N ow, for some fun! I have included here some of my favorite recipes, both from way back when my passion began and from now—some still calorie laden, but mostly not, which I use over and over again.

Just as I have changed since I founded Love and Quiches in my kitchen forty years ago, so has my cooking style. When I taught those classes so long ago almost everything was spilling over with butter, heavy cream, and starches; the more fat the better. I fried almost everything. Many of my techniques were overcomplicated, and I doubt that most of what I taught was incorporated into my students' everyday cooking.

I kept my saved notes from those classes, but they mostly stay behind the closed cabinet that I put them in when we moved to the city. I also rarely use my cookbooks any longer. I have learned not to be afraid of my own recipes; nowadays I mostly wing it. When I cook, I often vary my ingredients or method just a bit to keep it all interesting. Few recipes, I have found, are set in stone, and this helps keep the passion alive. For the most part, my new mantra is *easy does it!* So feel free to have fun with and put your own spin on the small selection of appetizers, main dishes, and desserts included below.

Long gone are the days when I would *never* buy anything *prepared, store bought* to serve at home. I had always made all my own stocks, my own mayonnaise, my own ice cream, and all my own sauces 100 percent from scratch. I even churned my own butter! I now realize that this may have been purely misplaced ego. I was trying to distinguish myself in some way, to prove something, but to whom I'm not quite sure.

Now I buy many of those things as components when I cook, although I vet them very carefully. Plenty of top-quality ingredients and prepared foods are available. I buy my fruit in one place, my meat in another; some cheeses in one place, others elsewhere; olive oil in one place, vinegars in another. That's my drill.

At home I still use only butter, never margarine or other substitutes, but I use less of it. I use olive oil more often in most of my cooking, but not too much; I add wines and broths to enhance the flavor without adding calories. When I'm tempted to use cream, I often use light cream instead, or even milk, with excellent results. Dijon mustard adds a lot of flavor to myriad foods without adding calories. I use a bit less salt, but only a bit: remember, salt is salt and there is no substitute to enhance flavor, at least for me. I use only Vidalia or other sweet onions when cooking; I use more shallots than I do garlic; I use wild mushrooms—all kinds—with reckless abandon. One inviolate rule is that I still make all my own salad dressings, *never* store bought, but I am not averse to finishing off a lively cauldron of pomodoro or bolognese sauce with a jar of Classico brand tomato and basil sauce to gather it all together.

A nice thing to do is have some friends in for dinner and cook it yourself. I can still manage to put together a dinner party that knocks it out of the ballpark, and I look forward to doing just that a few times each year for all my appreciative friends.

When I cook, I rarely use modern kitchen tools. They are much too much trouble to lug out of the closet (no room on the counter in my apartment) and to clean. Besides, they can't do anything that a knife, whisk, hand grater, eggbeater, or mandolin slicer can't do just as well. I donated my Cuisinart to the test kitchen at Love and Quiches twenty years ago and never replaced it. But I do have a blender, assorted mini-choppers, a spiral slicer, and other devices tucked away, just in case. Don't forget: I have been at this for a very long time.

And now for the recipes . . .

Quiche au Fromage (Cheese Quiche)

This is where I came in. Throughout the years, we have offered quiche in sizes ranging from bite-sized, to 4-inch for one, to 6 inches for two, to 8 inches for four, to 10 inches for eight, in numerous varieties from asparagus to olive . . . until we cried uncle. Now we offer just a few varieties in just a few sizes, and it does the job very well.

Serves 8 or 10

Crust

1½ cups	flour, all purpose
½ tsp.	salt
pinch	cayenne pepper
6 tbsp.	butter, sweet-unsalted, chilled and cut into pieces
3 tbsp.	shortening, all purpose
4–5 tbsp.	cold water

Combine the flour, salt, and pepper in a large bowl. Cut the chilled butter and shortening into the dry mixture with your fingers until the granules are the size of peas. Alternately, you can use a pastry cutter.

Add the chilled water one tablespoon at a time, mixing gently with a fork after each addition. Gently press the dough into a smooth ball.

Handle the dough as little as possible; overworking will make it tough. (The time of the year and humidity will determine how much water you will need: a bit more water on a dry day, a bit less on a humid day.) Flatten slightly and wrap in plastic wrap. Allow to rest in the refrigerator for at least 30 minutes; overnight is best. This allows the flour to absorb all of the liquid, as well as lets the dough relax and become more elastic, which will give the crust a lighter texture when it's baked.

Generously dust a clean, dry surface with flour. Flatten the dough slightly with your hands and dust the dough lightly with flour before rolling the dough out with a rolling pin.

Start rolling at the center of the dough and work outward. A good method is to roll out the dough between sheets of waxed paper, which allows an easier transfer into the pan. Working quickly, roll the dough into a circle ¼-inch thick. If not using waxed paper to roll it out, lift up an edge or move the dough to ensure that it's not sticking to the counter. Add flour as needed. The dough round should be about 4 inches wider in diameter than your pie pan. Use a dry pastry brush to sweep away any excess flour.

Carefully place rolled dough into a 10-inch deep-dish pie pan (or straight-sided fluted quiche pan, if you have one) so that the center point of dough is in the center of the pan. Pat into the pan all around, being careful not to tear dough. Crimp the edges with your fingers or a fork, as desired.

Filling

¾ cup	Swiss cheese, coarsely grated, top quality
¾ cup	fontina cheese, coarsely grated, top quality
¾ cup	mozzarella cheese, coarsely grated, top quality
¾ cup	cheddar cheese, coarsely grated, top quality
2 tsp.	cornstarch
3 cups	heavy cream (light cream or half milk & half cream may be used if preferred)
4 ea	large eggs
½ tsp.	salt
⅛ tsp.	nutmeg

Combine cheeses and blend together with cornstarch. Add heavy cream, eggs, salt, and nutmeg to the cheese mixture and whisk until completely incorporated.

Pour into prepared pie shell and bake at 375 degrees F for about 50–60 minutes, until puffy and golden brown. Allow to rest at least 15 to 30 minutes prior to serving to allow the custard to settle and for ease in cutting.

Notes: Use any other favorite cheeses as desired; add other complements, such as spinach, broccoli, artichokes, asparagus, crumbled bacon, or crabmeat to name just a few. Use your imagination.

In case you don't want to make your own crust, you can always buy a prepared shell, but the result won't be as good, and you will lose bragging rights.

Mesclun Green Salad with Goat Cheese Toasts and Balsamic Vinaigrette

I served this salad last summer at a dinner party at my summer home on Fire Island, and it was a big hit.

Serves 8 or 10

Mesclun Green Salad

2 oz.	pine nuts (about ½ cup)
2 oz.	macadamia nuts, chopped (about ½ cup)
4 oz.	pancetta, finely diced
1 lb.	mesclun greens, or other micro-greens if preferred
6 oz.	mini-plum tomatoes, halved lengthwise
2 oz.	dried cranberries (about ½ cup)
2 oz.	fresh figs (if in season), cut into ¼-inch dice

In a small fry pan over low heat, constantly stir both kinds of nuts until very lightly toasted. Be careful not to burn: 2 minutes at most.

In a small fry pan, fry pancetta bits until very crisp. Drain fat, pat dry with paper towel.

Combine all above ingredients in a salad bowl and toss well.

Balsamic Vinaigrette

½ cup	Balsamic vinegar
1 tsp.	Dijon mustard, optional
1 tsp.	sea salt, or more to taste
½ tsp.	fresh ground pepper, or more to taste
1 cup	extra virgin olive oil
1 ea	shallot, peeled and well diced (3 to 4 tbsp.)
1 tbsp.	extra virgin olive oil

In a bowl, whisk first four ingredients until very well combined.

In a steady stream, pour olive oil into vinegar mixture, stirring constantly. Set aside.

Sauté shallots in 1 tbsp. oil for a few minutes until translucent. They will turn very sweet. Be careful not to burn them.

Stir shallots into prepared dressing.

Dress salad with about half the dressing, and reserve the rest for another use.

Notes: This dressing complements almost any combination of greens. The mustard can be eliminated for a lighter dressing, and white balsamic vinegar can be used instead for another elegant twist.

Goat Cheese Toasts

1 loaf	French bread, long baguette, sliced thin (use about 8 to 10 of the slices for the salad)
1 can	olive oil spray
1 tsp.	salt
8 oz.	goat cheese log, ½-inch slices, cut while cold
½ tsp.	salad herbs

In a single layer, lay the bread slices side by side on a cookie sheet. Spray lightly with the oil; turn bread and lightly spray the other side. Sprinkle with the salt (regular salt broadcasts more evenly).

Bake in the oven at 200 degrees F for about 30 minutes, turning the slices halfway through until light in color but completely dry.

Place a goat cheese slice on each toast, and then allow cheese to come to room temperature.

Dust with the salad herbs.

To serve, divide the dressed salad among eight to ten plates, place a goat cheese toast on top of each portion, and serve. (Any extra toasts will keep well, covered tightly.)

Susan's Summertime Gazpacho

I make this at least once per summer, at my friend's insistence. With generous amounts of the optional garnishes, it is enough for a nice lunch as is.

Serves about 20

4 large	cucumbers, peeled, seeded, and diced
6 large	ripe tomatoes, dip in boiling water, slip skin off, and dice (leave in juice and seeds)
1 ea	red pepper, seeded and diced
1 ea	green pepper, seeded and diced
1 ea	yellow pepper, seeded and diced
1 ea	Vidalia onion, peeled and diced
2 cloves	garlic, diced finely
6 slices	white bread, good quality, torn into small pieces

Toss all of the above in a large bowl.

1 cup	beef broth (or chicken broth), homemade or good quality store bought
46 oz.	tomato juice (I prefer Sacramento brand)
½ cup	extra virgin olive oil

Pulse all of above chopped vegetables and liquids in a blender in batches, using some liquid, a bit of the oil, and some vegetables in each batch, until fine but *not* pureed. This takes practice! Collect each batch in another large bowl until complete.

4 tbsp.	red wine vinegar, or more to taste
4 tbsp.	Worcestershire sauce, or more to taste
2 tsp.	Tabasco sauce, or more to taste
2 tsp.	oregano, or more to taste
1 tbsp.	sea salt, or more to taste
2 tsp.	fresh ground pepper, or more to taste

Season soup with all of the above. This soup is bold; make *sure* to provide a good kick.

Chill to blend flavors at least 4 hours or overnight. Remove from fridge and stir well 1 hour before serving.

Garnish: Croutons

| 8 ea | slices good white bread: crusts removed, ½-inch dice |

Toast gently on cookie sheet for about ½ hour at 200 degrees until dry and light brown. Sprinkle a few on top of each serving (store any excess tightly covered).

Optional additional garnishes: Avocado and Fresh Crabmeat

Besides the croutons, you can also float 1 or 2 slices of avocado or 1 or 2 tablespoons of fresh crabmeat on top of the gazpacho. Choose one or both—I'm easy!

Notes: This recipe is not so easy (messy, too) because it involves a lot of peeling and dicing, but is well worth it, and no cooking is required. It keeps for at least two weeks in the fridge.

Because this recipe serves about twenty, feel free to cut it in half.

Caponata

I used to make this delicious Italian classic even before I taught those cooking classes; then I included it in my curriculum.

Yields about 4 lbs., enough for a crowd when served with other hors d'oeuvres

| 1¼ cups | extra virgin olive oil |
| 1½ lbs. | eggplant, unpeeled, cut into ¾-inch cubes, about 4 cups |

¾ cup	celery, thin sliced
1 ea	sweet onion, roughly chopped
1 ea	red pepper, ½-inch dice
14½ oz. can	diced tomatoes
1 tbsp.	sea salt, or more to taste
1 tsp.	cracked pepper, or more to taste
¼ cup	red wine vinegar, or more to taste
¼ cup	sugar, or up to 2 more tbsp. to taste
¼ cup	black olives, pitted and sliced
¼ cup	green olives, pitted and sliced
¼ cup	pine nuts
2 tbsp.	capers, small size and rinsed

Heat ¾ cup of the oil in a large saucepan and brown the eggplant over high heat, stirring constantly, for about 10 minutes until transparent but not too soft; then remove from pan and set aside.

Reduce the heat to medium high, and in the same pan add ½ cup more oil. Sauté the celery, onion, and red pepper for 5 to 8 minutes, until softened.

Add the tomatoes in their juice, the sea salt, and pepper, and simmer for about 10 to 15 minutes until most of the liquid dries out.

Add the vinegar, sugar, olives, pine nuts, and capers and cook for 5 minutes more over low heat.

Return the eggplant to the pan and cook for another 5 to 10 minutes. Remove from heat and allow to cool.

Serve at room temperature as hors d'oeuvres with homemade toasts (see recipe above with the mesclun salad), crackers, or crusty bread.

Caponata is traditionally served at room temperature, but it can also be served warm as a side dish for almost any protein, or as a sauce for your favorite pasta with grated cheese.

Notes: Eggplants, as recently available, are no longer bitter and need not be salted, drained, and squeezed. Also, feel free to cut this recipe in half if you are not entertaining a crowd, although it keeps well for up to a month in the refrigerator.

Oven-Dried Tomatoes

I prepare these tomatoes every time I entertain, serving them alongside cheeses, prosciutto, hummus, and so on. There are never any left, no matter how many tomatoes I use.

Yields 24 to 30 pieces

2½ lbs.	plum tomatoes, ripe (about 12 to 15)
¼ cup	extra virgin olive oil
½ cup	shallots, finely diced
¼ cup	sweet onion, finely diced
1 tsp.	oregano, fresh or dried
1 tsp.	sea salt
1 tsp.	cracked pepper, freshly ground

Preheat oven to 175 to 200 degrees F, depending on oven.

Cut tomatoes in half lengthwise; squeeze out some of the juice and seeds.

Toss the tomatoes with the remaining ingredients and marinate for about 15 minutes.

Set the tomatoes cut-side up on a baking sheet with low sides.

Spoon any remaining bits of shallots, etc., onto each tomato half.

Bake for about 4 hours, then turn oven off (do not open door or heat will escape) and leave overnight.

The tomatoes will appear shriveled when done, but will retain some moisture. When preparing, feel free to adjust the seasonings to taste. Serve at room temperature. Store in the refrigerator in airtight container with a bit more olive oil, if desired. They will keep well for three or four weeks.

Notes: These tomatoes will taste quite sweet. Serve on salads, with cheese, or anytime as an elegant replacement for store-bought sun-dried tomatoes.

Mixed Wild Mushrooms

I will now share one of my most versatile secrets, a recipe that can be used in a dozen different ways. The quantities can be doubled or tripled or quadrupled for larger gatherings. I adore mushrooms, any kind, and include them someplace with almost every meal, even in quiche.

1 ea	Vidalia onion, large, peeled, quartered and sliced thin
2 ea	shallots, peeled and chopped finely
2 ea	leeks, white part only, carefully cleaned of sand, sliced thin crosswise
¼ cup	extra virgin olive oil
1 oz.	dried porcini or any dried mushrooms, soak in hot water for 15 minutes, drain, reserve liquid
2 lbs.	mixed wild mushrooms, (e.g., shiitake, oyster, cremini, baby bella, or enoki), rinsed and dried
½ cup	ripe tomatoes, blanched and peeled, chopped, drained of juice and seeds for a bit of color (optional)
¾ cup	dry white wine
1 tsp.	sea salt, or more to taste
½ tsp.	white pepper
½ tsp.	dried or fresh thyme

Remove tough part of stems from the variety of mushrooms being used, and slice thin.

Sauté first three ingredients in the olive oil in large sauté pan until soft over medium heat for about 10 to 15 minutes.

Add mushrooms (and tomato if used) to sauté pan and continue cooking until mushrooms begin to give up liquid. Add wine and reserved soaking liquid (if desired) to pan; continue cooking until liquids reduce but mixture still retains some moisture.

Season to taste. When it tastes just right, it is finished!

To serve: Use ½ cup per serving as appetizer component, ¾ cup per side dish, 1 cup per main dish component (i.e., as a pasta sauce).

Notes: Other varieties of wild mushrooms such as chanterelles and morels are lovely, but they're not so easy to find and are sometimes very gritty and hard to clean. This delicious basic mixture can be used in a dozen different ways:

Wild Mushroom Ragu: Serve as is as a side dish with any roast, poultry, or fish. Complements almost anything very well. Add a handful of fresh chopped Italian parsley, if desired.

Warm Wild Mushroom Salad: Dress mixed baby greens, mache lettuce, or other elegant small greens with a little olive oil and white or dark balsamic vinegar, a bit of salt, and fresh ground pepper. Divide evenly among six plates; mound some of the wild mushrooms on top of each. *For added interest*, mix a few tablespoons of toasted pine nuts into the greens, and/or sprinkle some top-quality shaved Parmesan on top of each salad plate.

Wild Mushroom Soup: Transfer entire mushroom mixture to small stockpot. Add ½ cup of sherry and 3 cups of reduced salt chicken stock and simmer for about 20 minutes. Puree the mixture or leave as is, as desired. Add up to 1 cup light or heavy cream (I use light), simmer another few minutes, correct seasonings with a bit more sea salt and fresh ground black pepper, and serve.

Wild Mushroom Omelet: Use some of the wild mushroom mixture with some shredded Gruyère or fontina cheese folded in, one part mushrooms to two parts cheese or one to one, as a great filling for omelets with lightly dressed greens on the side for an elegant brunch or luncheon dish.

Wild Mushroom Risotto: Cook Arborio rice in broth, according to package instructions, using about ¼ cup dry rice per person. Fold into wild mushroom (to create a nice balance) in deep sauté pan, simmer a few minutes until heated through, adding a bit more broth as necessary to achieve a creamy and moist (but not soupy) consistency. Correct seasoning. Serve with fresh grated Parmesan cheese, if available, or good quality packaged, as a main dish (about 1½ cups risotto mixture) or as an appetizer (about ¾ cup risotto mixture).

Wild Mushroom Pasta: Boil orzo (a long grain rice–shaped pasta) in broth or water according to instructions, or thin spaghetti or linguini in water according to instructions. Use 2 to 3 oz. dry pasta per person (however, I use at least 3 oz. per person), drain (reserving a little cooking liquid), then stir into wild mushroom mixture (as noted above, about 1 cup mushroom mixture per portion of cooked pasta) and reheat for a few minutes on medium heat, adding some cooking liquid or broth as needed to keep the mixture loose but not too soupy. Toss in a handful of fresh chopped curly or Italian parsley. Adjust seasoning with salt and fresh ground black pepper, and serve as a main dish with freshly grated Parmesan cheese.

For added interest, sauté 4 to 6 oz. diced pancetta bacon or diced prosciutto until crisp; then drain away the rendered fat. Toss into wild mushroom mixture along with the cooked pasta while heating. Some finely diced fresh tomato, drained of liquid and seeds, is also very nice and adds a bit of color.

There are more ways to serve this delicious stuff. I have not been too specific on purpose. Be imaginative; *just do it. I* always have. The suggested quantities will vary depending upon who you are serving.

Whole Salmon Filet with Caramelized Onions and White Wine

This recipe is elegant and easy, and defers to all my friends that prefer to eat healthy. It is delicious.

Serves 6 generously

1 whole	wild caught salmon filet, 3 to 3½ lbs., 1 inch thick, skinless, rinsed and patted dry
1 tsp.	sea salt, or to taste
½ tsp.	white pepper, or to taste
1 cup	Japanese bread crumbs
1 can	olive oil spray
1½ cups	dry white wine, or up to ½ cup more, if desired
1 ea	Vidalia onion, large, peeled, halved and sliced thin
¼ cup	extra virgin olive oil
2 tsp.	sugar
¼ cup	parsley, fresh chopped

Preheat oven broiler until very hot.

Lay salmon filet into heavy oval ovenproof ceramic serving dish, large enough to lay filet flat, or rimmed broiling pan (although it is tricky to transfer whole onto serving platter).

Season with the salt and pepper.

Spread bread crumbs evenly over the filet.

Spray olive oil over entire surface of crumb-covered salmon to completely cover the bread crumbs (to avoid burning the crumbs).

Pour the wine all around the edges of the pan, but not *over* the salmon filet.

Sauté the onions in a frying pan in the oil until soft and translucent. Add the sugar and continue to sauté for a few more minutes. Set aside.

Place the salmon in top third of oven and broil for 5 minutes.

Pull the pan out and spoon the onion mixture over the white wine around the edges of the pan.

Return to the oven and broil the salmon for 4 or 5 more minutes *only* for medium rare. Do *not* overcook.

Serve at table, dividing into 6 slices and spooning some of the onion and white wine sauce onto each plate. Sprinkle a bit of the parsley over each serving.

Serve with mustard sauce, recipe below.

Mustard Sauce

One of my tried-and-true staples, good with almost any meat, fish, poultry, or vegetable.

1 cup	heavy cream (or light cream, if preferred)
1 cup	low salt chicken stock, homemade, supermarket, or from gourmet shop
⅓ cup	Dijon mustard
½ tsp.	sea salt, or to taste
¼ tsp.	white pepper, or to taste

Combine first two ingredients and simmer in saucepan (low heat to prevent burning) on stovetop until reduced by exactly half. Use a marked stick to keep track. This process takes time; be patient. Remove from heat.

Stir mustard into warm, reduced liquids.

Season with the salt and pepper, and serve.

Notes: Can be refrigerated for up to three or four weeks. Reheat *very* gently to avoid curdling. This recipe can be doubled, tripled, or quadrupled for larger gatherings, but increases the reduction time for the liquids quite a bit. Be patient.

Perfect Roast Chicken

This method will produce a crackly, dark skin. My friends and family are big eaters, and each chicken will feed no more than three, maybe four, tops.

So two chickens are a better bet, with leftovers for the next day. In my notes at the end, I'll give some quick instructions for Chicken Under a Brick for the more ambitious cook.

1 ea	whole chicken, free range, about 3½ lbs.
1 ea	lemon, halved
1 ea	orange, halved
2 tbsp.	sweet butter (or olive oil, if preferred)
2 tsp.	sea salt
1 tsp.	white pepper
½ ea	Vidalia onion
2 ea	shallots
1 tsp.	dried rosemary, or fresh sprigs if available

Preheat oven to 450 degrees F.

Remove any giblets from cavity; rinse and pat chicken dry. Rub with lemon and orange half and allow to air dry a few minutes.

Rub chicken inside and out with the butter, salt, and pepper.

Place the remaining lemon and orange halves, the onion half, the shallots, and rosemary in the cavity.

Place chicken breast-side up in a roasting pan, on a *rack* so that the back won't stew in its own juices. Bake for 40 minutes. Flip to breast-side down and continue to roast for another 15 minutes. Flip again to breast-side up for another 5 minutes—1 hour total. Remove from oven. Test for doneness by piercing flesh of the leg with a knife tip. If juices run clear, it is done (or instant read thermometer inserted into thickest part of leg reads no higher than 165 degrees F). Do *not* overcook or breast will be dry; cook just until done.

Carve chicken into 8 to 10 pieces, and serve with the sweet and tart barbeque sauce described below.

Notes: For **Chicken Under a Brick**, use one baby chicken or Cornish hen per person, cut in half down the back, backbone removed, opened like a book and flattened. Season with same ingredients for roasted chicken above, bake skin-side down in very hot 475-degree F oven in preheated cast iron skillet, weighted down with a preheated tinfoil-covered brick which conducts heat quite well (be very careful to use oven gloves to handle). Thirty minutes should be enough time to cook the birds through.

My Famous (but don't tell) Barbeque Sauce

This "no work" sauce keeps forever in the fridge and is always a big hit. Everybody loves it!

1 cup	ketchup
1 cup	"All Fruit" orange marmalade (I prefer the Polaner brand)
1 cup	dry white wine
½ cup	Dijon mustard

Combine all four ingredients in saucepan, mixing well.

Cook gently on stovetop over low heat, to prevent sputtering, for about 10 minutes.

Nothing else is needed for this perfect sauce.

Pasta with Shrimp and Spinach in White Wine Sauce

This is one of my favorite recipes, quite low in calories and easy to scale up for a crowd. I usually also throw in some shiitake mushrooms while sautéing the onions and leeks—not to sound too redundant or obsessive about my mushroom use.

Serves 6 generously

2 ea	Vidalia onion, large, peeled, quartered, and sliced thin
2 ea	leeks, rinsed thoroughly to remove sand, sliced cross-wise, white and light green part only
2 ea	shallots, peeled and diced (optionally substitute 2 garlic cloves if preferred)
¼ cup	extra virgin olive oil (more, if needed)
3 ea	bay leaves
1½ cups	dry white wine
2 cups	chicken stock, low salt, homemade, or store bought
2 cups	tomatoes, ripe fresh, seeded and diced; or 14 ½ oz. can good quality diced
2 tsp.	sea salt
2 tsp.	fresh ground pepper
1 tsp.	oregano, fresh or dried
1 tbs. ea	salt, olive oil, white vinegar (for pasta pot)
1 lb.	dried pasta (I use thin spaghetti, such as DeCecco Fedelini, but Penne or Orzo also work well)
2½ lbs.	raw shrimp, about 18 count per lb., peeled, cleaned, tail on
8 oz.	spinach, fresh, cleaned
1 cup	sweet greenpeas, fresh or good quality frozen
½ cup	parsley, fresh, chopped
¼ oz.	basil leaves, fresh, chopped

In a deep stockpot, over medium high heat, sauté first three ingredients in the oil until translucent and softened, but not too brown.

Add bay leaves and white wine and simmer for a few minutes.

Add the stock, tomatoes, salt, pepper, and oregano, and simmer for about ½ hour over low heat, adding a bit more wine or broth to keep the mixture soupy. Remove the bay leaves.

While the sauce is simmering, boil 4 qt. water in another deep pot, adding the salt, oil, and vinegar. Add pasta, stirring occasionally, and cook, al dente, as instructed. Drain, reserving some cooking liquid.

Meanwhile, add the shrimp to the sauce, raising the heat to medium, and cook until pink and just cooked through, about 5 to 8 minutes.

Add the spinach, peas, parsley, and basil and cook for only a minute or two longer. These should remain bright and green.

Toss with pasta (adding some of the retained cooking liquid, if needed) and serve immediately.

Note: Although the conventional wisdom says not to offer fresh grated Parmesan cheese with fish dishes, I disagree and always do so, offering my guests the option.

Bread and Chocolate

A classic French dessert and a conversation starter; something different. I served it twenty-five years ago at my daughter's wedding instead of the traditional offerings; nobody but me quite understood what I was trying to achieve, though. Maybe that was too much, too soon.

Serves 8

1 lb.	French bread, top-quality artisan bread, crusty, chewy, hand sliced
1 lb.	bittersweet chocolate, top quality, broken into random bite-sized pieces
1 cup	berries, any kind, or pomegranate seeds in season (optional)

Assemble this dessert on beautiful plates to serve, a little of each.

For larger crowds, increase the quantities.

Serve with strong coffee, champagne, or a fine dessert wine.

Scatter some berries, if desired.

Notes: Make sure to use the finest dark chocolate (no milk or white chocolate), and, for added interest, serve fresh figs (if in season) or other fruit (pears are nice) with this dessert. Fig jam, nuts, and crème fraîche are other elegant additions.

Avocado Cream

I demonstrated this dessert over forty years ago during one of my cooking classes, but it seems au courant to me, considering that even bacon, along with many other nontraditional ingredients, has become an "of the moment" dessert inclusion. It is very impressive and very easy to prepare.

Serves 6

2 large	avocados, peeled with pit removed
3 tbsp.	lime juice
½ cup	sugar
2 tbsp.	honey
¼ cup	heavy cream
pinch	salt

In a food processor, puree the avocados with the lime juice.

Add the next four ingredients and blend until very smooth, about 1 minute more.

Divide or pipe among six parfait glasses, and chill for at least 4 hours.

Serve garnished on top with a few berries or semisweet chocolate shavings. Or for something way out there, try garnishing with candied bacon. Also serve with shortbread cookies on the side.

Notes: I once learned a trick for keeping the vibrant green of the avocado from turning brown so quickly once cut: Rinsing or submerging in cold water prevents the fruit from browning for hours. But, even so, do not prepare this lovely dessert more than those few hours in advance.

Bittersweet Chocolate Truffle Cake

This timeless and elegant (flourless) cake was one of our first dessert products, introduced in 1974, and it has remained on our roster to this very day in several shapes and sizes.

Serves 8

1 lb.	bittersweet chocolate, chopped or broken into pieces

8 tbsp.	butter, sweet-unsalted (1 stick), softened
¼ cup	ground almonds
1 tbsp.	cocoa powder
½ tsp.	salt
1 tbsp.	strong coffee (or espresso)
6 ea	eggs, separated and at room temperature
2 tbsp.	sugar, granulated
1 tbsp.	rum
¾ tsp.	cream of tartar

Garnish: Dusting of confectioner's sugar

Melt chocolate and butter in a double boiler or microwave oven. Don't overheat or allow to burn. Remove from heat.

With rubber spatula, fold the almonds, cocoa, salt, and coffee into the chocolate and butter mixture.

In a separate deep bowl, whisk the yolks, sugar, and rum until they thicken and ribbon, appearing creamy and light in color. Then gently fold in the above chocolate mixture, being careful not to deflate the combined mixture.

Meanwhile, with an eggbeater, or in a stand mixer with the whisk attachment, whip whites with cream of tartar until stiff but not dry. Fold gently into chocolate mixture, being careful not to deflate whites. The mixture should remain soufflé-like in texture.

Wrap the bottom of a 9-inch springform pan with a double layer of tinfoil, sealing the bottom well. Butter the pan and line it with buttered parchment paper. Gently transfer the batter into prepared pan. Set on a cookie sheet and bake at 325 degrees F for 25 to 30 minutes just until set in center. Remove the cake from the oven; the center will appear underbaked but will continue to set as it cools. Allow to cool to room temperature. Once cooled, refrigerate in the pan for a few hours to aid in the unmolding process.

About 30 minutes before serving, run a thin knife between the cake and sides of the pan.

Carefully unmold and remove parchment, transfer to serving platter, sprinkle with confectioner's sugar, and serve at room temperature.

Note: Nice served with lightly whipped cream, vanilla (or coffee) ice cream, crème fraîche, and strawberries—or any ripe berries in season.

Bread and Butter Pudding

This easy, quintessential comfort food was also introduced in the 1970s and is still on our menu in one form or another, from praline to raspberry to maple.

Serves 8 to 12 generously

2 tbsp.	sugar, granulated
½ tsp.	cinnamon
1 ea	French bread, 8-oz. loaf, sliced thin crosswise or cubed, about a half lb. (substitute cubes of your favorite sourdough, walnut raisin, or even crusty white bread if preferred)
4 tbsp.	butter, melted
¼ cup	golden raisins, plumped in boiling water for a few minutes
1½ cups	milk
1½ cups	heavy cream (light cream or all milk can be used for a lighter version)
1 ea	vanilla bean (or 2 tsp. pure vanilla)
½ cup	sugar, granulated
3 ea	large eggs
2 ea	egg yolks
¼ tsp.	cinnamon
pinch	salt

Garnish: Dusting of confectioner's sugar

Combine 2 tbsp. sugar and ½ tsp. cinnamon completely in a small dish and set aside.

Arrange bread in 9 × 13 glass baking pan, or a deep-sided 10-inch round one.

Drizzle with the butter. Sprinkle with the raisins.

Scald milk and cream with the vanilla bean (if using one), remove from heat. Split the bean and scrape in some of the seeds. Add the sugar and vanilla (if no bean was used) and stir.

In separate bowl, beat the eggs and extra yolks lightly, then combine with the cream mixture and add the ¼ tsp. cinnamon and pinch of salt.

Pour custard over bread, patting down, and allow to soak for 5 minutes.

Sprinkle with reserved cinnamon sugar mixture and bake in pre-heated 350-degree F oven for approximately 45–50 minutes.

Dust with confectioner's sugar and serve warm or at room temperature.

Notes: Delicious served as a dessert or brunch item with ripe berries in season. Also nice accompanied by whipped cream, crème fraîche, or even maple syrup!

Nut Glacé (Brittle)

I used to make this confection to give as house gifts, wrapped up in a napkin, tied with ribbon, and placed in a pretty basket or bowl. This was before I started Love and Quiches. It occurs to me that it would make a nice dessert accompaniment served with ice cream, sorbet, or frozen yogurt; it's something different and easy to prepare. All you need is a candy (or frying) thermometer. Unlike traditional brittles, this confection is chock full of nuts.

1 cup	blanched slivered almonds
1 cup	walnuts, chopped coarsely into large pieces
1 cup	macadamia nuts, halves or chopped coarsely into large pieces
1 tsp.	table salt
1¼ cups	sugar
¾ cup	light corn syrup
⅓ cup	water
2 tbsp.	butter, in bits
2 tsp.	pure vanilla extract

In a 350-degree F oven, toast the nuts with the salt on a rimmed cookie sheet for 5 to 10 minutes. Remove from oven. Bring the sugar, corn syrup, and water to a boil in a heavy saucepan. Cook over moderately high heat, undisturbed, until candy thermometer reaches 290 degrees F. The mixture will have turned a light amber color. This will take about 15 minutes.

Take off heat and quickly stir in the butter, vanilla, and nuts.

Pour onto parchment-lined or lightly buttered cookie sheet and spread with a spatula or back of a greased spoon. Rest at room temperature until cool and hard. Break into random pieces, about 1½ inches each, to serve as candy or as a dessert accompaniment described above.

Notes: If desired, substitute any other favorite nuts, such as pecans or pistachios, or even peanuts. Also, this would be a great opportunity to try out your silicon liner, if you have one.

Killer Brownie Pie

We first baked this to be served at a dinner party at the home of Jacqueline Kennedy a very long time ago, and it has remained, in one form or another, on our menu ever since.

Serves 8 to 10

4 oz.	unsweetened chocolate (also known as baking chocolate), chopped or broken into pieces
8 oz.	butter, sweet-unsalted, melted (2 sticks)
4 ea	eggs, extra large
2 cups	sugar, granulated
1 tsp.	pure vanilla extract
¼ tsp.	salt
1 cup + 1 tbsp.	pastry flour (all purpose)
¾ cup	pecans, chopped

This recipe will fill one large 11-inch pie pan or an 8 × 8 deep square pan.

Preheat oven to 350 degrees F.

Coat the pan with cooking/baking spray.

Melt chocolate and butter in a double boiler or microwave oven. Don't overheat or allow to burn. Remove from heat.

Place chocolate mixture, eggs, sugar, vanilla, and salt in a bowl. With a stand mixer, hand mixer, or wooden spoon, mix well until all ingredients are fully incorporated. Blend in flour last and mix just until incorporated, being careful not to overmix. Gently fold ½ cup of the pecans into batter. Deposit into pan, sprinkle remaining ¼ cup pecans on top, and bake at 350 degrees F for approximately 45 minutes or until a toothpick inserted in the center comes out clean.

Cool and serve with your favorite ice cream, frozen yogurt, whipped cream, and berries.

Note: Mix in or top this brownie with your favorite chocolate or nuts . . . we add pecans.

Greek Yogurt Cheesecake with Honey Drizzle

We introduced this dessert very recently to keep up the demand for "all things yogurt."

Serves 8 to 12

Crust

1⅓ cups	graham cracker crumbs (plus some reserved for coating pan if desired)
¼ tsp.	cinnamon
⅓ cup	sugar, granulated
6 tbsp.	butter, melted

Place graham cracker crumbs, ground cinnamon, and sugar in a bowl and combine well. With a stand mixer, hand mixer, or spoon, pour in melted butter and stir until completely combined.

Wrap the bottom of a 10-inch springform pan with a double layer of tinfoil, sealing the bottom well. Press the graham crumb mixture evenly into the bottom of the pan. Grease the side of the pan with butter (and coat the sides with dry graham crumbs if desired).

Cheesecake Batter

24 oz.	cream cheese (Neufchatel cheese can be used for a lighter version)
2½ cups	sugar, granulated
¼ tsp.	salt
1½ tsp.	pure vanilla extract
9 oz.	yogurt, Greek (full fat, low fat, or nonfat can be used)
6 ea	eggs

Place cream cheese, sugar, and salt into a mixing bowl. With a stand mixer or hand mixer, blend together until mixture is fluffy and smooth. Add vanilla extract and Greek yogurt to cream cheese mixture. Beat together until incorporated. Add eggs one at a time until incorporated. Pour cheesecake batter over crust.

Set on rimmed cookie sheet and bake in a shallow water bath. Bake at 325 degrees F for 75–80 minutes or until set in center. Remove the cake from the oven and water bath, allowing the cake to cool to room temp. Chill in refrigerator for 8 hours prior to serving. About 30 minutes before serving, run a thin knife between the cake and sides of the pan.

Carefully unmold; transfer to serving platter.

Serve with a drizzle of honey—try some wild flower or orange blossom.

Note: For ease of cutting any cheesecake, use a hot, wet knife, wiping blade between slices.

Fresh Fruit Crisp

I prefer this fruit crisp with some nuts in the topping. You can certainly leave them out if you aren't a fan. If you prefer a more traditional topping with oatmeal, add ¾ cup of old-fashioned rolled oats. Use a 3-qt. (9 × 13) glass baking dish for this recipe.

Serves 10 to 12

Filling

1 cup	sugar, granulated
1 tbsp.	cinnamon
4 tbsp.	flour (all purpose)
4½ lbs.	apples, peeled, cored, and sliced ½-inch thick (to yield about 3 lbs. of apples)

Combine the sugar, cinnamon, and flour in a bowl. Toss the apples in the sugar mixture, ensuring that all of the apples are evenly covered. Spread into the bottom of baking dish.

Topping

½ cup	sugar, granulated
½ cup	sugar, light brown
1½ cups	flour (all purpose)
2 tbsp.	cinnamon
½ tsp.	salt
9 tbsp.	butter, sweet-unsalted, chilled and cut into small pieces
¾ cup	walnuts, chopped

Blend the sugars, flour, cinnamon, and salt in a bowl. Cut the chilled butter into the dry mixture with your fingers until the granules are the size of large peas. Alternately, you can use a pastry cutter. Mix together until crumbly and fully combined, adding the walnuts last. Do not overmix crumb topping. (If you are using oatmeal, you can add it with the dry ingredients.)

Sprinkle the crumb mixture evenly over the fruit and bake at 350 degrees F for about 45 minutes until the fruit bubbles.

Notes: This is a very simple apple crisp. You'll want to use flavorful and firm apples (Granny Smith are our go-to, or possibly Braeburn). You could even add a handful of blackberries, raisins, cranberries, or cherries. Or substitute summer fruit, such as peaches, for the apples. You can't go wrong . . . Serve warm with ice cream or with whipped cream.

Tiramisu

This favorite Italian dessert has become ubiquitous not only in Italian restaurants but also in all types of restaurants here and abroad, and it is one of our bestselling desserts everywhere.

As you might know, tiramisu means "pick me up" in Italian. It is so given the name from the flavors and ingredients. You will see that mine is made with freshly brewed espresso and liquor. If you prefer to have it a little sweeter or without the alcohol, just add some extra sugar to the syrup and/ or take out the alcohol.

Serves 10 to 12

36 ea	ladyfingers, dry Italian (also called Savoiardi cookies) cocoa, as needed, for dusting between layers and on top

Coffee Soaking Syrup

1½ cups	espresso, fresh brewed (or very strong coffee)
⅓ cup	sugar, granulated
¼ cup	dark rum, brandy, or coffee liquor (optional)

Place hot coffee in a bowl. Add sugar and stir to dissolve. Mix in liquor (if desired) and cool. Set aside to use at room temperature.

Mascarpone Cream

9 ea	eggs, separated
⅔ cup	sugar, granulated
½ cup	marsala wine
24 oz.	mascarpone cheese

With a hand mixer or stand mixer fitted with a whisk attachment, beat egg yolks with the sugar and marsala on medium high speed until light and foamy, up to 25 minutes. Gradually add in the mascarpone cheese and cream until smooth. In a separate clean bowl, whip the egg whites until firm peaks are formed, 5 to 7 minutes. Gently fold in the mascarpone cream mixture, a little at a time until fully incorporated.

Assembly: Use a 3-qt. (9 × 13) glass baking dish or a rectangular (straight-sided) decorative serving dish.

Place half of the ladyfingers on the bottom of the dish. Drizzle evenly with half of the coffee syrup. Spread half of the cream over the moistened ladyfingers. Sprinkle cocoa evenly over the top of the cream. Place the remaining ladyfingers evenly over the cocoa. Drizzle with the remaining coffee syrup and cover the top with the rest of the cream. Smooth evenly and cover the top with foil or plastic wrap. Refrigerate for at least 6 hours or overnight.

Sprinkle with cocoa prior to serving.

Note: For an even more elegant presentation, sprinkle dark chocolate shavings on top in addition to the cocoa.

About the Author

Susan Axelrod splits her time between New York City and Fire Island, New York, while continuing to run Love & Quiches Gourmet with the support of her husband, Irwin, and her children. On any given day, you can find Susan walking the production floor, reviewing formulas in the test kitchen, or mentoring her executive team. She is an avid reader, traveler, and lover of food as well as her New York hometown. Follow Susan on Facebook or on her blog, Susan's Sweet Talk (www.SusansSweetTalk.com).